THE NEW
SIGNET
WORLD
ATLAS

SIGNET
Published by New American Library, a division of
Penguin Putnam Inc., 375 Hudson Street,
New York, New York 10014, U.S.A.
Penguin Books Ltd, 27 Wrights Lane,
London W8 5TZ, England
Penguin Books Australia Ltd, Ringwood,
Victoria, Australia
Penguin Books Canada Ltd, 10 Alcorn Avenue,
Toronto, Ontario, Canada M4V 3B2
Penguin Books (N.Z.) Ltd, 182–190 Wairau Road,
Auckland 10, New Zealand

Penguin Books Ltd, Registered Offices:
Harmondsworth, Middlesex, England

First published by Signet, an imprint of New American Library,
a division of Penguin Putnam Inc.

First Printing (Revised and Updated Edition), August 1998
First Printing (Second Revised Edition), February 2000
10   9   8   7   6   5   4   3   2   1

THE NEW
SIGNET
WORLD
ATLAS

REVISED & UPDATED
EDITION

A SIGNET BOOK

Contents

vi–ix	World statistics
x–xi	Time zones
xii–xiii	Flight paths
xiv–xv	Climate
xvi–xvii	Wealth
xviii–xix	International organizations
xx–xxiv	World gazetteer

1	World Maps – general reference
2–3	Northern hemisphere 1:133.3M
4–5	Southern hemisphere 1:133.3M

EUROPE

6–7	Europe 1:26.7M
8–9	Scandinavia 1:13.3M
10–11	British Isles 1:6.7M
12–13	France 1:6.7M
14–15	Germany and Benelux 1:6.7M
16–17	Central Europe 1:6.7M
18–19	Spain and Portugal 1:6.7M
20–21	Italy and the Adriatic 1:6.7M
22–23	Greece and the Balkans 1:6.7M
24–25	Eastern Europe 1:13.3M

ASIA

26–27	Asia 1:67M
28–29	Western Russia and Central Asia 1:26.7M
30–31	Eastern Siberia 1:26.7M
32–33	Japan 1:6.7M Southern Honshu 1:13.3M
34–35	China 1:26.7M
36–37	South-east Asia 1:16.7M
38–39	Philippines and Eastern Indonesia 1:16.7M
40–41	Eastern India, Bangladesh and Burma 1:13.3M
42–43	Western India and Pakistan 1:13.3M
44–45	Iran, the Gulf and Afghanistan 1:13.3M
46–47	The Middle East and Turkey 1:13.3M
48–49	Arabia and the Horn of Africa 1:20M

AFRICA

50–51 Africa *1:56*M

52–53 North-east Africa *1:20*M

54–55 North-west Africa *1:20*M

56–57 Central Africa *1:20*M

58–59 Southern Africa *1:20*M

AUSTRALASIA

60–61 Australia *1:26.7*M

62–63 South-east Australia *1:10.7*M

64–65 New Zealand, Central and South-west Pacific *1:8*M

NORTH AMERICA

66–67 North America *1:46.7*M

68–69 Eastern Canada *1:20*M

70–71 Western Canada *1:20*M

72–73 North-east USA *1:8*M

74–75 South-east USA *1:8*M

76–77 North-central USA *1:8*M

78–79 Southern USA *1:8*M

80–81 North-west USA *1:8*M

82–83 South-west USA *1:8*M

84–85 Mexico *1:20*M

86–87 Caribbean and Central America *1:20*M

SOUTH AMERICA

88–89 South America *1:46.7*M

90–91 South America – North-west *1:21.3*M

92–93 South America – North-east *1:21.3*M

94–95 South America – South *1:21.3*M

POLAR REGIONS

96 Antarctica *1:46.7*M

INDEX

97–120 Index to World Maps

WORLD STATISTICS

Country/Territory	Area (1,000 sq km)	Area (1,000 sq miles)	Population (1,000s)	Capital City	Annual Income US$
AFGHANISTAN	652	252	24,792	KABUL	600
ALBANIA	28.8	11.1	3,331	TIRANA	750
ALGERIA	2,382	920	30,481	ALGIERS	1,490
AMERICAN SAMOA (US)	0.20	0.08	62	PAGO PAGO	2,600
ANDORRA	0.45	0.17	75	ANDORRA LA VELLA	16,200
ANGOLA	1,247	481	11,200	LUANDA	340
ANGUILLA (UK)	0.1	0.04	11	THE VALLEY	6,800
ANTIGUA & BARBUDA	0.44	0.17	64	ST JOHN'S	7,330
ARGENTINA	2,767	1,068	36,265	BUENOS AIRES	8,750
ARMENIA	29.8	11.5	3,422	YEREVAN	530
ARUBA (NETHERLANDS)	0.19	0.07	69	ORANJESTAD	15,890
AUSTRALIA	7,687	2,968	18,613	CANBERRA	20,540
AUSTRIA	83.9	32.4	8,134	VIENNA	27,980
AZERBAIJAN	86.6	33.4	7,856	BAKU	510
AZORES (PORTUGAL)	2.2	0.87	238	PONTA DELGADA	–
BAHAMAS	13.9	5.4	280	NASSAU	11,940
BAHRAIN	0.68	0.26	616	MANAMA	7,840
BANGLADESH	144	56	125,000	DHAKA	270
BARBADOS	0.43	0.17	259	BRIDGETOWN	6,560
BELARUS	207.6	80.1	10,409	MINSK	2,150
BELGIUM	30.5	11.8	10,175	BRUSSELS	26,420
BELIZE	23	8.9	230	BELMOPAN	2,700
BENIN	113	43	6,101	PORTO-NOVO	380
BERMUDA (UK)	0.05	0.02	62	HAMILTON	31,870
BHUTAN	47	18.1	1,908	THIMPHU	390
BOLIVIA	1,099	424	7,826	LA PAZ/SUCRE	950
BOSNIA-HERZEGOVINA	51	20	3,366	SARAJEVO	300
BOTSWANA	582	225	1,448	GABORONE	4,381
BRAZIL	8,512	3,286	170,000	BRASÍLIA	4,720
BRUNEI	5.8	2.2	315	BANDAR SERI BEGAWAN	15,800
BULGARIA	111	43	8,240	SOFIA	1,140
BURKINA FASO	274	106	11,266	OUAGADOUGOU	240
BURMA (= MYANMAR)	677	261	47,305	RANGOON	1,790
BURUNDI	27.8	10.7	5,531	BUJUMBURA	180
CAMBODIA	181	70	11,340	PHNOM PENH	300
CAMEROON	475	184	15,029	YAOUNDÉ	650
CANADA	9,976	3,852	30,675	OTTAWA	19,290
CANARY IS. (SPAIN)	7.3	2.8	1,494	LAS PALMAS/SANTA CRUZ	–
CAPE VERDE IS.	4	1.6	399	PRAIA	1,010
CAYMAN IS. (UK)	0.26	0.10	35	GEORGE TOWN	20,000
CENTRAL AFRICAN REPUBLIC	623	241	3,376	BANGUI	320
CHAD	1,284	496	7,360	NDJAMÉNA	240
CHILE	757	292	14,788	SANTIAGO	5,020
CHINA	9,597	3,705	1,236,915	BEIJING	860
COLOMBIA	1,139	440	38,581	BOGOTÁ	2,280
COMOROS	2.2	0.86	545	MORONI	450
CONGO	342	132	2,658	BRAZZAVILLE	660
CONGO (DEM. REP. OF THE)	2,345	905	49,001	KINSHASA	110
COOK IS. (NZ)	0.24	0.09	20	AVARUA	900
COSTA RICA	51.1	19.7	3,605	SAN JOSÉ	2,640
CROATIA	56.5	21.8	4,672	ZAGREB	4,610
CUBA	111	43	11,051	HAVANA	1,300
CYPRUS	9.3	3.6	749	NICOSIA	13,420
CZECH REPUBLIC	78.9	30.4	10,286	PRAGUE	5,200
DENMARK	43.1	16.6	5,334	COPENHAGEN	32,500

This alphabetical list includes all the countries and territories of the world. If a territory is not completely independent, then the country it is associated with is named. The area figures give the total area of land, inland water and ice. Units for areas and populations are in thousands.

Country/Territory	Area (1,000 sq km)	Area (1,000 sq miles)	Population (1,000s)	Capital City	Annual Income US$
DJIBOUTI	23.2	9	650	DJIBOUTI	850
DOMINICA	0.75	0.29	78	ROSEAU	3,090
DOMINICAN REPUBLIC	48.7	18.8	7,999	SANTO DOMINGO	1,670
ECUADOR	284	109	12,337	QUITO	1,590
EGYPT	1,001	387	66,050	CAIRO	1,180
EL SALVADOR	21	8.1	5,752	SAN SALVADOR	1,810
EQUATORIAL GUINEA	28.1	10.8	454	MALABO	530
ERITREA	94	36	3,842	ASMARA	570
ESTONIA	44.7	17.3	1,421	TALLINN	3,330
ETHIOPIA	1,128	436	58,390	ADDIS ABABA	110
FALKLAND IS. (UK)	12.2	4.7	2	STANLEY	–
FAROE IS. (DENMARK)	1.4	0.54	41	TÓRSHAVN	23,660
FIJI	18.3	7.1	802	SUVA	2,470
FINLAND	338	131	5,149	HELSINKI	24,080
FRANCE	552	213	58,805	PARIS	26,050
FRENCH GUIANA (FRANCE)	90	34.7	162	CAYENNE	10,580
FRENCH POLYNESIA (FRANCE)	4	1.5	237	PAPEETE	7,500
GABON	268	103	1,208	LIBREVILLE	4,230
GAMBIA, THE	11.3	4.4	1,292	BANJUL	320
GEORGIA	69.7	26.9	5,109	TBILISI	840
GERMANY	357	138	82,079	BERLIN/BONN	28,260
GHANA	239	92	18,497	ACCRA	370
GIBRALTAR (UK)	0.007	0.003	29	GIBRALTAR TOWN	5,000
GREECE	132	51	10,662	ATHENS	12,010
GREENLAND (DENMARK)	2,176	840	59	NUUK (GODTHÅB)	15,500
GRENADA	0.34	0.13	96	ST GEORGE'S	2,880
GUADELOUPE (FRANCE)	1.7	0.66	416	BASSE-TERRE	9,200
GUAM (US)	0.55	0.21	149	AGANA	6,000
GUATEMALA	109	42	12,008	GUATEMALA CITY	1,500
GUINEA	246	95	7,477	CONAKRY	570
GUINEA-BISSAU	36.1	13.9	1,206	BISSAU	240
GUYANA	215	83	820	GEORGETOWN	690
HAITI	27.8	10.7	6,781	PORT-AU-PRINCE	330
HONDURAS	112	43	5,862	TEGUCIGALPA	700
HONG KONG (CHINA)	1.1	0.40	6,707	–	22,990
HUNGARY	93	35.9	10,208	BUDAPEST	4,430
ICELAND	103	40	271	REYKJAVIK	26,580
INDIA	3,288	1,269	984,000	NEW DELHI	390
INDONESIA	1,905	735	212,942	JAKARTA	1,110
IRAN	1,648	636	64,411	TEHRAN	4,700
IRAQ	438	169	21,722	BAGHDAD	2,000
IRELAND	70.3	27.1	3,619	DUBLIN	18,280
ISRAEL	27	10.3	5,644	JERUSALEM	15,810
ITALY	301	116	56,783	ROME	20,120
IVORY COAST (CÔTE D'IVOIRE)	322	125	15,446	YAMOUSSOUKRO	690
JAMAICA	11	4.2	2,635	KINGSTON	1,560
JAPAN	378	146	125,932	TOKYO	37,850
JORDAN	89.2	34.4	4,435	AMMAN	1,570
KAZAKSTAN	2,717	1,049	16,847	ASTANA	1,340
KENYA	580	224	28,337	NAIROBI	330
KIRIBATI	0.72	0.28	85	TARAWA	920
KOREA, NORTH	121	47	21,234	PYONGYANG	1,000
KOREA, SOUTH	99	38.2	46,417	SEOUL	10,550
KUWAIT	17.8	6.9	1,913	KUWAIT CITY	17,390
KYRGYZSTAN	198.5	76.6	4,522	BISHKEK	440

The annual income is the Gross National Product per capita in US dollars. The figures are the latest available, usually 1997.

WORLD STATISTICS

Country/Territory	Area (1,000 sq km)	Area (1,000 sq miles)	Population (1,000s)	Capital City	Annual Income US$
LAOS	237	91	5,261	VIENTIANE	400
LATVIA	65	25	2,385	RIGA	2,430
LEBANON	10.4	4	3,506	BEIRUT	3,350
LESOTHO	30.4	11.7	2,090	MASERU	670
LIBERIA	111	43	2,772	MONROVIA	770
LIBYA	1,760	679	4,875	TRIPOLI	6,510
LIECHTENSTEIN	0.16	0.06	32	VADUZ	33,000
LITHUANIA	65.2	25.2	3,600	VILNIUS	2,230
LUXEMBOURG	2.6	1	425	LUXEMBOURG	45,360
MACAU (CHINA)	0.02	0.006	429	MACAU	7,500
MACEDONIA	25.7	9.9	2,009	SKOPJE	1,090
MADAGASCAR	587	227	14,463	ANTANANARIVO	250
MADEIRA (PORTUGAL)	0.81	0.31	253	FUNCHAL	–
MALAWI	118	46	9,840	LILONGWE	220
MALAYSIA	330	127	20,993	KUALA LUMPUR	4,680
MALDIVES	0.30	0.12	290	MALÉ	1,080
MALI	1,240	479	10,109	BAMAKO	260
MALTA	0.32	0.12	379	VALLETTA	12,000
MARSHALL IS.	0.18	0.07	63	DALAP-ULIGA-DARRIT	1,890
MARTINIQUE (FRANCE)	1.1	0.42	407	FORT-DE-FRANCE	10,000
MAURITANIA	1,030	412	2,511	NOUAKCHOTT	450
MAURITIUS	2.0	0.72	1,168	PORT LOUIS	3,800
MAYOTTE (FRANCE)	0.37	0.14	141	MAMOUNDZOU	1,430
MEXICO	1,958	756	98,553	MEXICO CITY	3,680
MICRONESIA, FED. STATES OF	0.70	0.27	127	PALIKIR	2,070
MIDWAY IS. (US)	0.005	0.002	2		–
MOLDOVA	33.7	13	4,458	CHIŞINĂU	540
MONACO	0.002	0.0001	32	MONACO	25,000
MONGOLIA	1,567	605	2,579	ULAN BATOR	390
MONTSERRAT (UK)	0.10	0.04	12	PLYMOUTH	4,500
MOROCCO	447	172	29,114	RABAT	1,250
MOZAMBIQUE	802	309	18,641	MAPUTO	90
NAMIBIA	825	318	1,622	WINDHOEK	2,220
NAURU	0.02	0.008	12	YAREN DISTRICT	10,000
NEPAL	141	54	23,698	KATMANDU	210
NETHERLANDS	41.5	16	15,731	AMSTERDAM/THE HAGUE	25,820
NETHERLANDS ANTILLES (NETHS)	0.99	0.38	210	WILLEMSTAD	10,400
NEW CALEDONIA (FRANCE)	18.6	7.2	192	NOUMÉA	8,000
NEW ZEALAND	269	104	3,625	WELLINGTON	16,480
NICARAGUA	130	50	4,583	MANAGUA	410
NIGER	1,267	489	9,672	NIAMEY	200
NIGERIA	924	357	110,532	ABUJA	260
NORTHERN MARIANA IS. (US)	0.48	0.18	50	SAIPAN	11,500
NORWAY	324	125	4,420	OSLO	36,090
OMAN	212	82	2,364	MUSCAT	4,950
PAKISTAN	796	307	135,135	ISLAMABAD	490
PALAU	0.46	0.18	18	KOROR	5,000
PANAMA	77.1	29.8	2,736	PANAMA CITY	3,080
PAPUA NEW GUINEA	463	179	4,600	PORT MORESBY	940
PARAGUAY	407	157	5,291	ASUNCIÓN	2,010
PERU	1,285	496	26,111	LIMA	2,460
PHILIPPINES	300	116	77,736	MANILA	1,220
PITCAIRN IS. (UK)	0.03	0.01	0.05	ADAMSTOWN	–
POLAND	313	121	38,607	WARSAW	3,590
PORTUGAL	92.4	35.7	9,928	LISBON	10,450
PUERTO RICO (US)	9	3.5	3,860	SAN JUAN	7,800
QATAR	11	4.2	697	DOHA	11,600
RÉUNION (FRANCE)	2.5	0.97	705	SAINT-DENIS	4,500
ROMANIA	238	92	22,396	BUCHAREST	1,420

Country / Territory	Area (1,000 sq km)	Area (1,000 sq miles)	Population (1,000s)	Capital City	Annual Income US$
RUSSIA	17,075	6,592	146,861	MOSCOW	2,740
RWANDA	26.3	10.2	7,956	KIGALI	210
ST HELENA (UK)	0.12	0.05	7	JAMESTOWN	–
ST KITTS & NEVIS	0.36	0.14	42	BASSETERRE	5,870
ST LUCIA	0.62	0.24	150	CASTRIES	3,500
ST VINCENT & GRENADINES	0.39	0.15	120	KINGSTOWN	2,370
SAN MARINO	0.06	0.02	25	SAN MARINO	20,000
SÃO TOMÉ & PRÍNCIPE	0.96	0.37	150	SÃO TOMÉ	330
SAUDI ARABIA	2,150	830	20,786	RIYADH	6,790
SENEGAL	197	76	9,723	DAKAR	550
SEYCHELLES	0.46	0.18	79	VICTORIA	6,850
SIERRA LEONE	71.7	27.7	5,080	FREETOWN	200
SINGAPORE	0.62	0.24	3,490	SINGAPORE	32,940
SLOVAK REPUBLIC	49	18.9	5,393	BRATISLAVA	3,700
SLOVENIA	20.3	7.8	1,972	LJUBLJANA	9,680
SOLOMON IS.	28.9	11.2	441	HONIARA	900
SOMALIA	638	246	6,842	MOGADISHU	500
SOUTH AFRICA	1,220	471	42,835	C. TOWN/PRET./BLOEM.	3,400
SPAIN	505	195	39,134	MADRID	14,510
SRI LANKA	65.6	25.3	18,934	COLOMBO	800
SUDAN	2,506	967	33,551	KHARTOUM	800
SURINAM	163	63	427	PARAMARIBO	1,000
SWAZILAND	17.4	6.7	966	MBABANE	1,210
SWEDEN	450	174	8,887	STOCKHOLM	26,220
SWITZERLAND	41.3	15.9	7,260	BERN	44,220
SYRIA	185	71	16,673	DAMASCUS	1,150
TAIWAN	36	13.9	21,908	TAIPEI	12,400
TAJIKISTAN	143.1	55.2	6,020	DUSHANBE	330
TANZANIA	945	365	30,609	DODOMA	210
THAILAND	513	198	60,037	BANGKOK	2,800
TOGO	56.8	21.9	4,906	LOMÉ	330
TONGA	0.75	0.29	107	NUKU'ALOFA	1,790
TRINIDAD & TOBAGO	5.1	2	1,117	PORT OF SPAIN	4,230
TRISTAN DA CUNHA (UK)	0.11	0.04	0.33	EDINBURGH	–
TUNISIA	164	63	9,380	TUNIS	2,090
TURKEY	779	301	64,568	ANKARA	3,130
TURKMENISTAN	488.1	188.5	4,298	ASHKHABAD	630
TURKS & CAICOS IS. (UK)	0.43	0.17	16	COCKBURN TOWN	5,000
TUVALU	0.03	0.01	10	FONGAFALE	600
UGANDA	236	91	22,167	KAMPALA	320
UKRAINE	603.7	233.1	50,125	KIEV	1,040
UNITED ARAB EMIRATES	83.6	32.3	2,303	ABU DHABI	17,360
UNITED KINGDOM	243.3	94	58,970	LONDON	20,710
UNITED STATES OF AMERICA	9,373	3,619	270,290	WASHINGTON, DC	28,740
URUGUAY	177	68	3,285	MONTEVIDEO	6,020
UZBEKISTAN	447.4	172.7	23,784	TASHKENT	1,010
VANUATU	12.2	4.7	185	PORT-VILA	1,290
VATICAN CITY	0.0004	0.0002	1	–	–
VENEZUELA	912	352	22,803	CARACAS	3,450
VIETNAM	332	127	76,236	HANOI	320
VIRGIN IS. (UK)	0.15	0.06	13	ROAD TOWN	–
VIRGIN IS. (US)	0.34	0.13	118	CHARLOTTE AMALIE	12,000
WALLIS & FUTUNA IS. (FRANCE)	0.20	0.08	15	MATA-UTU	–
WESTERN SAHARA	266	103	280	EL AAIÚN	300
WESTERN SAMOA	2.8	1.1	224	APIA	1,170
YEMEN	528	204	16,388	SANA	270
YUGOSLAVIA	102.3	39.5	10,500	BELGRADE	2,000
ZAMBIA	753	291	9,461	LUSAKA	380
ZIMBABWE	391	151	11,044	HARARE	750

TIME ZONES

The world is divided into 24 time zones, each centred on meridians at 15° intervals, which is the longitudinal distance the sun travels every hour. The meridian running through Greenwich in London, England, passes through the middle of the first time zone. Zones to the east of Greenwich are ahead of Greenwich Mean Time (GMT) by one hour for every 15° of longitude, while zones to the west are behind GMT by one hour.

When it is 12 noon at the Greenwich meridian, 180° east it is midnight of the same day, while at 180° west the day is only just beginning. To overcome this, the International Date Line was established in 1883 – an imaginary line which approximately follows the 180th meridian. Therefore, if one travelled eastwards from Japan (140° East) towards Samoa (170° West), one would pass from Sunday night straight into Sunday morning.

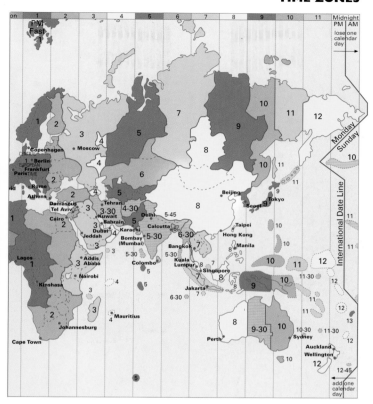

TIME DIFFERENCES FROM GMT (LONDON)

BEIJING	+8	BANGKOK	+7
CHICAGO	−6	DELHI	+5.30
JO'BURG	+2	LAGOS	+1
LOS ANGELES	−8	MEXICO CITY	−6
MOSCOW	+3	NEW YORK	−5
PARIS	+1	ROME	+1
SYDNEY	+10	TEHRAN	+3.30
TOKYO	+9	TORONTO	−5

KEY TO TIME ZONES MAP

Zones using GMT

Zones fast of GMT

Zones slow of GMT

Half-hour zones

- - - - - International boundaries

———— Time zone boundaries

10   Hours slow or fast of GMT

———— International Date Line

Actual Solar Time, when it is noon at Greenwich, is shown along the top of the map.

Note: Certain time zones are affected by the incidence of 'summer time' in countries where it is adopted.

FLIGHT PATHS

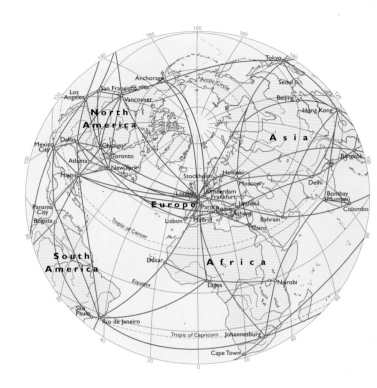

BUSIEST AIRPORTS

(TOTAL NUMBER OF PASSENGERS, 1997)

CHICAGO O'HARE	70,295,000
ATLANTA HARTSFIELD	68,206,000
DALLAS/FORT WORTH	60,489,000
LOS ANGELES INTL.	60,143,000
LONDON HEATHROW	57,975,000
TOKYO HANEDA	49,302,000
SAN FRANCISCO INTL.	40,500,000
FRANKFURT/MAIN	40,263,000
SEOUL/KIMPO INTL.	36,757,000

The flight paths shown on the maps above usually follow the shortest, most direct route from A to B, known as the *great-circle route*. A great circle is any circle that divides the globe into equal halves. Aircraft do not always fly along great-circle routes, however. Lack of search and rescue and emergency landing provisions, together with limits on fuel consumption and minimum flying altitudes, mean that commercial aircraft do not usually fly across Antarctica.

FLIGHT PATHS

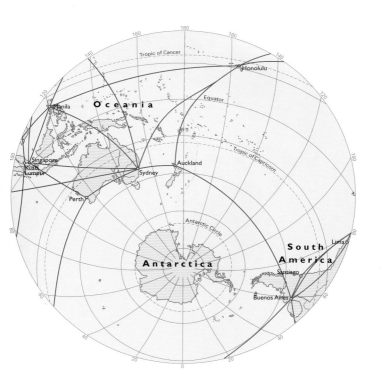

FLIGHT TIMES FROM NEW YORK			FLIGHT TIMES FROM LONDON		
FRANKFURT	8hrs	35mins	ATHENS	4hrs	05mins
JOHANNESBURG	17hrs	45mins	AUCKLAND	24hrs	20mins
MEXICO CITY	5hrs	45mins	BANGKOK	14hrs	30mins
PARIS	8hrs	15mins	BOMBAY (MUMBAI)	11hrs	15mins
ROME	9hrs	35mins	BUENOS AIRES	14hrs	20mins
SANTIAGO	12hrs	55mins	HONG KONG	14hrs	10mins
SINGAPORE	23hrs	10mins	LOS ANGELES	12hrs	00mins
TOKYO	14hrs	35mins	MOSCOW	3hrs	50mins
VANCOUVER	7hrs	25mins	NEW YORK	6hrs	50mins

CLIMATE

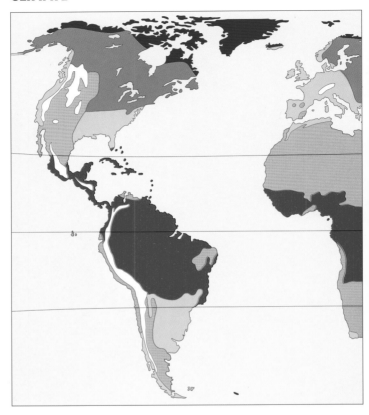

SEASONAL WEATHER EXTREMES

- **Caribbean**
  Hurricanes – August to October

- **Northern Latitudes**
  Blizzards – November to March

- **Southern Asia**
  Cyclones and typhoons – June to November

- **Southern Asia**
  Monsoon rains – July to October

Climate is weather in the long term: the seasonal pattern of temperature and precipitation averaged over a period of time. Temperature roughly follows latitude, warmest near the equator and coldest near the poles. The interplay of various factors, however, namely the differential heating of land and sea, the influence of landmasses and mountain ranges on winds and ocean currents, and the effect of vegetation,

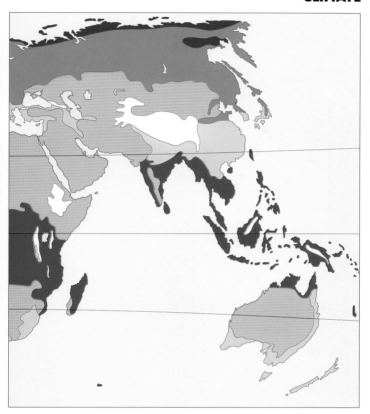

combine to add complexity. Thus New York, Naples and the Gobi Desert share almost the same latitude, but their resulting climates are very different.

Most scientists are now in agreement that the world's climate is changing, due partly to atmospheric pollution. By the year 2050 average world temperatures are predicted to rise by 1.5–2.8°C to make it hotter than at any time during the last 120,000 years.

CLIMATIC REGIONS

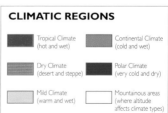

Tropical Climate (hot and wet)

Dry Climate (desert and steppe)

Mild Climate (warm and wet)

Continental Climate (cold and wet)

Polar Climate (very cold and dry)

Mountainous areas (where altitude affects climate types)

Note: Climate comprises a description of the condition of the atmosphere over a considerable area for a long time (at least 30 years).

WEALTH

The most commonly used method of classifying countries according to economic well-being is to calculate the Gross National Product (GNP) per capita (a measure of average income). The World Bank identifies three main groups according to GNP. These are known as high-income, middle-income and low-income economies. Sometimes low- and middle-income economies are referred to as developing countries.

Poverty in developing countries is often exacerbated by crippling debts. In these cases aid from abroad is vital to the population and the economy. The latest figures show that aid to Mozambique (the poorest country in the world with a GNP per capita of only US$90) amounts to more than 70% of its total GNP. In contrast, the country with the world's highest GNP per capita is Luxembourg with US$45,360.

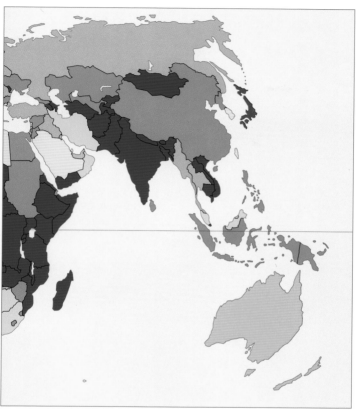

EXCHANGE RATES 2000
(UNITS PER US$)

AUSTRALIA	1.51	ISRAEL	4.09
BELGIUM	39.8	ITALY	1,913
CANADA	1.44	JAPAN	103
EGYPT	3.30	NORWAY	7.98
FRANCE	6.48	S. AFRICA	6.17
GERMANY	1.93	SPAIN	164
HONG KONG	7.73	SWEDEN	8.49
INDONESIA	7,527	UK	0.61

LEVELS OF INCOME

Gross National Product per capita: the value of total production divided by the population (1997)

- Over 400% of world average
- 200 – 400%
- 100 – 200%
- 50 – 100%
- 25 – 50%
- 10 – 25%
- Under 10%

[World average wealth per person US$6,316]

INTERNATIONAL ORGANIZATIONS

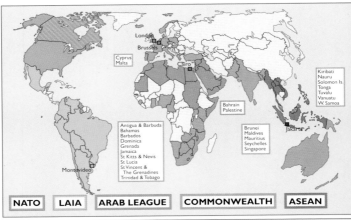

London
Brussels

Cyprus
Malta

Cairo

Kiribati
Nauru
Solomon Is.
Tonga
Tuvalu
Vanuatu
W Samoa

Bahrain
Palestine

Antigua & Barbuda
Bahamas
Barbados
Dominica
Grenada
Jamaica
St Kitts & Nevis
St Lucia
St Vincent &
  The Grenadines
Trinidad & Tobago

Brunei
Maldives
Mauritius
Seychelles
Singapore

Montevideo

Jakarta

| NATO | LAIA | ARAB LEAGUE | COMMONWEALTH | ASEAN |

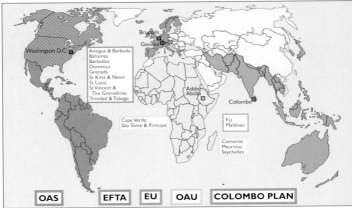

Washington D.C.

Brussels
Geneva

Antigua & Barbuda
Bahamas
Barbados
Dominica
Grenada
St Kitts & Nevis
St Lucia
St Vincent &
  The Grenadines
Trinidad & Tobago

Addis
Ababa

Colombo

Cape Verde
São Tomé & Príncipe

Fiji
Maldives

Comoros
Mauritius
Seychelles

| OAS | EFTA | EU | OAU | COLOMBO PLAN |

GLOSSARY OF ACRONYMS

ACP African-Caribbean-Pacific
ASEAN Association of South-east Asian Nations
CIS Commonwealth of Nations
EFTA European Free Trade Association
EU European Union
LAIA Latin American Integration Association

NATO North Atlantic Treaty Organization
OAS Organization of American States
OAU Organization of African Unity
OECD Organization for Economic Co-operation and Development
OPEC Organization for Petroleum Exporting Countries

INTERNATIONAL ORGANIZATIONS

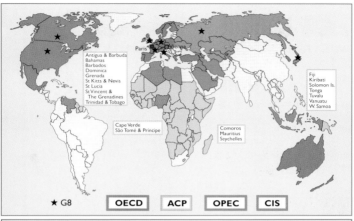

Antigua & Barbuda
Bahamas
Barbados
Dominica
Grenada
St Kitts & Nevis
St Lucia
St Vincent &
The Grenadines
Trinidad & Tobago

Paris Vienna

Fiji
Kiribati
Solomon Is.
Tonga
Tuvalu
Vanuatu
W. Samoa

Cape Verde
São Tomé & Príncipe

Comoros
Mauritius
Seychelles

★ G8   OECD   ACP   OPEC   CIS

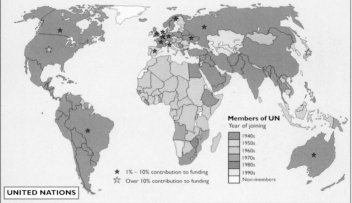

Members of UN
Year of joining

- 1940s
- 1950s
- 1960s
- 1970s
- 1980s
- 1990s
- Non-members

★ 1% – 10% contribution to funding
☆ Over 10% contribution to funding

UNITED NATIONS

THE UNITED NATIONS

Created in 1945 to promote peace and co-operation and based in New York, the UN is the world's largest international organization. The UN budget for 1996–7 was US$2.6 billion; the US contributed the most with 25.0%, followed by Japan 15.4%, then Germany 9.0%. From the original 51, membership of the UN has grown to 185. Recent additions include Andorra, Bosnia-Herzegovina, Moldova, Palau, San Marino and the Slovak Republic. There are only seven independent states which are not members – Kiribati, Nauru, Switzerland, Taiwan, Tonga, Tuvalu and the Vatican City.

WORLD GAZETTEER

AUSTRALIA

AREA 7,686,850 sq km / 2,967,893 sq mls
POPULATION 18,613,000
CAPITAL Canberra
GOVERNMENT Federal constitutional monarchy
LANGUAGES English (official)
CURRENCY Australian dollar
EMPLOYMENT Agriculture 5%, industry 16%, services 78%

BELGIUM

AREA 30,510 sq km / 11,780 sq mls
POPULATION 10,175,000
CAPITAL Brussels
GOVERNMENT Constitutional monarchy
LANGUAGES Dutch, French, German (all official)
CURRENCY Euro; Belgian franc
EMPLOYMENT Agriculture 3%, industry 20%, services 78%

BRAZIL

AREA 8,511,970 sq km / 3,286,472 sq mls
POPULATION 170,000,000
CAPITAL Brasília
GOVERNMENT Federal multiparty republic
LANGUAGES Portuguese (official)
CURRENCY Cruzeiro real
EMPLOYMENT Agriculture 29%, industry 16%, services 55%

CANADA

AREA 9,976,140 sq km / 3,851,788 sq mls
POPULATION 30,675,000
CAPITAL Ottawa
GOVERNMENT Federal constitutional monarchy
LANGUAGES English and French (official)
CURRENCY Canadian dollar
EMPLOYMENT Agriculture 3%, industry 19%, services 77%

CHINA

AREA 9,596,960 sq km / 3,705,386 sq mls
POPULATION 1,236,915,000
CAPITAL Beijing (Peking)
GOVERNMENT Single-party Communist state
LANGUAGES Mandarin Chinese (official)
CURRENCY Renminbi yuan
EMPLOYMENT Agriculture 74%, industry 14%, services 13%

CZECH REPUBLIC

AREA 78,864 sq km / 30,449 sq mls
POPULATION 10,286,000
CAPITAL Prague
GOVERNMENT Multiparty democratic republic
LANGUAGES Czech (official)
CURRENCY Czech koruna
EMPLOYMENT Agriculture 13%, industry 49%, services 37%

DENMARK

AREA 43,070 sq km/16,629 sq mls
POPULATION 5,334,000
CAPITAL Copenhagen
GOVERNMENT Democratic constitutional monarchy
LANGUAGES Danish (official)
CURRENCY Danish krone
EMPLOYMENT Agriculture 5%, industry 22%, services 60%

GERMANY

AREA 356,910 sq km/137,803 sq mls
POPULATION 82,079,000
CAPITAL Berlin/Bonn
GOVERNMENT Federal multiparty republic
LANGUAGES German (official)
CURRENCY Euro; Deutschmark
EMPLOYMENT Agriculture 4%, industry 30%, services 66%

EGYPT

AREA 1,001,450 sq km/386,660 sq mls
POPULATION 66,050,000
CAPITAL Cairo (El Qâhira)
GOVERNMENT Multiparty republic
LANGUAGES Arabic (official), French, English
CURRENCY Egyptian pound
EMPLOYMENT Agriculture 34%, industry 22%, services 60%

GREECE

AREA 131,990 sq km/50,961 sq mls
POPULATION 10,662,000
CAPITAL Athens
GOVERNMENT Multiparty democratic republic
LANGUAGES Greek (official)
CURRENCY Greek drachma
EMPLOYMENT Agriculture 25%, industry 19%, services 56%

FRANCE

AREA 551,500 sq km/212,934 sq mls
POPULATION 58,805,000
CAPITAL Paris
GOVERNMENT Multiparty democratic republic
LANGUAGES French (official)
CURRENCY Euro; French franc
EMPLOYMENT Agriculture 7%, industry 20%, services 74%

HUNGARY

AREA 93,030 sq km/35,919 sq mls
POPULATION 10,208,000
CAPITAL Budapest
GOVERNMENT Multiparty democratic republic
LANGUAGES Hungarian (official)
CURRENCY Hungarian forint
EMPLOYMENT Agriculture 6%, industry 28%, services 66%

WORLD GAZETTEER

INDIA

AREA 3,287,590 sq km/1,269,338 sq mls
POPULATION 984,000,000
CAPITAL New Delhi
GOVERNMENT Federal multiparty republic
LANGUAGES Hindi and English (both official)
CURRENCY Indian rupee
EMPLOYMENT Agriculture 63%, industry 11%, services 27%

JAPAN

AREA 377,800 sq km/145,869 sq mls
POPULATION 125,932,000
CAPITAL Tokyo
GOVERNMENT Democratic constitutional monarchy
LANGUAGES Japanese (official)
CURRENCY Japanese yen
EMPLOYMENT Agriculture 7%, industry 24%, services 69%

IRELAND

AREA 70,280 sq km/27,135 sq mls
POPULATION 3,619,000
CAPITAL Dublin
GOVERNMENT Multiparty democratic republic
LANGUAGES Irish and English (both official)
CURRENCY Euro; Irish pound (Punt)
EMPLOYMENT Agriculture 13%, industry 18%, services 69%

MEXICO

AREA 1,958,200 sq km/756,061 sq mls
POPULATION 98,553,000
CAPITAL Mexico City
GOVERNMENT Multiparty democratic republic
LANGUAGES Spanish (official)
CURRENCY Mexican peso
EMPLOYMENT Agriculture 23%, industry 20%, services 57%

ITALY

AREA 301,270 sq km/116,320 sq mls
POPULATION 56,783,000
CAPITAL Rome
GOVERNMENT Multiparty democratic republic
LANGUAGES Italian (official)
CURRENCY Euro; Italian lira
EMPLOYMENT Agriculture 9%, industry 20%, services 71%

NETHERLANDS

AREA 41,526 sq km/16,033 sq mls
POPULATION 15,731,000
CAPITAL Amsterdam/The Hague
GOVERNMENT Democratic constitutional monarchy
LANGUAGES Dutch (official)
CURRENCY Euro; Dutch guilder (florin)
EMPLOYMENT Agriculture 4%, industry 17%, services 78%

NEW ZEALAND

AREA 268,680 sq km/103,737 sq mls
POPULATION 3,625,000
CAPITAL Wellington
GOVERNMENT Parliamentary democracy
LANGUAGES English and Maori (both official)
CURRENCY New Zealand dollar
EMPLOYMENT Agriculture 10%, industry 20%, services 70%

RUSSIA

AREA 17,075,000 sq km/6,592,000 sq mls
POPULATION 146,861,000
CAPITAL Moscow
GOVERNMENT Federal multiparty republic
LANGUAGES Russian (official), Ukrainian, Belarussian and others
CURRENCY Russian rouble
EMPLOYMENT Agriculture 13%, industry 28%, services 59%

NIGERIA

AREA 923,770 sq km/356,668 sq mls
POPULATION 110,532,000
CAPITAL Abuja (Federal Capital Territory)
GOVERNMENT Transitional government
LANGUAGES English (official)
CURRENCY Nigerian naira
EMPLOYMENT Agriculture 45%, industry 4%, services 51%

SAUDI ARABIA

AREA 2,149,690 sq km/829,995 sq mls
POPULATION 20,786,000
CAPITAL Riyadh
GOVERNMENT Absolute monarchy (with a consultative assembly)
LANGUAGES Arabic (official)
CURRENCY Saudi riyal
EMPLOYMENT Agriculture 49%, industry 14%, services 37%

POLAND

AREA 312,680 sq km/120,726 sq mls
POPULATION 38,607,000
CAPITAL Warsaw
GOVERNMENT Multiparty democratic republic
LANGUAGES Polish (official)
CURRENCY Polish zloty
EMPLOYMENT Agriculture 28%, industry 28%, services 44%

SINGAPORE

AREA 618 sq km/239 sq mls
POPULATION 3,490,000
CAPITAL Singapore City
GOVERNMENT Multiparty republic
LANGUAGES Chinese, Malay, Tamil and English (all official)
CURRENCY Singapore dollar
EMPLOYMENT Agriculture 1%, industry 29%, services 71%

SOUTH AFRICA

AREA 1,219,916 sq km/470,566 sq mls
POPULATION 42,835,000
CAPITAL Cape Town/Pretoria/
Bloemfontein
GOVERNMENT Multiparty republic
LANGUAGES Afrikaans, English, 9 others
CURRENCY South African rand
EMPLOYMENT Agriculture 3%, industry
24%, services 68%

SPAIN

AREA 504,780 sq km/194,896 sq mls
POPULATION 39,134,000
CAPITAL Madrid
GOVERNMENT Constitutional monarchy
LANGUAGES Castilian Spanish (official),
Catalan, Galician, Basque
CURRENCY Euro; Spanish peseta
EMPLOYMENT Agriculture 11%, industry
21%, services 68%

SWEDEN

AREA 449,960 sq km/173,730 sq mls
POPULATION 8,887,000
CAPITAL Stockholm
GOVERNMENT Democratic constitutional
monarchy
LANGUAGES Swedish (official), Finnish
CURRENCY Swedish krona
EMPLOYMENT Agriculture 3%, industry
22%, services 75%

SWITZERLAND

AREA 41,290 sq km/15,942 sq mls
POPULATION 7,260,000
CAPITAL Bern
GOVERNMENT Federal republic
LANGUAGES French, German, Italian and
Romansch (all official)
CURRENCY Swiss franc
EMPLOYMENT Agriculture 6%, industry
30%, services 64%

UNITED KINGDOM

AREA 243,368 sq km/94,202 sq mls
POPULATION 58,970,000
CAPITAL London
GOVERNMENT Democratic constitutional
monarchy
LANGUAGES English (official)
CURRENCY Pound sterling
EMPLOYMENT Agriculture 2%, industry
20%, services 78%

UNITED STATES

AREA 9,372,610 sq km/3,618,765 sq mls
POPULATION 270,290,000
CAPITAL Washington, DC
GOVERNMENT Federal republic
LANGUAGES English (official) and over
30 others
CURRENCY US dollar
EMPLOYMENT Agriculture 3%, industry
18%, services 79%

WORLD MAPS – GENERAL REFERENCE

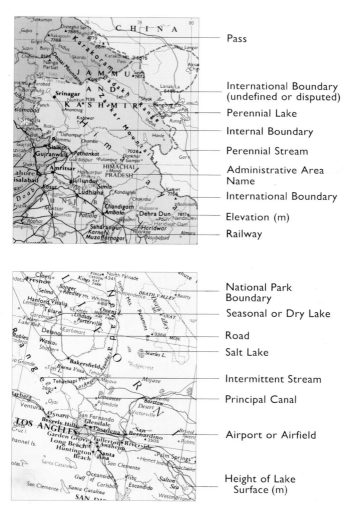

Pass

International Boundary
(undefined or disputed)

Perennial Lake

Internal Boundary

Perennial Stream

Administrative Area
Name

International Boundary

Elevation (m)

Railway

National Park
Boundary

Seasonal or Dry Lake

Road

Salt Lake

Intermittent Stream

Principal Canal

Airport or Airfield

Height of Lake
Surface (m)

Settlements

Settlement symbols and type styles vary
according to the scale of each map and
indicate the importance of towns rather
than specific population figures.

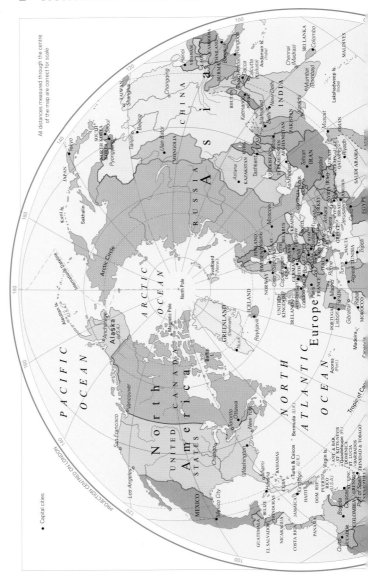

All distances measured through the centre of the map are correct for scale

PROJECTION CENTRED ON LONDON

• Capital cities

TIME ZONES

Zones using Greenwich Mean Time

Zones fast of Greenwich Mean Time

Zones slow of Greenwich Mean Time

Standard Time not the Zone hour

No Official Time

PROJECTION CENTRED ON CAPE TOWN

Cape Town

South Pole

Projection: Oblique Azimuthal Equidistant

PROJECTION CENTRED ON SAN FRANCISCO

San Francisco

North Pole

International Dateline

CARTOGRAPHY BY PHILIP'S

PROJECTION CENTRED ON THE ANTIPODES OF LONDON

All distances measured through the centre of the map are correct for scale

• Capital cities

P A C I F I C   O C E A N

Oceania

I N D I A N

A U S T R A L I A

NEW ZEALAND

Tropic of Cancer

Equator

Tropic of Capricorn

Antarctic Circle

International Dateline

West from Greenwich   East from Greenwich

Galapagos Is. *(Ecuador)*

Easter I. *(Chile)*

Hawaiian Is. *(U.S.A.)*

Marquesas Is. *(Fr.)*

Tuamotu Arch. *(Fr.)*

Pitcairn I. *(U.K.)*

Tahiti *(Fr.)*   FRENCH POLYNESIA

Cook Is. *(N.Z.)*

SAMOA

TONGA

FIJI

Kermadec Is. *(N.Z.)*

Chatham Is. *(N.Z.)*

Antipodes Is. *(N.Z.)*

Auckland

Wellington

Macquarie Is. *(Austral.)*

Auckland Is. *(N.Z.)*

New Caledonia *(Fr.)*

VANUATU

SOLOMON IS.

TUVALU

KIRIBATI

MARSHALL IS.

Midway I. *(U.S.A.)*

Wake I. *(U.S.A.)*

FED. STATES OF MICRONESIA

Northern Marianas (U.S.A.)

Guam *(U.S.A.)*

Bonin Is. *(Japan)*

PHILIPPINES

PALAU

PAPUA NEW GUINEA

Port Moresby

Brisbane

Sydney

Canberra

Tasmania

Adelaide

Perth

VIETNAM

Ho Chi Minh City

BRUNEI

Borneo

MALAYSIA

SINGAPORE

Kuala Lumpur

I N D O N E S I A

Jakarta

Chiang Palyang

Cocos Is. *(Austral.)*

Manila

Magnetic Pole

Victoria Land

Bali

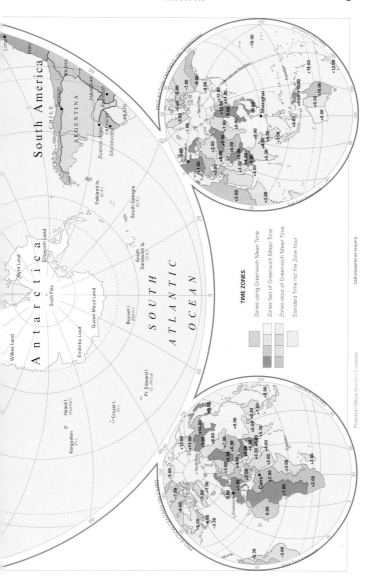

South America

PERU
BOLIVIA
La Paz
PARAGUAY
Santiago
CHILE
ARGENTINA
Buenos Aires
URUGUAY
Montevideo
BRAZIL
Asunción

Falkland Is. *(U.K.)*
South Georgia *(U.K.)*
South Sandwich Is. *(U.K.)*
Bouvet I. *(Nor.)*

Antarctica
Byrd Land
Ellsworth Land
Wilkes Land
Queen Maud Land
Enderby Land
South Pole

SOUTH ATLANTIC OCEAN

Pr. Edward I. *(S. African)*
Crozet I. *(Fr.)*
Heard I. *(Austral.)*
Kerguelen *(Fr.)*

TIME ZONES

Zones using Greenwich Mean Time
Zones fast of Greenwich Mean Time
Zones slow of Greenwich Mean Time
Standard Time not the Zone hour

Shanghai

North Pole
Greenwich
International Dateline
Equator

Cairo
Greenwich
North Pole
Equator

Projection Oblique Azimuthal Equidistant

CARTOGRAPHY BY PHILIP'S

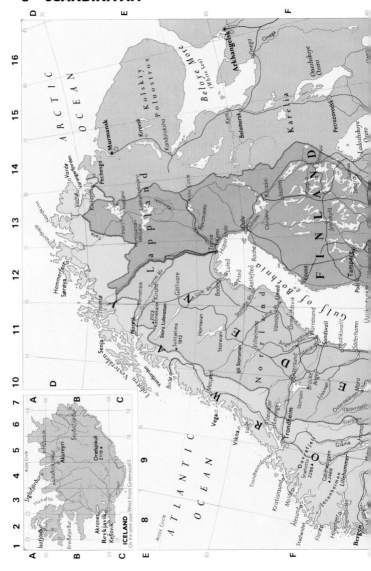

ARCTIC OCEAN

Norway
Sweden
Finland
Lappland
Karélia
Kolskiy Poluostrov

Beloye More (White Sea)

Arkhangelsk
Onega
Onezhskoye Ozero
Petrozavodsk
Ladozhskoye Ozero

Murmansk
Kirovsk
Kandalaksha
Kem
Belomorsk

Vardø
Vadsø
Varangerfjorden
Pechenga
Kirkenes
Inari
Ivalo
Sodankylä

Arctic Circle

Hammerfest
Sørøya
Nordkapp
Tana
Nordkinn

Rovaniemi
Kemijärvi
Kittilä
Kemi
Tornio
Haparanda
Oulu
Oulujoki
Kajaani
Iisalmi
Kuopio
Jyväskylä
Tampere

FINLAND

Gulf of Bothnia

Vaasa
Pori
Uusikaupunki

Narvik
Tromsø
Senja
Vesterålen
Lofoten
Kebnekaise 2123
Torne älv
Kiruna
Gällivare
Storaván
Boden
Luleå
Luleå älv
Piteå
Skellefteå
Umeå
Vindeln

Stora Lulevatten
Sulitjelma 1913
Hornaván

Norrland

Vännäs
Örnsköldsvik
Härnösand
Sundsvall
Hudiksvall
Söderhamn

Bodø
Storuman
Mospell
Vega
Vikna

SWEDEN

Ammarnäs
Wilhelmina
Ångermanälven
Ådalsliden
Sollefteå
Ånge
Östersund
Storsjön
Bräcke
Ljusdal

Trondheim
Trondheimsfjorden
Stenkjer
Levanger
Dovrefjell
Snøhetta 2286
Galdhøpiggen 2469
Glåma

Österdalälven
Klarälven
Västerdalälven

Kristiansund
Molde
Åndalsnes
Ålesund
Stadlandet
Florø
Høyanger
Sognefjord
Sognefjorden
Bergen

NORWAY

Jotunheimen
Lillehammer
Hamar

ARCTIC OCEAN

ATLANTIC OCEAN

Arctic Circle

ATLANTIC OCEAN

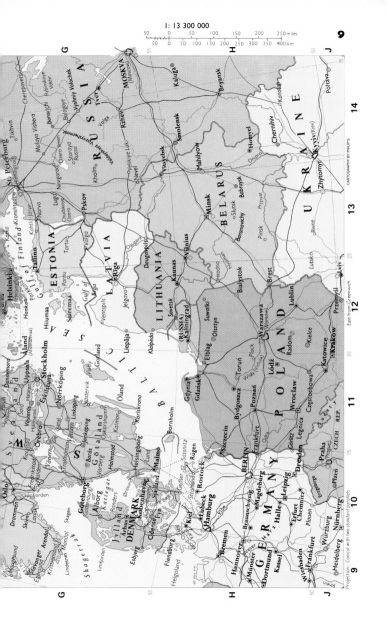

1: 13 300 000

50   0   50   100   150   200   250 miles
50   0   50   100   150   200   250   300   350   400 km

9

CARTOGRAPHY BY PHILIP'S

Projection: Conical with two standard parallels

East from Greenwich

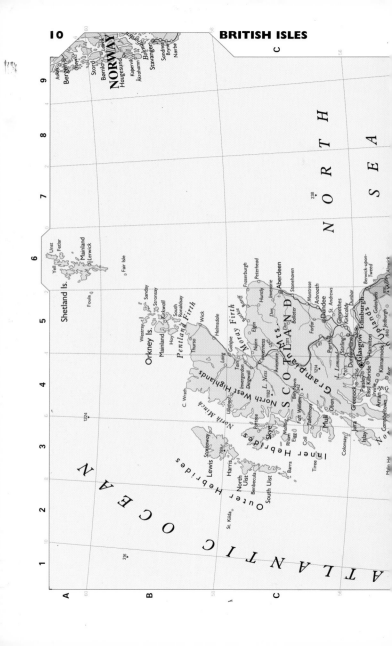

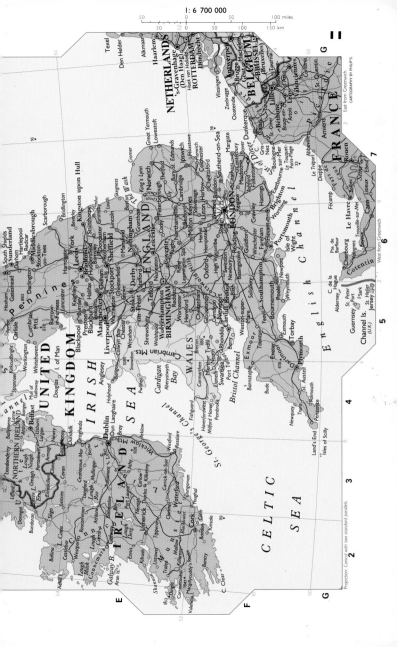

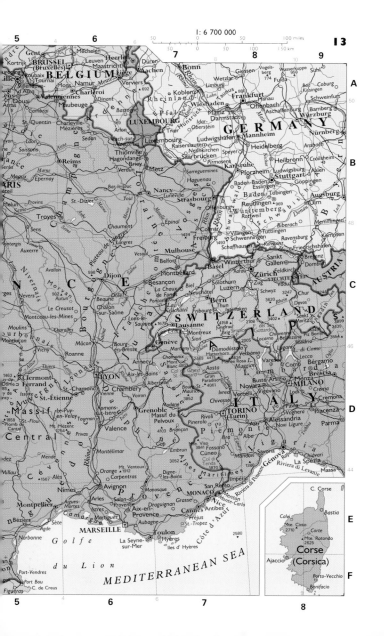

Projection: Conical with two standard parallels

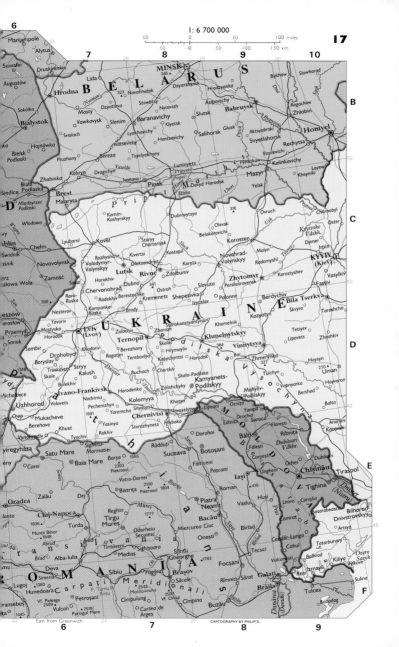

1: 6 700 000

50   0   50   100 miles

50   0   50   100 150 km

FRANCE

Montpellier   Arles   Camargue

Graulhet   1266

Auch   Castres   Béziers   Sète

Dax   Orthez   Toulouse   Canal du Midi   Agde   Golfe du Lion

Biarritz   Bayonne   Pau   Béarn   Carcassonne   Narbonne

San Sebastián   Renteria   Lourdes   Pamiers   Saint-Gaudens   Limoux

Eibar   V a s   Pamplona   Pyrénées   2872   Foix   Perpignan   Roussillon   Port-Vendres   A

Vitoria   Afaniz   Navarra   Puerto de   Jaca   3355   Pico del   3080   Andorra la   Mt. Canigou   Port Bou   C. de Creus

Somport   Mte. Perdido   Aneto   3404   Vella   Puigcerdá   Figueras   G. de Rosas

Logroño   Tafalla   Argüís   ANDORRA   Seo de Urgel   Olot   42

Calahorra   Tudela   Huesca   Tremp   Berga   Gerona   San Feliú de Guixols

Tarazona   Barbastro   Manresa   Vich   Costa Brava

Sierra del Moncayo   2316   Monzón   1677   Igualada   Granollers   Blanes   Lloret de Mar

Almazán   Zaragoza   Balaguer   Cervera   Tarrasa   Sabadell   Badalona   Mataro

Calatayud   Lérida   Hospitalet de   Santa Coloma de Gramanet   B

Sigüenza   Caspe   Valls   Llobregat   BARCELONA

Calamocha   Alcañiz   Reus   Sitges   El Prat de Llobregat

Montalbán   Tortosa   Tarragona   Villanueva y Geltrú   Costa Dorada

Teruel   2019   Morella   G. de   San Jorge   C. de Tortosa   2410

Cuenca   Castellón de la Plana   40

Orden   Onda   Is. Columbretes   1700   C. de Formentor   Mahón

Vall de Uxó   Villarreal   Sóller   1445   Inca   Menorca

Lliria   Sagunto   Baleares   Palma de   Manacor

Requena   Torrente   VALENCIA   Golfo de   Mallorca   Calviá   Lluchmayor   Mallorca

La Albufera   B. de Palma   Cabrera   C

Algemesí   Sueca   Valencia   Ibiza

Albacete   Alcira   Cullera   San Antonio   Ibiza

Játiva   Gandía   Formentera

Almansa   Alcoy   Denia   C. de la Nao

Villarrobledo   Yecla   1558   Altea

La Roda   Jumilla   Elda   Benidorm   SEA

Hellín   Cieza   Elche   Villajoyosa

Murcia   Orihuela   Alicante

Caravaca   2001   Alcantarilla   Torrevieja   Costa Blanca

Mula   Murcia   Mar Menor

Vélez   Lorca   Cartagena   C. de Palos

Rubio   Mazarrón

Baza   Almanzora   Aguilas

Cuevas del   Vera   ALGERIA

Almanzora   2700   ALGIERS   D

Almería   Birkhadem   Bordj el Kifan

Roquetas   C. de Gata   Ain Benian   Koléa   Maison   Bordj Menaiel

de Mar   Cherchell   Bou Ismael   Boufarik   El Arba

Fourches   C. Kramis   Gouraya   Djendel   Medéa   Sour el Ghozlane

Oran   Arzew   Massif de Dahra   1146   Miliana   Berrouaghia   Sidi-Aissa   36

C. Falcon   Ech Cheliff   Blida   Ksar el Boukhari

Mostaganem   Ain Tédelès   Chliff   Khemis   Theniet   Chabounia   Ain Oussera

Hammam   Mohammadia   Oued Rhiou   1986   Miliana   el Had   Zahrez   E

Bouhadjar   Relizane   Tissemsilt   Hamodia   Ksar Chergui

Beni Saf   Mascara   Tiaret   Chellala

Ain Témouchent   Sougueur

Ghazaouet   Remchi

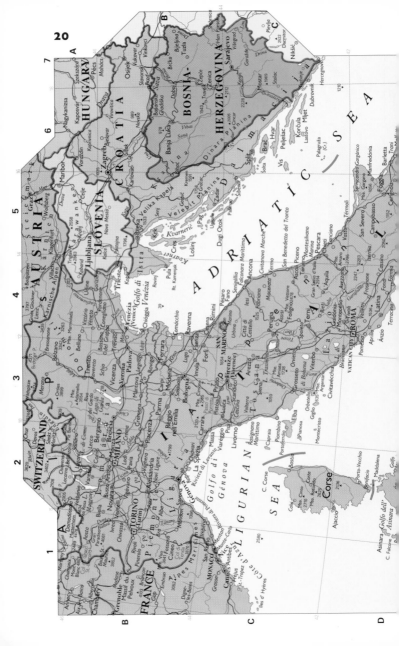

1: 6 700 000

50 0 50 100 miles
50 0 50 100 150 km

Projection: Conical with two standard parallels

East from Greenwich

IONIAN SEA

TYRRHENIAN SEA

MEDITERRANEAN SEA

Sardegna

NAPOLI

Str. di Messina

MALTA

ALGERIA

TUNISIA

Tunis

Golfe de Tunis

Golfe de Hammamet

Reggio di Calàbria

Catània

Siracusa

Isole Éolie

Monti Nebròdi

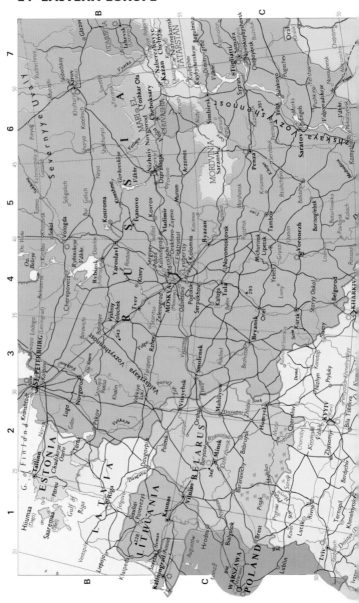

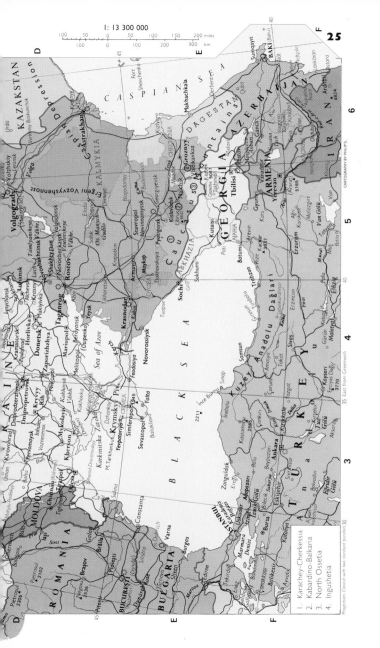

25

1: 13 300 000

Projection: Conical with two standard parallels 30
CARTOGRAPHY BY PHILIP'S

1. Karachey-Cherkessia
2. Kabardino-Balkana
3. North Ossetia
4. Ingushetia

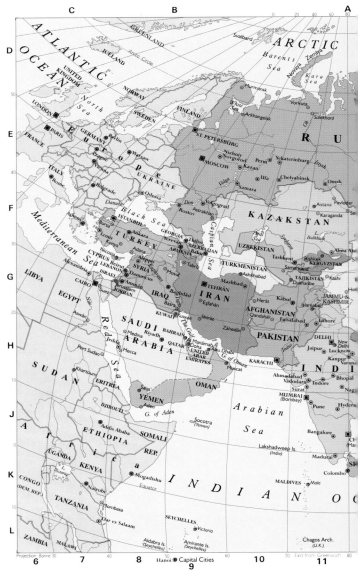

Hanoi ● Capital Cities

1: 67 000 000

200   0   200   400   600   800   1000   1200 miles
200   0   400   800   1200   1600   2000 km

B   C   D

120   140   160   180

OCEAN

Severnaya
Zemlya

Laptev
Sea

New
Siberian
Is.

Wrangel
Is.

ALASKA
(U.S.A.)

Bering
Sea

Aleutian Is.
(U.S.A.)

50

Khatanga

Verkhoyansk

Gizhiga

...sk

Lena

Yakutsk

Sea of
Okhotsk

Magadan

Okhotsk

E

Krasnoyarsk   Bratsk   L. Baikal

Angara

Chita

Ulan Ude

Amur

Blagoveshchensk

Khabarovsk

Sakhalin

Komsomolsk

40

Yuzhno-
Sakhalinsk

Kuril
Is.

Hokkaidō

Sapporo

Petropavlovsk-
Kamchatsky

sibirsk
Novokuznetsk

Irkutsk

Hailar

Qiqihar

Harbin

Changchun

Vladivostok

F

Ürümqi   Hami

Ulan Bator

MONGOLIA

Baotou

Yumen

Lanzhou

Huang-ho

Xi'an

Taiyuan

BEIJING   TIANJIN

Jinan

SHENYANG   Anshan

Jinzhou   Dalian

NORTH
KOREA

Pyongyang

SEOUL   SOUTH
KOREA

Pusan

Sea of
Japan

Honshū

TŌKYŌ

Yokohama

Kyōto

Nagoya   JAPAN

Hiroshima   Ōsaka

Kyūshū

Sapporo

30

Bonin Is.
(Japan)

G

TIBET

Lhasa

Chengdu

Yangtze

Wuhan

Nanjing

SHANGHAI

HANGZHOU   East

Nanchang   China

Fuzhou

Changsha

CHONGQING

CHINA

Kunming

Si Kiang

GUANGZHOU

HONG KONG

Macau

Taipei   RYUKYU
Is.

TAIWAN

Sea

Yellow
Sea

Volcano Is.
(Japan)

Tropic of Cancer

20

H

Thimphu

BHUTAN

Brahmaputra

...ndu

Ganges

Patna

BANGLADESH

DACCA

CALCUTTA

Kolka(a)

BURMA
(MYANMAR)

Chittagong

Hanoi   Haiphong

Hainan

LAOS

Vientiane

VIETNAM

Luzon

MANILA   PHILIPPINES

Mindanao

Davao

GUAM
(U.S.A.)

FED. STATES
OF MICRONESIA

PALAU

10

J

Bay of
Bengal

Rangoon

Andaman Is.
(India)

THAILAND

BANGKOK

CAMBODIA

Phnom Penh

G. of
Thailand

Ho Chi Minh
City

South China Sea

Palawan

Sulu
Sea

Zamboanga

Celebes   Sea

Manado

BRUNEI   SABAH

Bandar Seri Begawan

0

K

Nicobar Is.
(India)

Medan

Str. of Malacca

PEN.
MALAYSIA

Kuala Lumpur

SINGAPORE

MALAYSIA

SARAWAK

Sumatra

Borneo

Celebes

INDONESIA

Ujung Pandang

Banda   Sea

Ambon

Ceram

Halmahera

IRIAN

JAYA

10

L

OCEAN

Palembang

Banjarmasin

Java   Sea

JAKARTA   Bandung

Java

Semarang   Surabaya

Sumba

Flores

EAST
TIMOR

Timor

Timor Sea

Arafura Sea

AUSTRALIA

12   13   14   15   16   17

90   100   110   120   130   140

CARTOGRAPHY BY PHILIP'S

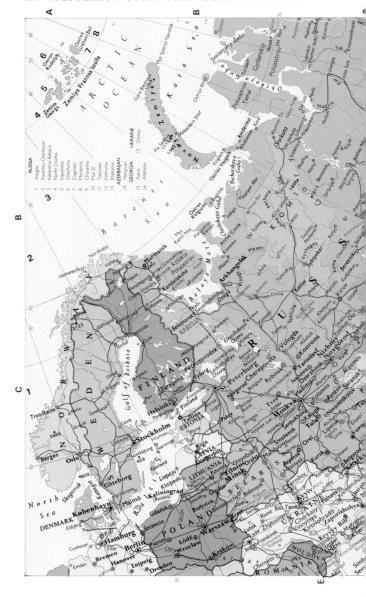

100   0   100   200   300   400   500 miles
100   0   200   400   600   800 km

East from Greenwich

Projection: Conical Orthomorphic with two standard parallels

CARTOGRAPHY BY PHILIP'S

A

1 Zemlya
Georga
2 Ostrov
Rudolfa 3
Ostrov Graham Bell
Zemlya Frantsa Iosifa
4
5
6 Ostrov
Pioner
7
Mys Arkticheskiy
8
Ostrov
Komsomolets
9
Ostrov Oktyabrskoy
Revolyutsii
965
10
11 2800
12
13

B

ARCTIC OCEAN

Severnaya
Zemlya
Proliv Vilkitskogo
Ostrov Bolshevik

Laptev
Sea
Ostrov Novosi

Gora Bolshaya
Novaya Zemlya
Mys Sporyy Navolok
Kara Sea
Ostrov Belyy

Poluostrov
Gory Byrranga 1146
Taymyr
Oz. Taymyr
Nordvik
Ostrov Bolshoy
Begichev

70

Amderma
Poluostrov Yamal
Obskaya Guba
Yuribey
Gydanskiy
Nosok
Poluostrov
Ust Port
Karaul
Dickson
Pyasina
Agapa
Volochanka
Kheta
Khatanga
Popigay
Novorybnoye
Nyurung Kyuyol
Saskylakh
Bulun
Kyusyur

Khalmer Yu
Novyy Port
Tazovskiy
(Khalmer-Sede)
Nyda
Norilsk
Gory
Putorana
1701
Potapovo
Ust Olenek
Anabar
Olenek
Dzhardzh

C

Nadym
Urengoy
Tarko Sale
Pur
Taz
Krasnoselkupsk
Igarka
Karasino
Turukhansk
Noginsk
Nizhnyaya Tunguska
Tura
Vilyuy
962
Stolgontsy
Arctic Circle
S
I
A
Ugolyoye
Vilyu

60

Surgut
Nizhne-
Vartovsk
Aleksandrovskoye
Laryak
Strezhevoy
Taylakova
Podkamennaya
Tunguska
Boykit
Kuyumba
Mutoray
Verkhneye
Kalinino
Yerbogachen
Kurya
Romano
Vitim
Nokh

Kargasok
Kolpashevo
Belyy Yar
Maksimkin
Yar
Kel
Katanga
Sym
1104
Yartsevo
Severo-
Yeniseyskiy
Kezhma
Dubrovskoye
Karshunovo
Kirensk

Tara
Tomsk
Bakchar
Molchanovo
Chulym
Yenisey
Strelka
Usye
Angara
Kondratyevo
Ust-Ilimsk
Zheleznogorsk
Makarovo
Nizhneangarsk

D

Novosibirsk
Anzhero Sudzhensk
Kemerovo
Leninsk Kuznetskiy
Belovo
Kiselevsk
Prokopyevsk
Novo-
Kuznetsk
Asino
Bogotol
Achinsk
Kansk
Vostochnyy
Marinsk
Krasnoyarsk
Nevanka
Ilanskiy
Tayshet
Zayarsk
Bratsk
Ust-Kut
Ust-Ilga

Barnaul
Biysk
HAKASSIA
Minusinsk
Abakan
Artemovsk
Voznesenka
Tulun
Zima
Nizhneudinsk
Angara
2840

Pavlodar
Rubtsovsk
Gorno-Altaysk
(Gorn-Altay)
Zapadnyy
Sayan
Turan
TUVA
Munku Sardyk
3491
Cheremkhovo
Usolye Sibirskoye
Irkutsk
Angarsk
1620
Ulan Ude
Chita

50

Semey
Oskemen
Belukha
4506
GORNO-ALTAY
Kyzyl
Chadan
Khem
Kyzyl
Hovsgol
Nuur
Gusinoozersk
Kyakhta
Petrovsk
Zabaykalskiy
Khilok

E

Narymskaya
Uss Nuur

6
7
8

100
110

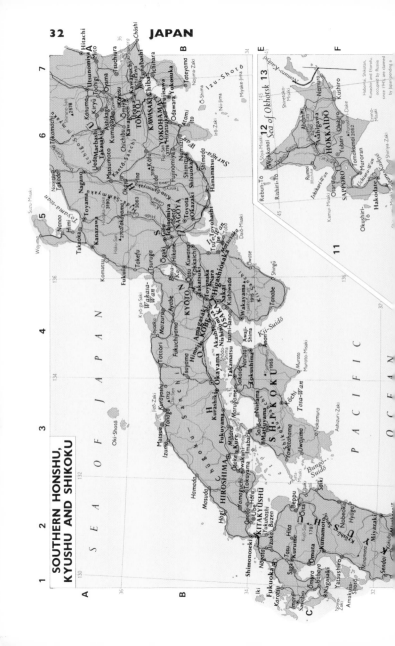

SOUTHERN HONSHU, KYUSHU AND SHIKOKU

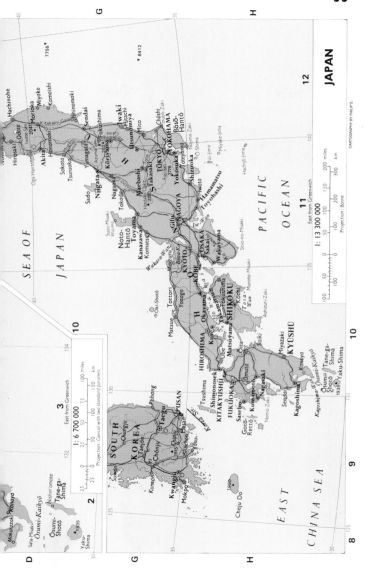

33

CARTOGRAPHY BY PHILIP'S

SEA OF

JAPAN

PACIFIC

OCEAN

EAST

CHINA SEA

SOUTH

KOREA

KYUSHU

SHIKOKU

HIROSHIMA

KITAKYUSHU

FUKUOKA

Nagasaki

Kagoshima

Kumamoto

NAGOYA

KYOTO

OSAKA

KOBE

TOKYO

YOKOHAMA

Niigata

Sendai

Akita

1 : 13 300 000

East from Greenwich

Projection: Bonne

1 : 6 700 000

East from Greenwich

Projection: Conical with two standard parallels

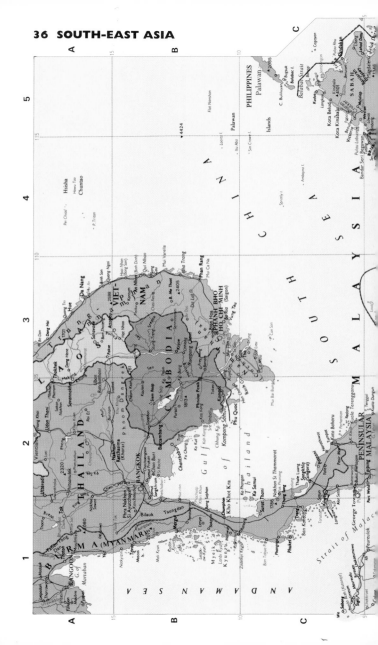

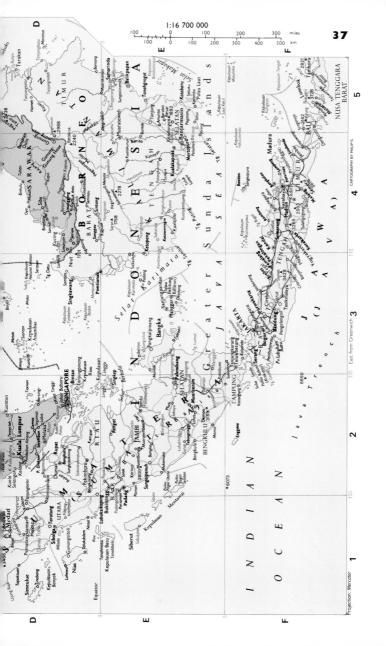

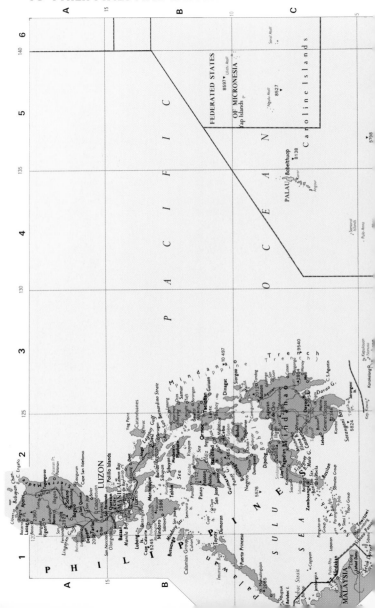

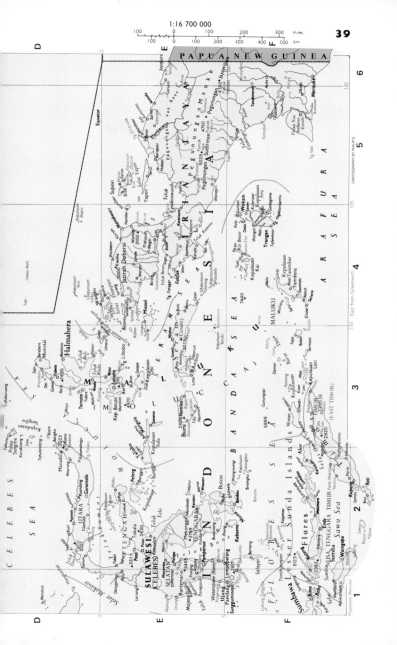

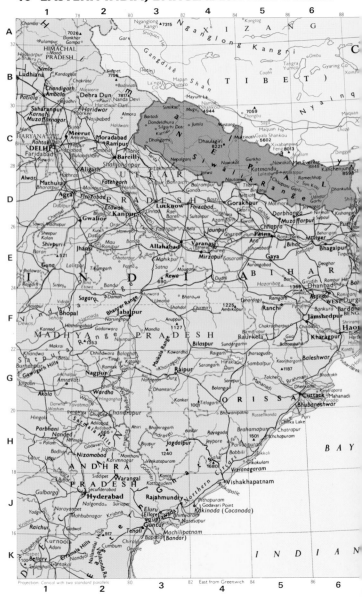

Projection: Conical with two standard parallels

East from Greenwich

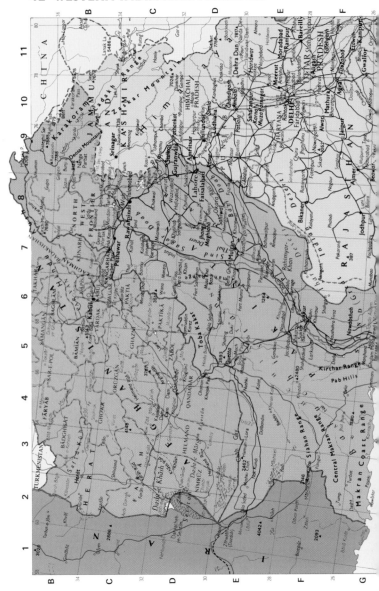

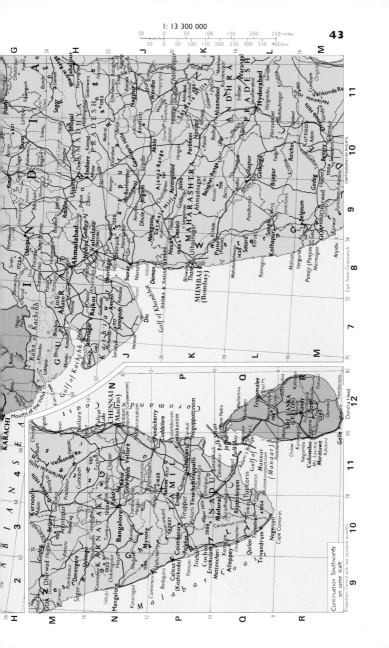

1: 13 300 000

50   0   50   100   150   200   250 miles
50   0   50 100 150 200 250 300 350 400 km

5   6   68   7   8

UZBEKISTAN

Bukhoro
Chärjew
(Chardzhou)

Qarshi Kasansay Shakhrisabz
Guzar Denau Ordzhonikidzeabad

Dushanbe TAJIKISTAN
Qŭrghonteppa Kŭlob Khorog
Pamir

B

Chamkhakly Kerki
Mary Andkhvoy Aqchah
Bayramaly Iolotan Shebarghan
Murgab Mazār-e Sharīf
Khōlm
Termiz
BALKH
Baghlān
TAKHAR
BADAKHSHAN 7690 7709
Feyzābād

36

Mary (Mesbed) Tashkepri Meymaneh SAR-E-POL SAMANGAN
FARYĀB Sayghān
Sang-e-Māsheh KAPISA Kābul NANGARHAR
Peshawar Islāmābād Rawal-
pindi

C

Herāt 3588 Owbeh Safīd Kūh Kohi-Bābā 8143
Chaghcharān Shamālū VARDAK LOWGAR
Gardēz PAKTIĀ Khōwst
Spin Ghar WEST Salt Range Sargodha

32

AFGHANISTAN ORŪZGĀN GHAZNĪ Ghaznī
PAKTIKĀ FRONTIER
4148 3787
Mūsā Qal'eh Qalāt-e Ma'rūf Toba Kakar
Hindu Bagh
Quetta 3593
Multān

D

QANDAHĀR Qandahār Chaman
Kūshkak Arghandāb
HELMAND Rīgestān
ZĀBOL Zaranj NĪMRŪZ Dasht-e Mārgow
Hāmūn-i Lora

Seistan Chāh Gay 2462
Kalāt
BALUCHISTAN

28

Dasht-i-Tahlab 2480
PAKISTAN
Jacobābād Sukkur
INDIA 387
GREAT INDIAN DESERT

E

SISTĀN VA BALŪCHISTĀN Siahan Range Kohān
Panguras 2146 Pab Hills 1980
Central Makran Range Makran Coast Range
Hyderabad

ARABIAN SEA 4122
KARACHI
Mouths of the Indus
Rann of Kachchh
KACHCHH
Gulf of Kachchh
Jamnagar

F

Tropic of Cancer

Oman Masqat (Muscat) Al Qurayyāt

24

20

60   5   64   6   CARTOGRAPHY BY PHILIP'S.   7

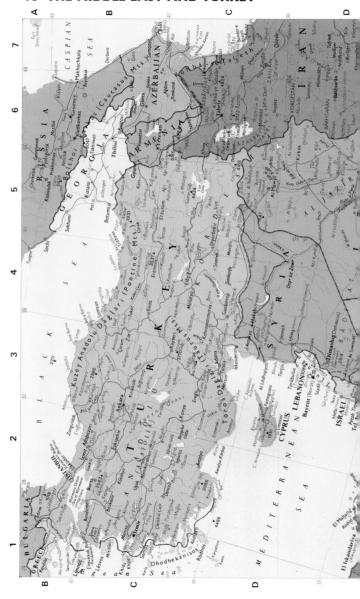

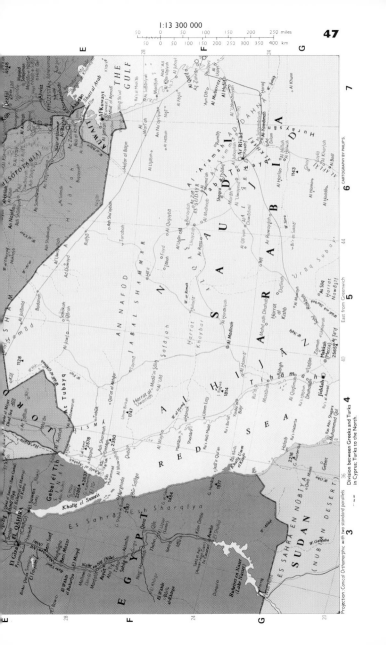

1:13 300 000

50   0   50   100   150   200   250 miles
50 0 50 100 150 200 250 300 350 400 km

E   F   G

7

CARTOGRAPHY BY PHILIPS.

6

East from Greenwich

5

Projection Conical Orthomorphic with two standard parallels

3   Division between Greeks and Turks 4
- - - in Cyprus: Turks to the North.

THE GULF

KUWAIT
Al Kuwayt

Sharaz al Arab

KHUZISTAN
Ahraz

MESOPOTAMIA
(IRAQ)

AL HAJARA

AD DAHNA

SAUDI

ARABIA

Ar Riyad

NAJD

AN NAFUD

JABAL SHAMMAR

Buraydah

Al Madinah

HIJAZ

Tihama

Makkah
(Mecca)
2665

RED SEA

Jiddah

Ras Abu Shagara
C. Muhammad Qol

SINAI
Gebel el Tih

SHAM

AT TUBAYQ

Dead Sea

EGYPT

EL QAHIRA
(Cairo)
Pyramids

Khalig el Suweis

Es Sahra esh Sharqiya

SUDAN
ES SAHRA EN NUBIA
(NUBIAN DESERT)

Buheiret en Nasir
(Lake Nasser)

28   E

F   24

G   20

AFGHANISTAN

Zābol

Bīrjand

Dasht-e Lūt

Kermān

I R A N

Yazd

Kavīr

Eşfahān

Kāshān

Shīrāz

Borūjerd

Dezfūl

Ahvāz

Khorramshahr

Bandar-e Khomeynī

Būshehr

Bandar 'Abbās

Str. of Hormuz

Gulf of Oman

Masqaţ (Muscat)

O M A N

Maşīrah

THE GULF

Ad Dammām

Al Hufūf

Ash Shāriqah

Dubayy (Dubai)

Abū Zaby (Abu Dhabi)

UNITED ARAB EMIRATES

Al Kuwayt (Kuwait)

Al Başrah

Baghdād

Al Jazīrah (Mesopotamia)

Karbalā'

Al Hillah

I R A Q

SYRIA

Dimashq (Damascus)

Bayrūt

LEBANON

ISRAEL

Tel Aviv

Ammān

JORDAN

EGYPT

El Suweis (Suez)

Aswān

Bahra en Nasir (Lake Nasser)

Es Sahrâ esh Sharqîya

Es Sahra en Nûbîya (Nubian Desert)

An Nafūd

Ar Riyāḑ (Riyadh)

S A U D I   A R A B I A

Al Madīnah

Makkah (Mecca)

Jiddah

Aţ Ṭā'if

Tropic of Cancer

A S Ī R

Bur Sūdān

Suakin

R E D   S E A

Rub' al Khali

A R A B I A N   S E A

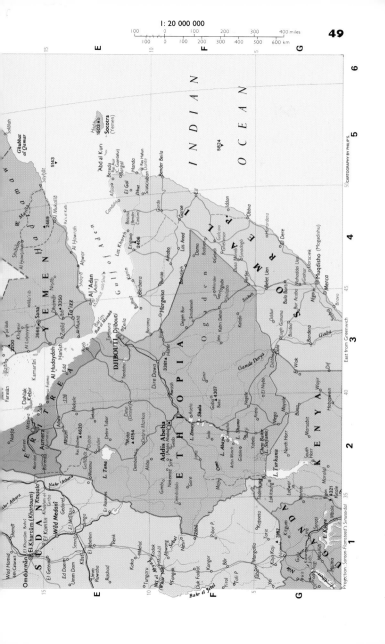

100   0   100   200   300   400 miles
100 0 100 200 300 400 500 600 km

INDIAN

OCEAN

Socotra
(Yemen)
Abd al Kuri

Soqatra

Ghubbat
al Qamar

W. Maşîla

Shiḥan

Al Ḥulaymah

Sayḥût

5143

Al Mukallā

2469

Ra's al Kalb

Al Ḥawrah

Shabwah

Al Luḥayyah

Ra's al Hadn
Dante

Bereda
Ras Hafun
(Guardafui)
Burgao

Aluula

El Gal
Dhut

Hondo

5824

Bargal

Scauscuban
Dante

Bender Beila

YEMEN

'Uzho

Khudur

2000

Şan'ā'
3666
Dhamār
3350
Ta'izz

Zabîd
3194

Jīzān

oLodar

Al 'Adan
(Aden)

Balhaf

Shuqrā'

Aşyân

Karîn

Gulf   of   Aden

Alula

Candala

Bosaso
(Bender
Cassim)

Gardo

Iskushuban

Obbia

YEMEN

Farasān

Dahlak
Kebir

Kamarân

Hanîsh

Al Ḥudaydah
Edd

Bāb al Mandab

Zeila
Berbera

Borama

Hargeisa

Erigavo
2406

Las Khoreh

Burao

Mt Kebri Dehar
Galcaio

Eyl

Hargeisa

Harardera

Ras Hadu

El Dere

SUDAN

Shendi

Omdurmân
El Khartûm Bahri
El Khartûm (Khartoum)
Wâd Medanî

En Nahud

Kassala

Gedaref

El Obeid

Sennar

Nahr el Atbara
Atbara

Ed Damer

Keren
Asmera

Barentu

Mitsiwa
Zula

Adwa
Adigrat

Ra's Kasar

Mek'elē

Aksum

Nakfa

ERITREA

DJIBOUTI
Djibouti

Dire Dawa

Harar

Jijiga

Tendaho

Dese
(Dessye)

Debre Markos

Woldia
4154

Debre Tabor

L. Tana

Addis Abeba
(Addis Ababa)
Nazret

Debre Zeyit

ETHIOPIA

3381

Aware

Degeh Bur

Imi

Scusciuban

Werder

Gerlogubi
Shilabo

Kebri Dehar

K'elafo

Dolo

Bardera

Belet Uen

Bulo Burti

Galcaio

Obbia

S   O   M   A   L   I   A

Hobyo

Harardera

El Dere

Bulaxar

Algoi

Brava

Merca

Muqdisho
(Mogadishu)

Marka

Mareb

Aksum

Gonder

Goba
4307
Bati

Asela

Metu

Gimbi

Nek'emte

Jima

Shashemenē

L. Abaya

Ch'ew Bahir
(L. Stefanie)

Soddo

L. Zway

Wonji

Shala

Neghelli

Wag

Ganale Dorya

Dolo

Juba
Lugh Ganana

El Wak

Giamame

Bur Acaba

Baidoa

Dinsor

Audegle

Bur Hacaba

SUDAN

Malakâl

Renk

Kôdok

Kaka

Melut

Abwong

Nâsir
Wât el Abyad
Ayod

KENYA

Mandera

Wajir

Habaswein

Buna

El Wak

Mado
Gashi

L. Turkana

North Horr

Marsabit

Bahr el Jebel

Bor

Nagishot

Kapoeta

Lokichokio

Lokitaung

Kangen

Dûk Faidît

Kongor

Pibor P.

Pibor

Lotagipi

Lodwar

Tirol

Moyale

4321

Lokwar

Jerer

Wabe Gestro

Dawa

UGANDA

Mongalla

Nimule

3187

Kitgum

Gulu

Kotido

Moroto

Koji Koji

Kaberamaido

Soroti

INDIAN

OCEAN

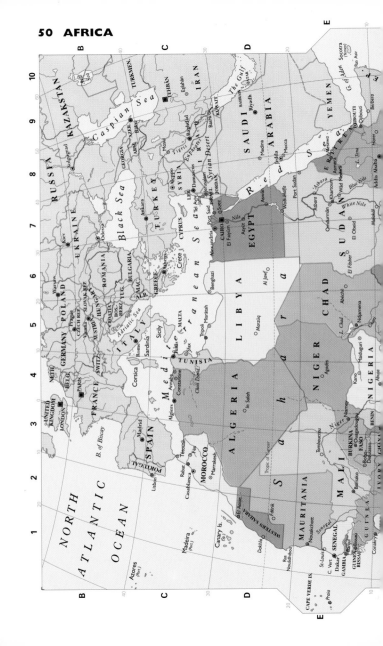

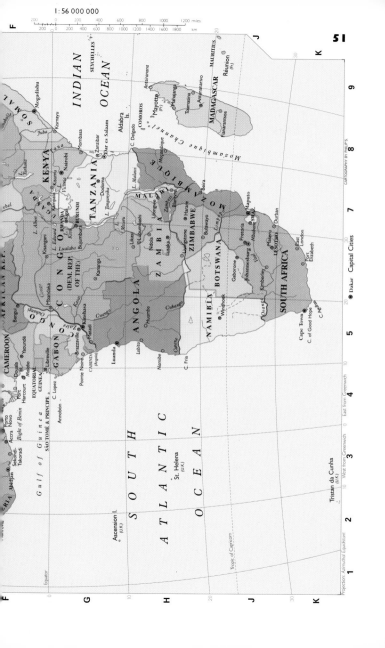

1 : 56 000 000

200 0 200 400 600 800 1000 1200 miles
200 0 200 400 600 800 1000 1200 1400 1600 1800 km

51

CARTOGRAPHY BY PHILIP'S

● Dakar Capital Cities

Projection: Azimuthal Equidistant

Equator

Tropic of Capricorn

West from Greenwich   East from Greenwich

INDIAN OCEAN

SEYCHELLES

Aldabra Is.

COMOROS Mayotte

MAURITIUS Réunion (Fr.)

MADAGASCAR

Antsiranana
Mahajanga
Toamasina
Antananarivo
Fianarantsoa

SOMALI

Mogadishu

Kismayu

Mombasa
Dar es Salaam
Zanzibar
C. Delgado

KENYA
Nairobi
Nakuru
Kisumu
L. Turkana
L. Edward
L. Victoria

UGANDA
Kampala

RWANDA Kigali
BURUNDI Bujumbura

TANZANIA
Dodoma

MOZAMBIQUE
Nampula
Mozambique
Beira
Maputo

MALAWI
Lilongwe
Blantyre
L. Malawi

Mozambique Channel

CONGO (DEM. REP. OF THE)
Zaïre
Kinshasa
Brazzaville
Kananga
Mbandaka
Kisangani
Lubumbashi
Likasi
L. Tanganyika

ZAMBIA
Lusaka
Ndola
Kitwe

ZIMBABWE
Harare
Bulawayo

BOTSWANA
Gaborone

Livingstone

ANGOLA
Luanda
Lobito
Benguela
Huambo
Namibe
CABINDA (Angola)

GABON
Libreville
Port Gentil
C. Lopez

CAMEROON
Douala
Yaoundé

EQUATORIAL GUINEA
Malabo
Bata

SAO TOMÉ & PRÍNCIPE
Annobón

GHANA
Accra

NIGERIA
Port Harcourt

Lagos
Porto Novo
Abidjan
Sekondi-Takoradi

Gulf of Guinea
Bight of Benin

NAMIBIA
Windhoek

SOUTH AFRICA
Pretoria
Johannesburg
Kimberley
Cape Town
C. of Good Hope
Port Elizabeth
East London
Durban
Bloemfontein

LESOTHO Maseru
SWAZILAND Mbabane

SOUTH ATLANTIC OCEAN

Ascension I. (U.K.)

St. Helena (U.K.)

Tristan da Cunha (U.K.)

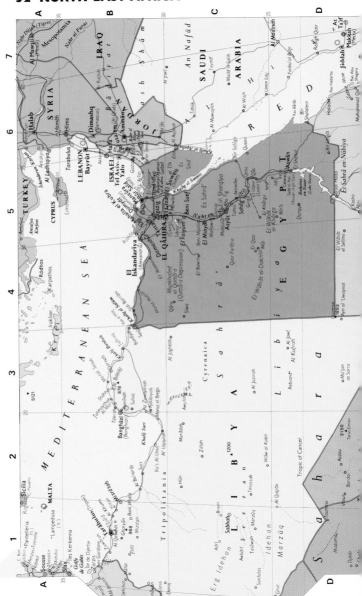

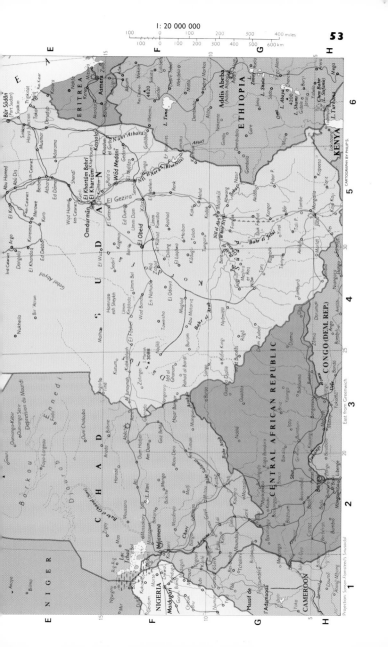

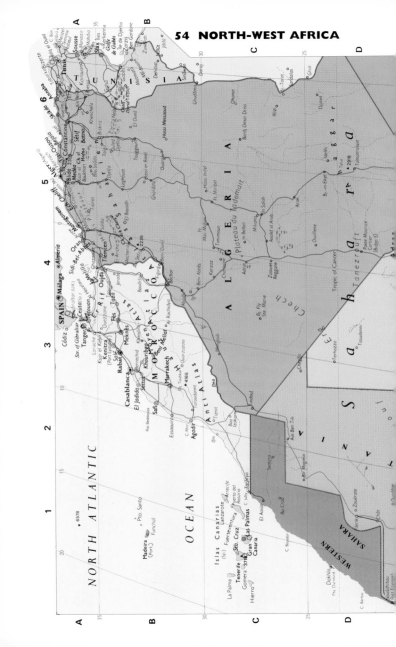

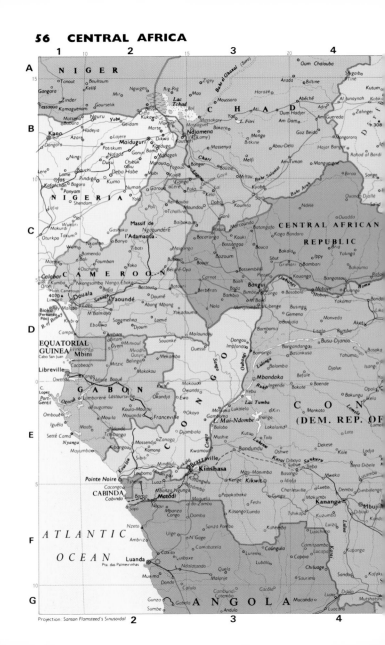

Projection: Sanson Flamsteed's Sinusoidal

1: 20 000 000

100   0   100   200   300   400 miles
100   0   100   200   300   400   500   600 km

5   30   **6**   35   **7**   40   **8**

Kipushi   Lubumbashi   Mpika   Bandawe   Cóbuè   Metangula   A
Solwezi   Chililabombwe   Lundazi   Nkhota Kota   Marrupa   Montepuez   Pemba   Quissanga
Kasempa   Chingola   Kitwe   Ndola   Serenje   Chipata   Lichinga   Marrupa   Montepuez   Pemba
Lukanga   Mufulira   Lilongwe   Mangoche   Namapa   Memba
Luanshya   Kapiri Mposhi   Mbeya   Cuamba   Meconta   Mossuril
Mumbwa   Kabwe   Petauke   Nampula   Moçambique   15

Namwala   Chisamba   Lusaka   Fingoè   Cahora Bassa   Aïto Molocue   Anchoge
Monze   Mazabuka   Kariba Dam   Zumbo   Zambezi   Blantyre   Chiúta   Metil   Mocuba   Moma
Kalomo   Kariba   Kariba Lake   Mt. Darwin   Tete   3000   Morrumbala   V. da Maganja
Livingstone   Kariba Gorge   Bindura   Shamva   Sena   Mocurra   Quelimane   B
Victoria Falls   Chitungwiza   Cheguta   **Harare**   Chembo   Velha   Morrombé
Hwange   Nata   Kadoma   Marondera   Chinhoyi   Rusape   Nhaminga   Chinde
  Gwaai   **ZIMBABWE**   Mutare   Dondo
Sawhili   Gweru   Mvuma   Gutu   **INDIAN**
  Plumtree   **Bulawayo**   Zvishavane   **Beira**
Francistown   Gwanda   W. Nicholson   Mwenezi   Nova Sofala   20   **OCEAN**
Shashi   Selebi   Pikwe   Tuli   Beitbridge   Massingir   Pafuri
Serowe   Palapye   Messina   Nova Mambone
Mahalapye   Soutpansberg   Funhalouro   Pta. da Barra Falsa   C
  Louis Trichardt   Massinga
Gaborone   Thabazimbi   Pietersburg   Olifants   Marromeu   Inhambane
  Nylstroom   Tzaneen   Inharrime
Rustenburg   Lydenburg   Chicualacuala   Chibuto   25   Ile Europa (Réunion)
  Nelspruit   Xai-Xai
Johannesburg   **Pretoria**   W. Ibank   Komatipoort   **Maputo**   D

Bassas da India (Réunion)

MADAGASCAR

On same scale as General Map

CARTOGRAPHY BY PHILIP'S.

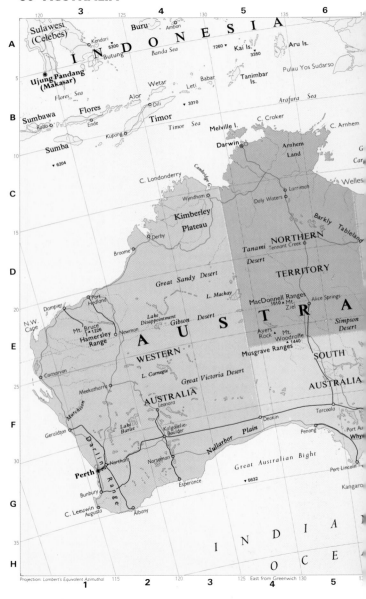

1: 26 700 000

PAPUA NEW GUINEA

Mount Hagen o
4508 ▲ Mt.
Wilhelm
Lae
Owen Stanley Range
Fly
Gulf of
Papua
Port
Moresby
Torres Strait

New Britain
9140
Solomon
Sea
D'Entrecasteaux Arch.
Louisiade
Archipelago

Mt.
Balbi
Bougainville
Choiseul

**SOLOMON
ISLANDS**

Santa Isabel
New
Georgia
Honiara
Guadalcanal
San Cristobal
Rennell

▲ 2331
Malaita

C. York

Weipa o Cape
York
Peninsula

Cooktown o

Cairns

Bartle Frere
1611 ▲

Great Barrier

Normanton o
Forsayth o

Reef

Coral Sea

P A C I F I C

O C E A N

Chesterfield Is.

Coral
Sea
Islands
Territory

Mitchell

Flinders

Mount Isa o

Charters Towers
Hughenden o

Townsville

Winton o
Longreach o

Diamantina

QUEENSLAND

Mackay

Rockhampton

L I A

Great Dividing

Yaraka o

Gladstone

Bundaberg

Tropic of Capricorn

Barcoo Creek

Grey Range

Cooper Creek

Charleville o
Quilpie o

Cunnamulla o

Thargomindah o

Roma o

Maryborough

Gympie o

Warrego

Dirranbandi o

BRISBANE
Toowoomba o
Ipswich
Gold
Coast

Lismore

Eyre

Narree

Bourke o

Walgett o

Tamworth

Round
Mt.
▲ 1615

Cabar o

Broken Hill o

NEW SOUTH

Darling

Dubbo o

Taree

Port Pirie o

Flinders Range

Orange o

WALES

Bathurst o

Newcastle

Adelaide

Murray

Mildura o

Wagga Wagga o

Goulburn o

SYDNEY
Wollongong
Shellharbour

Canberra
AUSTRALIAN
CAPITAL TERRITORY

Encounter B.

Shepparton o
Horsham o

Albury o

Murray Mt.
Kosciuszko
2237 ▲

Alps

o Bombala

T a s m a n   S e a

Mount Gambier o

VICTORIA
Bendigo o
Ballarat o
MELBOURNE
Geelong

Warrnambool o

Australian

C. Howe

Lord Howe
(Austr.)
▼ 734

Bass Strait

King I.

Furneaux Group

▼ 5267

Burnie o

Launceston

TASMANIA

Mt.Ossa
1617 ▲

Hobart

S.E. Cape

NORTH ISLAND

Three Kings Is.
C. Reinga
North C.
C. Maria van Diemen
Houhora
Ahipara B.
Kaitaia
Taurus Pt.
Kaikohe
Hokianga Harb.
Dargaville
Donnelly's Crossing
Kaipara Harb.
Helensville
Whangarei
Bream Hd.
Bream Bay
Lt. Barrier I.
Gt. Barrier I.
C. Rodney
C. Colville
Hauraki Gulf
Takapuna Devonport
Auckland
Onehunga
Coromandel
Whitianga
Waiuku
Waikato
Mayor I.
Cambridge
Hamilton
Huntly
Te Kuiti
Waihi
Tauranga
Bay of Plenty
Te Puke
Whakatane
East C.
Te Araroa
Hicks Bay
Te Kaha
Opotiki
Gisborne
Tolaga Bay
Poverty Bay
Mahia Peninsula
Napier
Hastings
Hawke Bay
C. Kidnappers
Waipukurau
Dannevirke
Woodville
Pahiatua
C. Turnagain
Palmerston North
Foxton
Wanganui
Patea
Hawera
South Taranaki Bight
New Plymouth
North Taranaki Bight
Mt. Egmont (Taranaki)
Stratford
Inglewood
Waitara
Taumarunui
Taupo
L. Taupo
Rotorua
Murupara
Wairoa

SOUTH-WEST PACIFIC

1:72 000 000

Mariana Trench
NORTHERN MARIANAS (U.S.)
Saipan
GUAM (U.S.)
Caroline Islands
FEDERATED STATES OF MICRONESIA
Chuuk
Pohnpei
MARSHALL IS.
Bikini Atoll
Enewetak Atoll
Ailinglapalap
Majuro
Micronesia
Equator
NAURU
Banaba
Butaritari
Tarawa
KIRIBATI
Gilbert Is.
TUVALU
Baker I. (U.S.)
International Date Line
Melanesia
Admiralty Is.
Bismarck Arch.
New Ireland
New Britain
Rabaul
PAPUA NEW GUINEA
Port Moresby
Lae
Louisade Arch. (Austr.)
SOLOMON IS.
Guadalcanal
Honiara
Sta. Cruz I.
VANUATU
Coral Sea
Is. Chesterfield
NEW CALEDONIA (Fr.)
Nouméa
Is. Loyauté
Rotuma
FIJI
Vanua Levu
Viti Levu
Suva
Wallis & Futuna (Fr.)
Tropic of Capricorn
Norfolk I. (Aust.)
Kermadec Is. (N.Z.)
NEW ZEALAND
AUSTRALIA
Cairns
Townsville
Rockhampton
Brisbane
Great Divide
Great Dividing Range

N

500 miles
500 0 500 1000 km

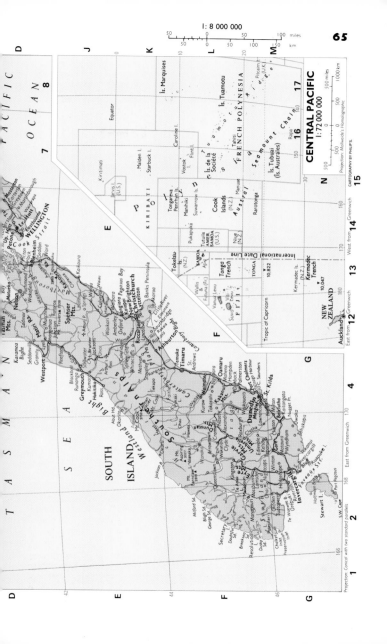

1:8 000 000

CENTRAL PACIFIC
1:72 000 000

FRENCH POLYNESIA

KIRIBATI

Cook Islands (N.Z.)

SAMOA

TONGA

International Date Line

NEW ZEALAND

SOUTH ISLAND

WELLINGTON

Christchurch

Dunedin

Invercargill

TASMAN SEA

PACIFIC OCEAN

Tropic of Capricorn

Equator

West from Greenwich

East from Greenwich

Projection: Conical with two standard parallels

CARTOGRAPHY BY PHILIPS

Projection: Mollweide's Homolographic

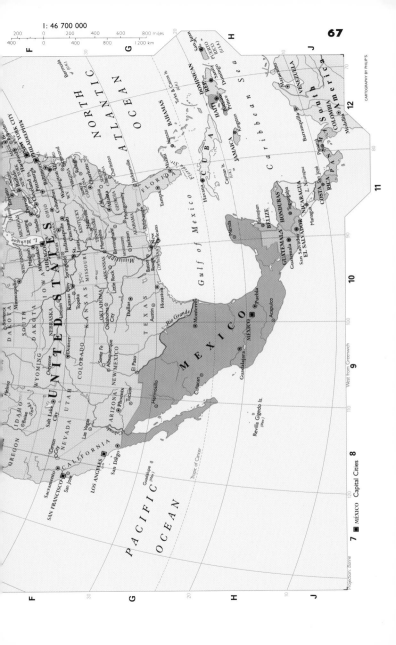

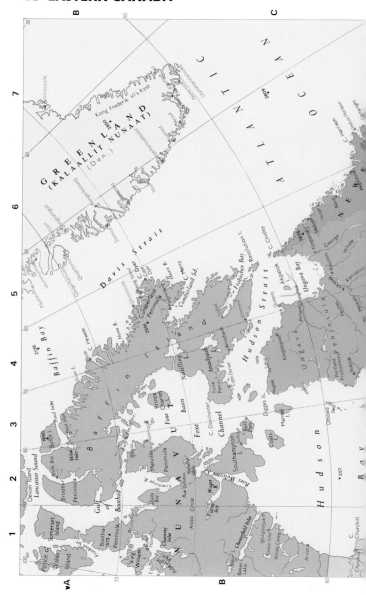

1 : 20 000 000

Projection Bonne

West from Greenwich

CARTOGRAPHY BY PHILIP'S

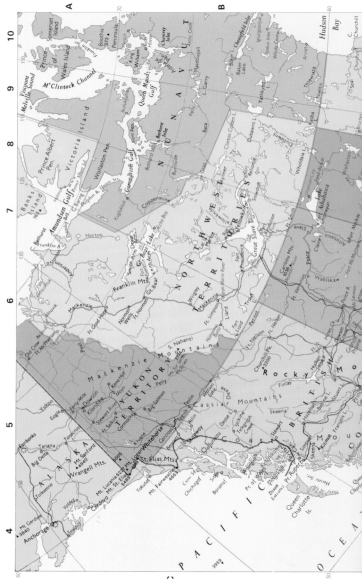

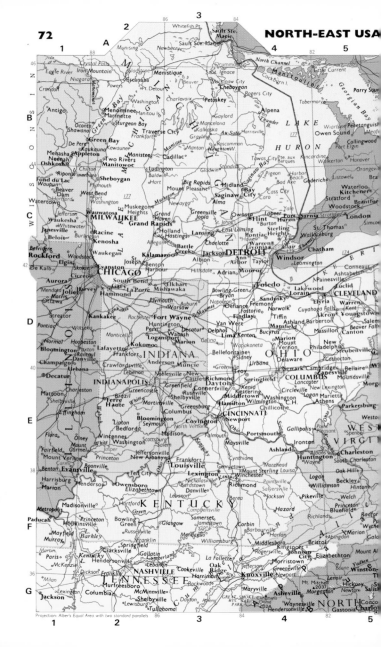

Projection: Alber's Equal Area with two standard parallels

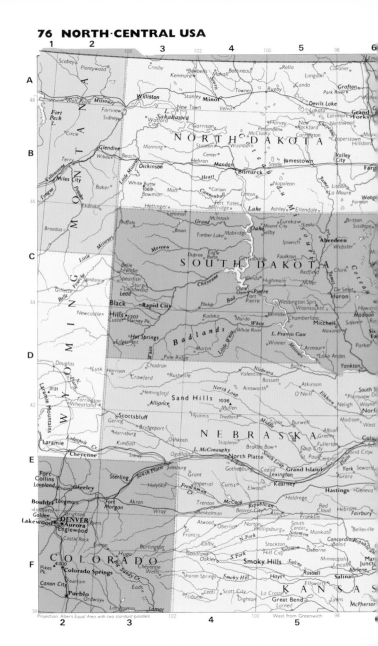

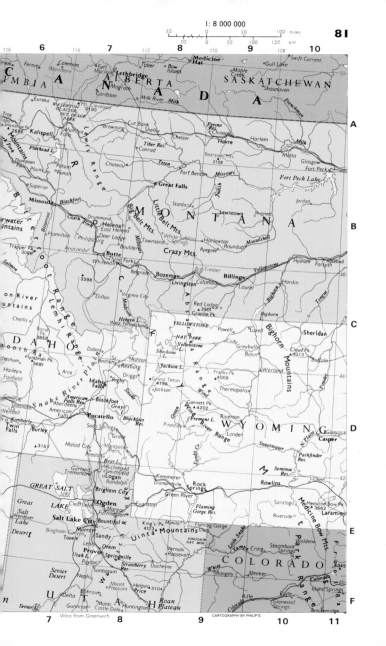

1 122 **2** 120 **3** 118 **4** 116 **5**

N E V A D A

Pancake Ra.
Grant Ra. ▲3444
Snake Ra.
Tonopah
°Goldfield
Pahute Mesa
Pioche
Caliente
Beatty
Las Vegas Lake
Paradise Mead
Henderson
Boulder City
Hoover

C A L I F O R N I A

A Oakland Stockton Sonora Bridgeport
SAN FRANCISCO Tuolumne YOSEMITE NAT. PARK Mono Lake
Redwood City Tremont Modesto Turlock Mariposa
Sunnyvale Merced ▲4341 Bishop White Mtn.
B SAN JOSE Atwater Chowchilla North Palisade ▲4341
Santa Cruz Los Banos Madera KINGS CANYON NAT. PARK Independence
Watsonville Hollister Mendota Clovis Fresno DEATH VALLEY NAT.
Salinas Gilroy Fresno Sanger Mt. Whitney ▲4418 3021
Monterey Gonzales Selma Reedley SEQUOIA NAT. PARK Panamint Spring Mts. ▲3633
Pacific Grove Soledad Hanford Visalia Exeter ▲3366 MON.
Pt. Sur King City Lemoore Tulare Lindsay Porterville Searles L.
Coalinga Corcoran Earlimart Mojave
Cambria Paso Robles Wasco Delano Ridgecrest Soda L.
Morro Bay Atascadero Shafter Bakersfield Davis Dam Kingman
San Luis Obispo Guadalupe Arroyo Grande Buena Vista Tehachapi Mts. Mojave Needles Lake Havasu City
C Santa Maria Tehachapi ▲2693 Barstow Bristol L. Parker Dam
Lompoc Santa Barbara Ojai Lancaster Palmdale Victorville Providence Mts. Twentynine Palms Parker
Pt. Arguello Pt. Conception Ventura Oxnard San Fernando Colorado R. Aqueduct Blythe
D Santa Rosa I. LOS ANGELES Glendale Pasadena San Bernardino Palm Springs Quartzsite
Santa Cruz I. Beverly Hills Garden Grove Fullerton Riverside Cahuilla Mts. Sonora
Channel Is. Long Beach Anaheim Santa Ana Indio Desert
San Nicolas I. Huntington Beach San Clemente Hemet Coachella Chocolate Mts.
Oceanside Vista Salton Imperial Dam
San Clemente Carlsbad Escondido Sea Westmorland Gila
Santa Catalina El Cajon Brawley
D SAN DIEGO La Mesa El Centro
Chula Vista Calipatria
Tijuana Tecate Calexico All American Canal
Mexicali Yuma
San Luis Somerton
Rio Colorado
E P A C I F I C Ensenada Sierra de Juarez Gran Desierto
O C E A N Pta. Sto. Tomas Santo Tomas
Cabo Colonet Cerro de la Encantada ▲3078 San Felipe Bahia de San Jorge
Puerta Peñasco
F 120 118 Pta. Baja
C.S. Quintin Pta. San Antonio
San Luis
B A J A Punta Prieta I. Angel de la Guarda
C A L I F O R N I A Golfo de California
I. Cedros Canal de Ballenas
Bahia Sebastián
Vizcaino

5 114 **6**

1: 20 000 000

100   0   100   200   300   400 miles
100   0   100   200   300   400   500   600 km

6   7   8   9

UNITED STATES

Gainesville
Dallas
Marshall
Tyler
Shreveport
Jacksonville
Alexandria
Monroe
Meridian
Birmingham
Jackson
Vicksburg
Montgomery
Columbus
Macon
Atlanta
Augusta
Columbia
C. Royal
Charleston
Natchez
Hattiesburg
Beaumont
Lake Charles
Lafayette
Baton Rouge
Mobile
Dothan
Albany
Savannah
Altamaha
Port Arthur
Galveston
New Orleans
Pensacola
Tallahassee
Jacksonville
Matagorda I.
Corpus Christi
Mississippi Delta
C. San Blas
Apalachee B.
Daytona Beach
C. Canaveral
Grande del Norte
Orlando
Tampa
Lakeland
St. Petersburg
Sarasota
Palm Beach
Grand Bahama I.
Fort Lauderdale
L. Okeechobee
Madre

GULF OF MEXICO

Miami
C. Sable
Key West
Florida Str.
Andros I.

Tropic of Cancer

La Habana (Havana)
Matanzas
Cárdenas
Sagua la Grande
Sta. Clara
Caibarién
Canal de Yucatan
C. Catoche
El Cuyo
Marianao
Pinar del Río
San Antonio
G. de Batabanó
C U B A
Cienfuegos
Trinidad
Sancti Spiritus
Ciego de Ávila
Progreso
Tizimin
El Díoz
Puerto Morelos
I. de Juventud
Golfo de Campeche
Mérida
Peto
Valladolid
I. de Cozumel
Vigía Chico
Grand Cayman (U.K.)
Veracruz
Campeche
Campeche
Felipe Castillo Puerto
Alvarado
Yucatan
Ciudad del Carmen
Ciudad Chetumal
Tlacotalpan
Coatzacoalcos
Laguna de Terminos
Corozal
Ambergris Cay
Villahermosa
me de huantepec
Turtla Gutierrez
Belize
Turneffe Is.
Chiapa
San Cristobal
BELIZE
Belmopan
Middlesex
Pto. Barrios
Golfo de Hondu
Juchitan
Chiapa
Tonala
GUATEMALA
Pto. Cortés
Tela
Trujillo
Iriona
G. de Huixtla
huantepec
Guatemala
Zacapa
Piedra Sula
La Ceiba
Caratasca
San José
Sta. Rosa
HONDURAS
C. Gracias á Dios
Comayagua
Wanks or Coco
Chiquimula
Tegucigalpa
Jinotega
Puerto Cabezas
Sta. Ana
San Vicente
Nacaome
Matagalpa
El Gallo
Providencia (Col.)
San Salvador
San Miguel
Choluteca
EL SALVADOR
G. de Fonseca
NICARAGUA
San Andrés (Col.)
Chinandega
León
Mosqua
Granada
Bluefields
Managua
L. Nicaragua
San Juan
Irazú
Pen. de Nicoya
COSTA RICA
Limón
Colón
Puntarenas
San José
Alajuela
Chitré
Cartago
PANAMA
3374
Panama
La Palma
El Real
Arch. de las Perlas
Coiba
Pen. de Azuero
G. de Panama

A
B
C
D
E
F

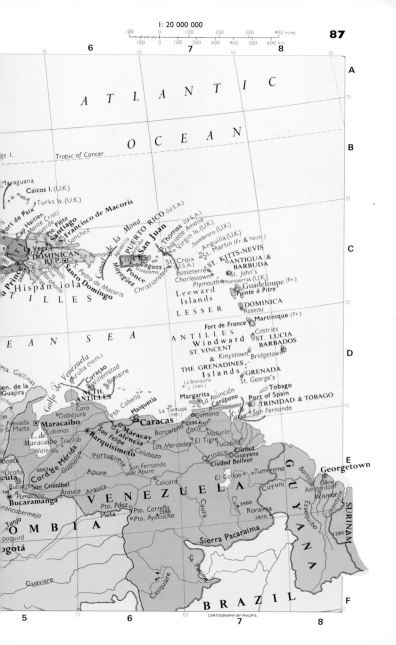

NORTH

ATLANTIC

OCEAN

Tropic of Cancer

BAHAMAS

Turks & Caicos Is. (U.K.)

CUBA

Havana

HAITI

DOMINICAN REP.

Port-au-Prince

JAMAICA

Kingston

Virgin Is. (U.K.)

Puerto Rico (U.S.A.)

San Juan

ANTIGUA & BARBUDA

ST. KITTS-NEVIS

GUADELOUPE (Fr.)

Basse-Terre

DOMINICA

MARTINIQUE (Fr.)

Fort-de-France

ST. LUCIA

Castries

ST. VINCENT

Kingstown

BARBADOS

Bridgetown

GRENADA

St. George's

TRINIDAD & TOBAGO

Port of Spain

Caribbean Sea

Aruba

Curaçao

MEXICO

GUATEMALA

Guatemala

BELIZE

HONDURAS

Tegucigalpa

EL SALVADOR

San Salvador

NICARAGUA

Managua

COSTA RICA

San José

PANAMA

Panamá

Gulf of Panama

G. of Darién

C. de la Aguja

Barranquilla

Cartagena

Maracaibo

Valencia

Caracas

VENEZUELA

Ciudad Guayana

Cúcuta

Bucaramanga

San Cristóbal

Medellín

Bogotá

Cali

Magdalena

COLOMBIA

ECUADOR

Quito

Guayaquil

G. of Guayaquil

Galápagos Is. (Ecuador)

Chimbote

Callao

LIMA

PERU

Cuzco

Trujillo

Chiclayo

Iquitos

Napo

Marañón

Ucayali

Amazon

Japurá

Putumayo

Negro

Orinoco

Meta

Guaviare

GUYANA

Georgetown

SURINAM

Paramaribo

FRENCH GUIANA

Cayenne

C. Orange

RORAIMA

Branco

Essequibo

AMAZONAS

ACRE

RONDÔNIA

Pôrto Velho

Manaus

Madeira

Purus

Juruá

Tapajós

Xingu

Santarém

Marajó

Belém

PARÁ

AMAPÁ

Tocantins

MARANHÃO

São Luís

PIAUÍ

Teresina

Parnaíba

CEARÁ

Fortaleza

C. de São Roque

Campina Grande

Natal

Recife

BRAZIL

MATO GROSSO

BAHÍA

Salvador

Maceió

Aracaju

Rio São Francisco

Equator

Mamoré

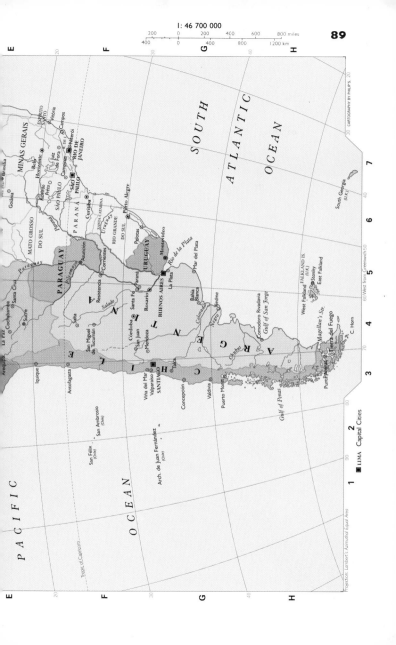

1: 46 700 000

200   0   200   400   600   800 miles
400   0   400   800   1200 km

CARTOGRAPHY BY PHILIP'S

PACIFIC

OCEAN

Tropic of Capricorn

San Félix
(Chile)

San Ambrosio
(Chile)

Arch. de Juan Fernández
(Chile)

■ LIMA   Capital Cities

Projection: Lambert's Azimuthal Equal Area

SOUTH

ATLANTIC

OCEAN

South Georgia
(U.K.)

MINAS GERAIS

ESPÍRITO
SANTO

Brasília

Goiânia

Belo
Horizonte

Campos

Vitória

Juiz
de Fora

Niterói

RIO DE
JANEIRO

Ouro
Prêto

Campinas

SÃO PAULO

SÃO
PAULO

MATO GROSSO
DO SUL

PARANÁ

Curitiba

SANTA CATARINA

PARAGUAY

Asunción

Pilcomayo

Paraguay

RIO GRANDE
DO SUL

Pôrto Alegre

Pelotas

URUGUAY

Montevideo

Río de la Plata

Mar del Plata

Santa Cruz

Cochabamba

Sucre

La Paz

Arequipa

Iquique

Antofagasta

Salta

San Miguel
de Tucumán

Córdoba

San Juan

Mendoza

Viña del Mar
Valparaíso

SANTIAGO

Concepción

Valdivia

Puerto Montt

Gulf of Penas

Salado

Santa Fe

Paraná

Resistencia

Corrientes

Rosario

BUENOS
AIRES

La Plata

Bahía
Blanca

Río Negro

Colorado

Nueve

A R G E N T I N A

C H I L E

Río Chubut

Comodoro Rivadavia

Gulf of San Jorge

West Falkland

FALKLAND IS.
(U.K.)

Stanley

East Falkland

Magellan's Str.

Punta Arenas

Tierra del Fuego

C. Horn

20° West from Greenwich

50°

60° West from Greenwich

40°

30°

30°

40°

50°

60°

20°

20°

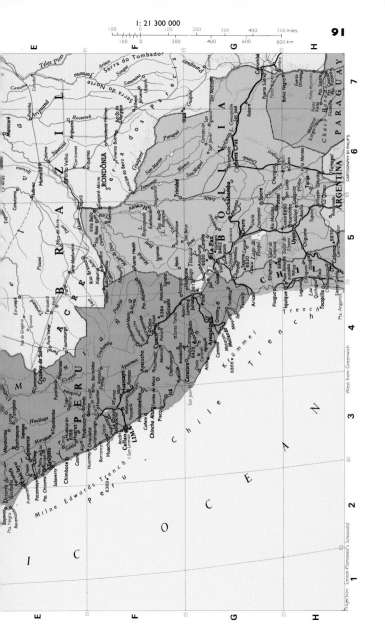

CARTOGRAPHY BY PHILIPS

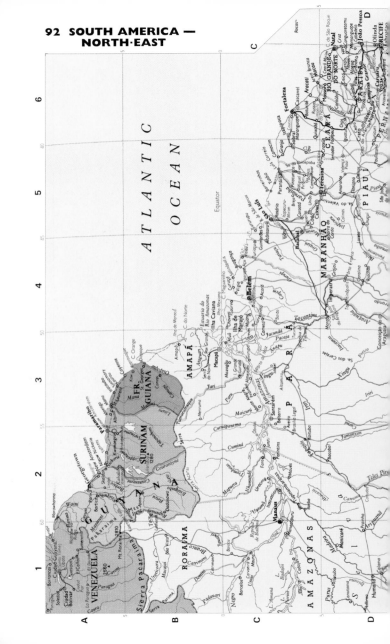

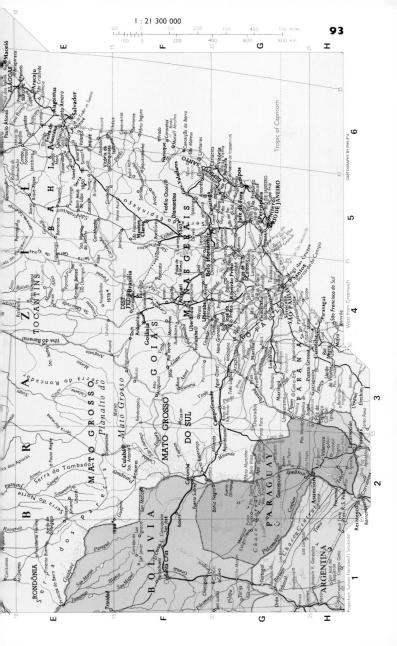

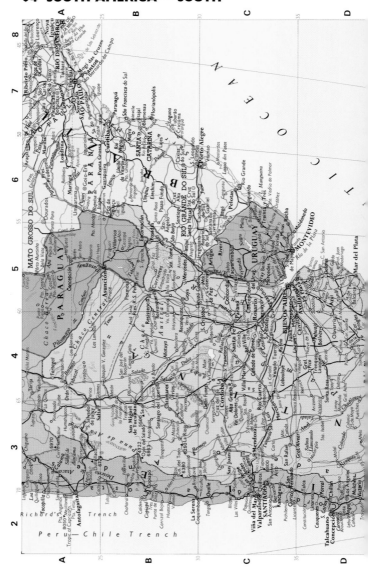

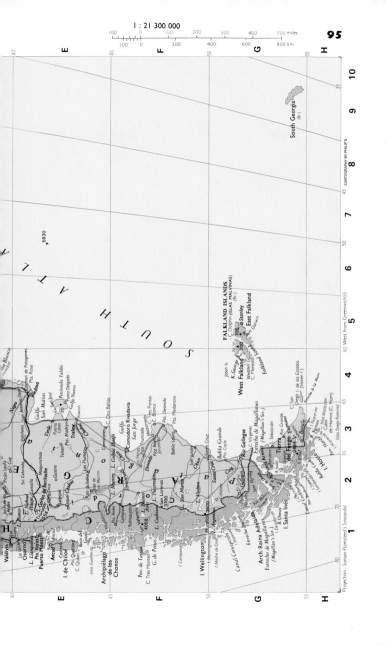

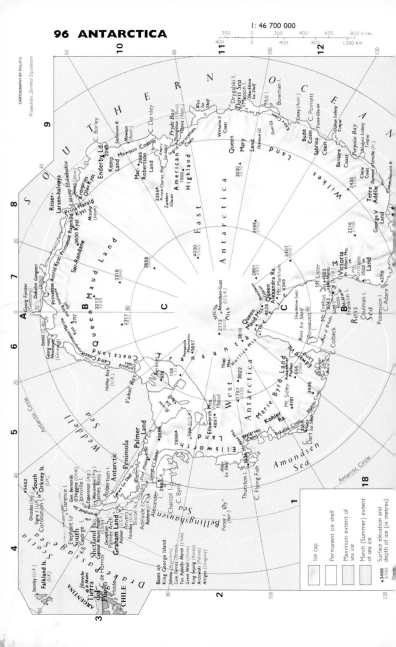

Index to Map Pages

The index contains the names of all principal places and features shown on the maps. Physical features composed of a proper name (Erie) and a description (Lake) are positioned alphabetically by the proper name. The description is positioned after the proper name and is usually abbreviated:

Erie, L. **72 C5**

Where a description forms part of a settlement or administrative name however, it is always written in full and put in its true alphabetical position:

Lake Charles **79 D7**

Names beginning St. are alphabetized under Saint, but Sankt, Sint, Sant, Santa and San are all spelt in full and are alphabetized accordingly.

The number in bold type which follows each name in the index refers to the number of the map page where that feature or place will be found. This is usually the largest scale at which the place or feature appears.

The letter and figure which are in bold type immediately after the page number give the grid square on the map page, within which the feature is situated.

Rivers carry the symbol → after their names. A solid square ■ follows the name of a country while an open square □ refers to a first order administrative area.

Aachen	14 C4	Au Dawhah . . . 44 E2	Agadir 54 B3
Aalen	14 D6	Ada 79 B5	Agartala 41 F8
Aarau	13 C8	Adaja → . . . 18 B3	Agde 13 E5
Aare →	13 C8	Adamaoua,	Agen 12 D4
Ābādān	47 E7	Massif de l' 53 G1	Agra 42 F10
Abakan	30 D7	Adamello,	Ağri 21 D6
Abashiri	32 F12	Mte. 20 A3	Ağri Daği . . . 46 C6
Abbeville . . .	12 A4	Adam's	Al Başrah . . . 47 E6
Abéché	53 F3	Bridge . . . 43 Q11	Agrigento . . . 21 F4
Abeokuta . . .	55 G5	Adams Mt. . . 80 B3	Agrinion 23 E3
Aberdeen,		Adana 46 C3	Aguascalientes
U.K.	10 C5	Adapazari . . . 46 B2	. . . . 84 C4
Aberdeen,		Adare, C. . . . 96 B15	Aguilas 19 D5
S. Dak.,		Adda → . . . 20 B2	Agulhas, C. . . 58 E4
U.S.A. . . .	76 C5	Addis Abeba . 53 G6	Ahaggar 54 D6
Aberdeen,		Adelaide . . . 62 B2	Ahmadabad . . 43 H8
Wash.,		Adelaide I. . . 96 A3	Ahmadnagar . . 43 K9
U.S.A. . . .	80 B2	Adelaide Pen. 70 B10	Ahmadpur . . . 42 E7
Aberystwyth	11 E4	Adélie, Terre 96 A14	Ahvāz 47 E7
Abidjan	55 G4	Aden = Al	Aigues-Mortes 13 E6
Abilene	78 C4	'Adan . . . 49 E4	Aiken 75 C7
Abitibi L. . . .	69 D3	Aden, G. of . 49 E4	Ain → 13 C6
Abkhazia □ .	11 E1	Adige → . . . 20 B4	Aisne → . . . 13 B5
Abohar	42 D9	Adirondack	Aix-en-
Absaroka		Mts. 73 C8	Provence . 13 E6
Range . . .	81 C9	Admiralty I. . 71 C6	Aix-les-Bains . 13 D6
Abu Dhabi =		Admiralty Is. . 64 K9	Aiyion 23 E4
Abū Ẓāby .	44 E3	Ado-Ekiti . . . 55 G6	Ajaccio 13 F8
Abū Ẓāby . .	44 E3	Adoni 43 M10	Ajanta Ra. . . 43 J9
Abuja	55 G6	Adour → . . . 12 E3	Ajaria □ . . . 25 E5
Abukuma-		Adra 18 D4	Ajmer 42 F9
Gawa → . .	33 G12	Adrano 21 F5	Ajo, C. de . . 18 A4
Acapulco . . .	84 D5	Adrar 54 C4	Akashi 32 B4
Accra	55 G4	Adriatic Sea . 20 C5	Akharnaí . . . 23 E4
Achill I.	11 E1	Ægean Sea . . 23 E5	Akhelóös → . . 23 E3
Achinsk	30 D7	Aerhtai Shan 34 B4	Akhisar 23 E6
Acireale	21 F5	Afghanistan ■ 45 C6	Akimiski I. . . 69 C2
Acklins I. . . .	86 B5	'Afif 47 G5	Akita 33 G12
Aconcagua,		Afyonkarahisar	'Akko 46 D3
Cerro	94 C3	. . . . 46 C2	Aklavik 70 B6
Acre □	91 E4	Agadez 55 E6	Akola 43 J10
Ad Dammām .	47 F7	Agadir 54 B3	Akpatok I. . . 68 B4
Akron 72 D5		Albany,	
Aksaray 46 C3		Australia . . 60 H2	
Aksehir 46 C2		Albany, Ga.,	
Aktsyabrski . . 17 B9		U.S.A. . . 75 D5	
Al 'Adan . . . 49 E4		Albany, N.Y.,	
Al Başrah . . . 47 E6		U.S.A. . . 73 C9	
Al Hijāz 47 F4		Albany, Oreg.,	
Al Hudaydah 49 E3		U.S.A. . . 80 C2	
Al Hufūf . . . 47 F7		Albany → . . 69 C2	
Al Jawf 47 F4		Albemarle . . . 75 B7	
Al Jazirah . . 46 C5		Alberche → . 18 C3	
Al Kūt 47 D6		Albert L. . . . 57 D6	
Al Kuwayt . . 47 E7		Albertville . . 13 D7	
Al Lādhiqīyah 46 D3		Albi 12 E5	
Al Madīnah . 47 F4		Ålborg 9 G9	
Al Manāmah 44 E2		Alborz,	
Al Mawsil . . 46 C5		Reshteh-ye	
Alamosa . . . 83 B10		Kūhhā-ye . 44 B3	
Alania =		Albuquerque . 83 C9	
North		Albury 63 C4	
Ossetia □ . 25 E5		Alcalá de	
Alanya 46 C2		Henares . . 18 B4	
Alaşehir 23 E7		Alcalá la Real 18 D4	
Alaska □ . . . 71 B4		Alcamo 21 F4	
Alaska, G. of 71 C5		Alcañiz 19 B5	
Alaska		Alcántara,	
Peninsula . 71 C4		Embalse de 18 C2	
Alaska Range 71 B4		Alcantarilla . 19 D5	
Alba 20 B2		Alcaraz, Sierra	
Alba-Iulia . . 17 E6		de 19 C4	
Albacete . . . 19 C5		Alcaudete . . 18 D3	
Albania ■ . . 23 D3		Alcázar de	
		San Juan . 18 C4	
		Alchevsk . . . 25 D4	
		Alcira 19 C5	
		Alcoy 19 C5	
		Aldabra Is. . . 51 G8	
		Aldan 31 C10	
		Alderney . . . 11 G5	
		Alençon . . . 12 B4	
		Aleppo =	
		Halab . . . 46 C4	

Alès

Alès 13 D6
Alessándria . 20 B2
Ålesund 8 F9
Aleutian Is. . 71 C2
Alexander
  Arch. 71 C6
Alexander I. . 96 A3
Alexandria =
  El
  Iskandarîya 52 B4
Alexandria,
  Canada ... 71 C7
Alexandria,
  S. Africa .. 59 E5
Alexandria,
  La., U.S.A. 79 D7
Alexandria,
  Va., U.S.A. 73 E7
Alexandroúpolis
  .... 22 D5
Algarve ... 18 D1
Algeciras .. 18 D3
Algemesí .. 19 C5
Alger 54 A5
Algeria ■ .. 54 C5
Alghero .. 21 D2
Algiers =
  Alger 54 A5
Algoa B. .. 59 E5
Aliağa ... 23 E6
Alicante .. 19 C5
Alice Springs 60 D5
Aligarh ... 42 F11
Alipur Duar . 41 D7
Aliwal North 59 E5
Aljustrel ... 18 D1
Alkmaar .. 14 B3
All American
  Canal 82 D6
Allahabad .. 40 E3
Allegheny → 73 D5
Allegheny
  Plateau .. 73 F5
Allentown .. 73 D8
Alleppey ... 43 Q10
Aller → 14 B5
Allier → ... 13 C5
Alma Ata =
  Almaty ... 29 E8
Almada ... 18 C1
Almadén ... 18 C3
Almansa ... 19 C5
Almanzor,
  Pico del
  Moro 18 B3
Almanzora → 19 D5
Almaty ... 29 E8
Almazán ... 19 B4
Almelo ... 14 B4
Almendralejo 18 C2
Almería ... 19 D4
Alnwick ... 11 D6
Alor 39 F2
Alps 14 E5
Alsace ... 13 B7
Alsask ... 71 C9
Alsásua ... 19 A4
Altai =
  Aerhtai
  Shan ... 34 B4
Altamura .. 21 D6
Altay 34 B3
Altea 19 C5
Alton 77 F9
Altoona ... 73 D6
Altun Shan . 34 C3
Alwar 42 F10
Amadjuak .. 68 B3
Amadjuak L. 68 B3
Amagasaki . 32 B4
Amakusa-
  Shotō ... 32 C2
Amaliás ... 23 F3

Amarillo 78 B3
Amaro, Mte. . 20 C5
Amasra 46 B3
Amasya ... 46 B3
Amazon =
Amazonas →
  .... 92 C3
Amazonas □ 90 D6
Amazonas → 92 C3
Ambala ... 42 D10
Amberg ... 15 D6
Ambikapur . 40 F4
Amboise ... 12 C4
Ambon ... 39 E3
Amchitka I. . 71 C1
Ameland ... 14 B3
American
  Highland . 96 B10
American
  Samoa ■ . 65 L13
Americus .. 75 C5
Amery ... 71 C10
Ames 77 D8
Amherst ... 69 D4
Amiata, Mte. . 20 C4
Amiens ... 12 B5
Amirante Is. . 26 K9
'Ammān ... 47 E3
Amorgós ... 23 F5
Amper → ... 15 D6
Amravati ... 43 J10
Amreli ... 43 J7
Amritsar ... 42 D9
Amroha ... 42 E11
Amsterdam . 14 B3
Amstetten .. 15 D8
Amudarya → 29 E6
Amundsen
  Gulf 70 A7
Amundsen
  Sea 96 B1
Amur → ... 31 D12
An Nafūd ... 47 E5
An Najaf ... 47 D6
An Nhon ... 36 B3
Anaconda .. 81 B7
Anadolu ... 46 C2
Anaheim ... 82 D4
Anambas,
  Kepulauan 37 D3
Anamur ... 46 C3
Anan 32 C4
Anantnag .. 42 C9
Ananyiv ... 17 E9
Anápolis .. 93 F4
Anār 44 D3
Anatolia =
  Anadolu .. 46 C2
Anchorage .. 71 B5
Ancona ... 20 C4
Andalucía □ . 18 D3
Andalusia .. 74 D4
Andaman Is. . 27 H13
Anderson .. 72 D3
Anderson → 70 B7
Andes, Cord.
  de los ... 91 G3
Andhra
  Pradesh □ . 43 L11
Andijon ... 29 E8
Andikíthira . 23 G4
Andorra ■ .. 19 A6
Andreanof Is. 71 C2
Ándria ... 20 D6
Ándros ... 23 F5
Ándros I. ... 86 B4
Andújar ... 18 C3
Aneto, Pico de 19 A6
Angara → ... 30 D7
Angarsk ... 30 D8
Ånge 8 F11
Ångermanälven →
  .... 8 F11

Angers ... 12 C3
Anglesey ... 11 E4
Angola ■ .. 58 A3
Angoulême . 12 D4
Angoumois . 12 D4
Anguilla ■ .. 87 C7
Anhui □ ... 35 C6
Anjou ... 12 C3
Ankara ... 46 C3
Ann Arbor .. 72 C4
Annaba ... 54 A6
Annan ... 11 D5
Annapolis .. 73 E7
Annecy ... 13 D7
Anniston ... 74 C5
Annobón ... 51 G4
Ansbach ... 14 D6
Anshun ... 35 D5
Antakya ... 46 C4
Antalya ... 46 C2
Antalya
  Körfezi .. 46 C2
Antananarivo 59 H9
Antarctic Pen. 96 A4
Antarctica .. 96 C
Antequera .. 18 D3
Antibes ... 13 E7
Anticosti, I. d' 69 D4
Antigua &
  Barbuda ■ 87 C7
Antofagasta . 94 A2
Antrim ... 11 D3
Antsiranana . 59 G9
Antwerpen .. 14 C3
Anvers =
  Antwerpen 14 C3
Anyang ... 35 C6
Anzhero-
  Sudzhensk 29 D9
Ánzio ... 20 D4
Aomori ... 33 F12
Aoraki Mt.
  Cook 65 E4
Aosta ... 20 B1
Apalachicola →
  .... 74 E5
Aparri ... 38 A2
Apeldoorn .. 14 B3
Apia 65 L13
Appalachian
  Mts. 73 F5
Appennini .. 20 B3
Appleton ... 72 B1
Aprilia ... 20 D4
Aqmola =
  Astana ... 29 D8
Aqtöbe ... 29 D6
Aquitain,
  Bassin ... 12 D3
Ar Ramādī .. 46 D5
Ar Riyāḍ ... 47 F6
Ara 40 E5
Arabian Gulf
  = Gulf, The 44 E2
Araban Sea . 26 H10
Araç 46 B3
Aracaju ... 93 E6
Araçatuba .. 93 G3
Aracena ... 18 D2
Arad 16 E5
Arafura Sea . 39 F4
Aragón □ ... 19 B5
Aragón → .. 19 A5
Araguaia → . 92 D4
Arakan Yoma 41 H10
Aral 29 E7
Aral Sea ... 29 E6
Aran I. ... 10 D2
Aran Is. ... 11 E2
Aranda de
  Duero ... 18 B4
Aranjuez ... 18 B4
Arapgir ... 46 C4

Arapiraca .. 93 D6
Ararat ... 62 C3
Ararat, Mt. =
  Ağrı Dağı . 46 C6
Arbatax ... 21 E2
Arbīl 46 C6
Arbroath ... 10 C5
Arcachon ... 12 D3
Arcos de la
  Frontera .. 18 D3
Arctic Bay . 68 A2
Arctic Red
  River 70 B6
Ardabīl ... 46 C7
Ardahan ... 46 B5
Ardenne ... 14 D3
Ardmore ... 78 B5
Arendal ... 9 G9
Arequipa ... 91 G4
Arévalo ... 18 B3
Arezzo ... 20 C3
Arganda ... 18 B4
Argentan ... 12 B3
Argentário,
  Mte. 20 C3
Argentina ■ . 94 D3
Argolikós
  Kólpos ... 23 F4
Árgos ... 23 F4
Argostólion . 23 E3
Århus 9 G10
Arica ... 91 G4
Arizona □ .. 83 C7
Arkansas □ . 79 B7
Arkansas → 79 C8
Arkansas City 78 A5
Arkhangelsk . 28 C5
Arklow ... 11 E3
Arlanzón → . 18 A3
Arlberg P. .. 14 E6
Arles 13 E6
Arlington, Va.,
  U.S.A. ... 73 E7
Arlington,
  Wash.,
  U.S.A. ... 80 A2
Arlon ... 14 D3
Armagh ... 11 D3
Armenia ... 90 C3
Armenia ■ .. 25 E5
Armidale ... 63 B5
Armstrong .. 69 C2
Arnaud → .. 68 B3
Arnhem ... 14 C3
Arnhem Land 60 C5
Arno → ... 20 C3
Arnsberg ... 14 C5
Arran ... 10 D4
Arras 13 A5
Arrée, Mts. d' 12 B2
Árta 23 E3
Artois ... 12 A5
Artsyz ... 17 E9
Artvin ... 46 B5
Aru,
  Kepulauan 39 F4
Aruba ■ ... 87 D6
Arunachal
  Pradesh □ . 41 C10
Arusha ... 57 E7
Arviat ... 70 B10
Asahigawa .. 32 F12
Asansol ... 40 F6
Ascension I. . 51 G2
Aschaffenburg 14 D5
Aschersleben 15 C6
Áscoli Piceno 20 C4
Ash Shām,
  Bādiyat .. 47 D4
Ash Shāriqah 44 E3
Ashburton .. 65 E4
Ashcroft ... 71 C7
Asheville .. 75 B6

Ashford ... 11 F7
Ashgabat .. 29 F6
Ashikaga .. 32 A6
Ashizuri-Zaki 32 C3
Ashkhabad =
  Ashgabat . 29 F6
Ashmyany .. 17 A7
Ashqelon .. 47 E3
Ashtabula .. 72 D5
Ashuanipi, L. 69 C4
Asifabad ... 43 K11
Asinara ... 20 D2
Asinara, G.
  dell' ... 20 D2
Asipovichy .. 17 B9
'Asīr □ ... 48 D3
Asir, Ras ... 49 E5
Asmera ... 53 E6
Assam □ ... 41 D9
Assen 14 B4
Assiniboia .. 71 D9
Assiniboine →
  .... 71 D10
Assisi ... 20 C4
Astana ... 29 D8
Asti 20 B2
Astipálaia .. 23 F6
Astorga ... 18 A2
Astoria ... 80 B2
Astrakhan .. 25 D6
Asturias □ .. 18 A3
Asunción ... 94 B6
Aswân ... 52 D5
Atacama,
  Desierto de 94 A3
Atami ... 32 B6
Atbara ... 53 E5
Atbara → ... 53 E5
'Atbara → .. 53 E5
Athabasca .. 71 C8
Athabasca → 70 C8
Athabasca, L. 70 C8
Athens =
  Athínai .. 23 F4
Athens, Ala.,
  U.S.A. ... 74 B4
Athens, Ga.,
  U.S.A. ... 75 C6
Athínai ... 23 F4
Athlone ... 11 E3
Áthos ... 23 D5
Athy 11 E3
Atlanta ... 75 C5
Atlantic City . 73 E8
Atlas Mts. =
  Haut Atlas 54 B3
Attawapiskat →
  .... 69 C2
Atyraū ... 29 E7
Aubagne ... 13 E6
Aube → ... 13 B5
Auburn ... 74 C5
Aubusson .. 12 D5
Auch 12 E4
Auckland ... 64 B6
Aude → ... 13 E5
Augsburg ... 14 D6
Augusta, Italy 21 F5
Augusta, Ga.,
  U.S.A. ... 75 C7
Augusta,
  Maine,
  U.S.A. ... 73 B11
Aunis ... 12 C3
Aurangabad,
  Bihar, India 40 E5
Aurangabad,
  Maharashtra,
  India 43 K9
Aurich ... 14 B4
Aurillac ... 12 D5
Aurora, Colo.,
  U.S.A. ... 76 F2

Aurora, Ill.,
  U.S.A. ... 72 D1
Austin, Minn.,
  U.S.A. ... 77 D8
Austin, Tex.,
  U.S.A. ... 78 D5
Australia ■ ... 60 E6
Australian
  Alps 63 C4
Australian
  Capital
  Territory □ 63 C4
Austria ■ ... 15 E8
Autun 13 C6
Auvergne ... 13 D5
Auvergne,
  Mts. d' ... 13 D5
Auxerre ... 13 C5
Avallon ... 13 C5
Aveiro 18 B1
Avellino ... 21 D5
Aversa 21 D5
Avezzano ... 20 C4
Aviemore ... 10 C5
Avignon ... 13 E6
Ávila 18 B3
Avilés 18 A3
Avola 21 F5
Avranches ... 12 B3
Axiós → ... 23 D4
Ayabe 32 B4
Ayamonte ... 18 D2
Aydın 23 F6
Ayers Rock .. 60 F5
Áyios
  Evstrátios . 23 E5
Aylmer, L. .. 70 B8
Ayr 10 D4
Ayvacık ... 23 E6
Ayvalık ... 23 E6
Az Zarqā ... 46 D4
Azamgarh ... 40 D4
Azerbaijan ■ 25 C1
Azores 50 C1
Azov, Sea of 25 D4
Azuaga ... 18 C3
Azuero, Pen.
  de 86 E3

Baba Burnu . 23 E6
Babaeski ... 22 D6
Bābol 44 B3
Babruysk ... 17 B9
Babuyan
  Chan. 38 A2
Bacabal ... 92 C5
Bacău 17 E8
Back → ... 70 B9
Bacolod ... 38 B2
Bad Ischl ... 15 E7
Bad Kissingen 14 C6
Bad Lands ... 76 D3
Badajoz ... 18 C2
Badalona ... 19 B7
Baden 15 D9
Baden-Baden 14 D5
Baden-
  Württemberg □
  ...... 14 D5
Badgastein ... 15 E7
Baena 18 D3
Baeza 18 D4
Baffin B. ... 68 A4
Baffin I. ... 68 B3
Bafra 46 B3
Baghdād ... 46 D6
Bagheria ... 21 E4
Baguio 38 A2
Baharampur . 40 E7
Bahawalpur . 42 E7
Bahía □ ... 93 E5

Bahía Blanca 94 D4
Bahraich ... 40 D3
Bahrain ■ ... 44 E2
Baia Mare .. 17 E6
Baie Comeau 69 D4
Baikal, L. =
  Baykal, Oz. 30 D8
Baird Mts. .. 71 B3
Baja California 84 A1
Baker, L. ... 70 B10
Baker Lake . 70 B10
Baker Mt. ... 80 A3
Baker's Dozen
  Is. 69 C3
Bakersfield . 82 C3
Bākhtarān .. 46 D6
Bakı 25 E6
Bakony
  Hegyseg . 16 E3
Baku = Bakı . 25 E6
Balabac Str. . 36 C5
Balaguer ... 19 B6
Balaklava ... 25 E3
Balaton ... 16 E3
Baleares, Is. . 19 C7
Baleshwar ... 40 G6
Bali 37 F5
Balıkeşir ... 23 E6
Balikpapan . 37 E5
Balkan Mts. =
  Stara
  Planina .. 22 C4
Ballarat ... 62 C3
Ballater ... 10 C5
Ballina 11 D2
Ballinasloe . 11 E2
Ballymena ... 11 D3
Balqash ... 29 E8
Balqash Köl . 29 E8
Balrampur ... 40 D4
Balsas → ... 84 D4
Balta 17 D9
Bălți 17 E8
Baltic Sea .. 9 G11
Baltimore ... 73 E7
Baluchistan □ 42 F4
Balya 23 E6
Bam 44 D4
Bamako ... 55 F3
Bamberg ... 14 D6
Bamenda ... 55 G7
Banda,
  Kepulauan 39 E3
Banda Aceh . 36 C1
Banda Sea .. 39 F3
Bandar 'Abbās 44 E4
Bandar-e
  Khomeyni . 47 E7
Bandar Seri
  Begawan . 36 D4
Bandırma ... 23 D7
Bandon ... 11 F2
Bandundu ... 56 E3
Bandung ... 37 F3
Banff, Canada 71 C8
Banff, U.K. .. 10 C5
Bangalore .. 43 N10
Banggai,
  Kepulauan 39 E2
Banghāzi ... 52 B3
Bangka, P. .. 37 E3
Bangka, Selat 37 E3
Bangkok ... 36 B2
Bangladesh ■ 41 E7
Bangor,
  Down, U.K. 11 D4
Bangor,
  Gwynedd,
  U.K. ... 11 E4
Bangor,
  U.S.A. ... 73 B11
Bangui 56 D3
Bangweulu, L. 57 G6

Banja Luka .. 20 B6
Banjarmasin . 37 E4
Banjul 55 F1
Banks I. ... 70 A7
Banks Pen. .. 65 E5
Bankura ... 40 F6
Bannu 42 C7
Banská
  Bystrica .. 16 D4
Bantry 11 F2
Banyak,
  Kepulauan 37 D1
Baoding ... 35 C6
Baoji 35 C5
Baotou ... 35 B6
Bar-le-Duc . 13 B6
Baracaldo ... 19 A4
Baramula ... 42 B9
Baran 43 G10
Baranavichy . 17 B8
Baranof I. ... 71 C6
Barbados ■ . 87 D8
Barberton ... 19 A6
Barberton ... 59 D6
Barcelona
  Pozzo di
  Gotto ... 21 E5
Barcelona ... 19 B7
Barddhaman 40 F6
Bareilly ... 42 E11
Barfleur, Pte.
  de 12 B3
Barhi 40 E5
Bari 20 D6
Bari Doab .. 42 D8
Baring, C. ... 70 B8
Barisal ... 41 F8
Barito → ... 37 E4
Barkly
  Tableland . 60 D6
Barletta ... 20 D6
Barmer ... 42 G7
Barnaul ... 29 D9
Barnsley ... 11 E6
Barnstaple .. 11 F4
Barquisimeto 90 A5
Barra 10 C3
Barra
  ...... 90 B2
Barrancos ... 18 C2
Barranquilla . 90 A4
Barreiro ... 18 C1
Barrow 71 A4
Barrow-in-
  Furness ... 11 D5
Barry 11 F5
Barstow ... 82 C4
Bartin 46 B3
Bartlesville .. 79 A6
Barysaw ... 17 A9
Barsarabeasca 17 E9
Basel 14 E4
Bashkortostan □
  ...... 29 D6
Basilan ... 38 C2
Basildon ... 11 F7
Basingstoke . 11 F6
Basque
  Provinces =
  Pais
  Vasco □ . 19 A4
Basra = Al
  Başrah ... 47 E6
Bass Str. ... 61 H8
Bassano ... 20 B4
Bassano del
  Grappa ... 20 B4
Bassein ... 41 J10
Basseterre ... 87 C7
Basti 40 D4
Bastia 13 E8
Bastogne ... 14 C3

Bata 56 D1
Batangas ... 38 B2
Bath 11 F5
Bathurst,
  Australia . 63 B4
Bathurst,
  Canada ... 69 D4
Bathurst, C. . 70 A7
Bathurst Inlet 70 B9
Batman ... 46 C5
Batna 54 A6
Baton Rouge 79 D8
Battambang . 36 B2
Battipáglia .. 21 D5
Battle Creek . 72 C3
Battle Harbour 69 C5
Battleford ... 71 C9
Batu,
  Kepulauan 37 E1
Batu Pahat .. 37 D2
Batumi ... 25 E5
Bauru 93 G4
Bautzen ... 15 C8
Bavaria =
  Bayern □ . 15 D6
Bawean ... 37 F4
Bay City ... 72 C4
Bayamo ... 86 B4
Bayan Har
  Shan ... 34 C4
Bayburt ... 46 B5
Bayern □ ... 15 D6
Bayeux ... 12 B3
Bayındır ... 23 E6
Baykal, Oz. .. 30 D8
Bayonne ... 12 E3
Bayramiç ... 23 E6
Bayreuth ... 15 D6
Bayrūt ... 46 D3
Baytown ... 79 E6
Baza 19 D4
Beagle, Canal 95 G3
Beardmore
  Glacier ... 96 C14
Béarn 12 E3
Beauce, Plaine
  de la ... 12 B4
Beaufort Sea 66 B6
Beaufort West 58 E4
Beaumont ... 79 D6
Beaune ... 13 C6
Beauvais ... 12 B5
Beauval ... 71 C9
Beaver → ... 71 B5
Beaver ... 71 B5
Beawar ... 42 F9
Béchar ... 54 B4
Bedford ... 11 E6
Be'er Sheva . 47 E3
Be'an 35 B7
Beijing ... 35 C6
Beira 59 B6
Beirut =
  Bayrūt ... 46 D3
Beja 18 C2
Béjar 18 B3
Békéscsaba . 16 E5
Bela 42 F5
Belarus ■ ... 24 C2
Belcher Is. .. 69 C3
Belém 92 C4
Belfast ... 11 D4
Belfort ... 13 C7
Belgaum ... 43 M9
Belgium ■ .. 14 C3
Belgorod ... 24 C4
Belgrade =
  Beograd ... 22 B3
Belitung ... 37 E3
Belize ■ ... 85 D7
Belize City .. 85 D7
Bell Peninsula 68 B2
Bellary ... 43 M10

Belle-Ile ... 12 C2
Belle Isle ... 69 C5
Belle Isle, Str.
  of 69 C5
Belleville,
  Canada ... 69 D3
Belleville,
  U.S.A. ... 77 F10
Bellingham . 80 A2
Bellingshausen
  Sea 96 A2
Bellinzona ... 13 C8
Belluno ... 20 A4
Belmopan ... 85 D7
Belo Horizonte 93 F5
Beloit 77 D10
Belokorovichi 17 C9
Belonia ... 41 F8
Belorussia ■
  = Belarus ■ 24 C2
Beloye More . 28 C4
Belukha ... 29 E9
Bemidji ... 77 B7
Ben Nevis ... 10 C4
Benalla ... 63 C4
Benares =
  Varanasi ... 40 E4
Benavente ... 18 A3
Benbecula ... 10 C3
Bend 80 C3
Bendigo ... 63 C3
Benevento ... 20 D5
Bengal, Bay of 41 J7
Bengbu ... 35 C6
Benghazi =
  Banghāzi . 52 B3
Bengkulu ... 37 E2
Beni Suef ... 52 C5
Benidorm ... 19 C5
Benin ■ ... 55 G5
Benin, Bight
  of 55 H5
Benin City ... 55 G6
Benoni ... 59 D5
Benton Harbor 72 C2
Benue → ... 55 G6
Benxi 35 B7
Beograd ... 22 B3
Beppu 32 C2
Berber 53 E5
Berbera ... 49 E4
Berbérati ... 56 D3
Berdyansk ... 25 D4
Berdychiv ... 17 D9
Berehove ... 17 D6
Berestechko . 17 C7
Bereznik ... 28 C5
Berezniki ... 28 D6
Berga 19 A6
Bergama ... 23 E6
Bérgamo ... 20 B2
Bergen ... 8 F9
Bergerac ... 12 D4
Berhala, Selat 37 E2
Bering Sea .. 71 C1
Bering Strait 71 B3
Berja 19 D4
Berkeley ... 80 G2
Berkner I. ... 96 B4
Berlin 15 B7
Bermuda ■ . 67 F13
Bern 13 C7
Bernburg ... 15 C6
Bernina, Piz . 13 C8
Beroun ... 16 D2
Berry 12 C5
Bershad ... 17 D9
Berwick-upon-
  Tweed ... 10 D6
Besançon ... 13 C7
Besni 46 C4
Bessarabiya . 17 E9
Bessemer ... 74 C4

Betanzos

Betanzos ... 18 A1
Bethel 71 B3
Bethlehem,
 S. Africa .. 59 D5
Bethlehem,
 U.S.A. 73 D8
Béthune 13 A5
Betsiamites . 69 D4
Bettiah 40 D5
Betul 43 J10
Beverley 11 E6
Beverly Hills 82 C3
Beypazarı .. 46 B2
Beyşehir Gölü 46 C2
Béziers 13 E5
Bhagalpur .. 40 E6
Bhandara ... 43 J11
Bhanrer Ra. 43 H11
Bharatpur .. 42 F10
Bhatpara ... 41 F7
Bhavnagar .. 43 J8
Bhilwara ... 43 G9
Bhima → ... 43 L10
Bhimavaram 40 J3
Bhiwani 42 E10
Bhopal 43 H8
Bhubaneshwar
 .... 40 G5
Bhuj 43 H6
Bhusaval ... 43 J9
Bhutan ■ ... 41 D8
Biała Podlaska 17 B6
Białystok ... 17 B6
Biarritz 12 E3
Biberach ... 14 D5
Biddeford .. 73 C10
Bié, Planalto
 de 58 A3
Biel 13 C7
Bielefeld ... 14 B5
Biella 20 B2
Bielsko-Biała 16 D4
Bien Hoa ... 36 B3
Bienville, L. 69 C3
Big Spring .. 78 C3
Big Trout L. 69 C2
Biğa 23 D6
Bigadiç 23 E7
Biggar 71 C9
Bighorn → .. 81 B10
Bighorn Mts. 81 C10
Bihać 20 B5
Bihar 40 E5
Bihar □ 40 E5
Bijeljina ... 20 B7
Bikaner 42 E8
Bikini Atoll . 64 H11
Bila Tserkva . 17 D10
Bilaspur ... 40 F4
Bilbao 19 A4
Bilecik 46 B2
Bilhorod-
 Dnistrovskyy
 .... 25 D3
Billings 81 C9
Biloxi 79 D9
Bina-Etawah 43 G11
Bingham
 Canyon ... 81 E7
Binghamton . 73 C8
Bingöl 46 C5
Binjai 37 D1
Bioko 56 D1
Birecik 46 C4
Birmingham,
 U.K. 11 E6
Birmingham,
 U.S.A. 74 C4
Birr 11 E3
Biscay, B. of . 12 D2
Bishkek 29 E8
Biskra 54 B6
Bismarck ... 76 B4

Bismarck
 Arch. 64 K9
Bissau 55 F1
Bitlis 46 C5
Bitola 22 D3
Bitterfontein . 58 E3
Bitterroot
 Range 81 B6
Biwa-Ko ... 32 B5
Biysk 29 D9
Bjelovar ... 20 B6
Black Forest =
 Schwarzwald
 .... 14 D5
Black Hills . 76 D3
Black Sea .. 25 E3
Black
 Volta → .. 55 G4
Blackburn .. 11 E5
Blackpool .. 11 E5
Blackwater → 11 E2
Blagoveshchensk
 .... 31 D10
Blairmore .. 71 D8
Blanc, Mont . 13 D7
Blanca Peak . 83 B10
Blanes 19 B7
Blantyre ... 59 B6
Blenheim ... 65 D5
Bloemfontein 59 D5
Bloemhof ... 59 D5
Blois 12 C4
Bloomington,
 Ill., U.S.A. 77 E10
Bloomington,
 Ind., U.S.A. 72 E2
Blue Mts.,
 Oreg.,
 U.S.A. 80 C4
Blue Mts., Pa.,
 U.S.A. 73 D7
Blue Nile =
 Nîl el
 Azraq → .. 53 E5
Blue Ridge
 Mts. 75 A6
Bo Hai 35 C6
Bobo-
 Dioulasso . 55 F4
Boca Raton .. 75 F7
Bochum 14 C4
Boden 8 E12
Bodensee .. 13 C8
Bodø 8 E10
Bodrog → .. 16 D5
Bodrum 23 F6
Bogalusa ... 79 D9
Bogotá 90 C4
Bogra 41 E7
Böhmerwald 15 D7
Bohol 38 C2
Bohol Sea .. 38 C2
Boise 80 D5
Boise City .. 78 A2
Bolbec 12 B4
Bole 55 G4
Bolhrad ... 17 F9
Bolivia ■ ... 91 G6
Bologna ... 20 B3
Bolsena, L. di 20 C3
Bolshevik,
 Ostrov ... 30 B8
Bolton 11 E5
Bolu 46 B2
Bolvadin ... 46 C2
Bolzano ... 20 A3
Boma 56 F2
Bombay =
 Mumbai .. 43 K8
Bonavista .. 69 D5
Bonifacio .. 13 F8
Bonn 14 C4

Bonny, Bight
 of 56 D1
Boothia, Gulf
 of 68 A2
Boothia Pen. 70 A10
Borås 9 G10
Bordeaux .. 12 D3
Borger 78 B3
Borkum 14 B4
Borneo 37 D4
Bornholm .. 9 G11
Borysław ... 17 D6
Bosa 21 D7
Bosanska
 Gradiška . 20 B6
Bosna → ... 20 B7
Bosnia-
 Herzegovina ■
 .... 20 B6
Bosporus =
 Karadeniz
 Boğazı ... 22 D7
Boston, U.K. 11 E6
Boston, U.S.A. 73 D10
Bothnia, G. of 8 F12
Botletle → .. 58 C4
Botoşani ... 17 E8
Botswana ■ . 58 C4
Bouaké 55 G3
Bouar 56 C3
Boulder 76 E2
Boulogne-sur-
 Mer 12 A4
Bourbonnais 13 C5
Bourg-en-
 Bresse ... 13 C6
Bourg-St.-
 Maurice .. 13 D7
Bourges 12 C5
Bourgogne . 13 C6
Bourke 63 B4
Bournemouth 11 F6
Boyne → ... 11 E3
Boz Dağları . 23 E7
Bozburun .. 23 F7
Bozcaada .. 23 E6
Bozeman ... 81 C8
Bra 20 B1
Brač 20 C6
Bracciano, L.
 di 20 C4
Bräcke 8 F11
Bradenton .. 75 F6
Bradford ... 11 E6
Braga 18 B1
Bragança .. 18 B2
Brahmapur . 40 H5
Brahmanbaria 41 E8
Brahmani → 40 G6
Brahmaputra →
 .... 41 F7
Bräila 17 F8
Branco → .. 90 D6
Brandenburg 15 B7
Brandenburg □
 .... 15 B7
Brandon ... 71 D10
Brandvlei .. 58 E4
Brantford .. 69 D2
Brasília ... 93 F4
Braşov 17 F7
Brassey,
 Banjaran . 36 D5
Bratislava .. 16 D3
Bratsk 30 D8
Braunau ... 15 D7
Braunschweig 14 B6
Brawley 82 D5
Bray 11 E3
Bray, Pays de 12 B4
Brazil ■ 93 E4
Brazos → .. 79 E6

Brazzaville . 56 E3
Brčko 20 B7
Brecon 11 F5
Breda 14 C3
Bredasdorp . 58 E4
Bregenz ... 14 E5
Bremen 14 B5
Bremerhaven 14 B5
Bremerton . 80 B2
Brenner P. .. 15 E6
Bréscia 20 B3
Bressanone . 20 A3
Brest, Belarus 17 B6
Brest, France 12 B1
Bretagne ... 12 B2
Briançon ... 13 D7
Bridgeport .. 73 D9
Bridgetown . 87 D8
Bridgewater . 69 D4
Bridlington . 11 D6
Brig 13 C7
Brigham City 81 F7
Brighton ... 11 F6
Brindisi ... 21 D6
Brisbane ... 63 A5
Bristol, U.K. 11 F5
Bristol, U.S.A. 75 A6
Bristol B. .. 71 C3
Bristol
 Channel .. 11 F4
Britstown .. 58 E4
Brittany =
 Bretagne . 12 B2
Brive-la-
 Gaillarde . 12 D4
Brno 16 D3
Brodeur Pen. 68 A2
Brody 17 C7
Broken Hill . 62 B3
Brooks Ra. . 71 B5
Broughton
 Island =
 Qikiqtarjuaq 68 B4
Brownsville . 78
Brownwood . 78 D4
Bruay-en-
 Artois ... 13 A5
Bruce, Mt. . 60 E2
Bruck an der
 Mur 15 E8
Brugge 14 C2
Brunei ■ ... 36 D4
Brunswick . 75 D7
Brussel 14 C3
Bryan 79 D5
Bryansk ... 24 C3
Bucak 46 C2
Bucaramanga 90 B4
Buchach ... 17 D7
Buchans ... 69 D5
Bucharest =
 Bucureşti . 22 B6
Buckie 10 C5
Bucureşti .. 22 B6
Budapest ... 16 E4
Bude 11 F4
Buenaventura 90 C3
Buenos Aires 94 C5
Buffalo 73 C6
Bug → 16 B5
Buh → 25 D3
Bujumbura . 57 E5
Bukavu 57 E5
Bukhoro ... 29 F7
Bukittinggi . 37 E2
Bulandshahr 42 E10
Bulawayo .. 59 C5
Buldan 23 E7
Bulgaria ■ .. 22 C5
Bunbury ... 60 G2
Buncrana .. 11 D3
Bundaberg . 63

Bundi 43 G9
Bundoran .. 11 D2
Bungo-Suidō 32 C3
Bür Sa'īd .. 52 B5
Bür Südân .. 53 E6
Buraydah ... 47 F6
Burdur 46 C2
Burgas 22 C6
Burgersdorp 59 E5
Burgos 18 A4
Burgundy =
 Bourgogne 13 C6
Burhaniye . 23 E6
Burkina
 Faso ■ ... 55 F4
Burlington,
 Iowa, U.S.A. 77 E9
Burlington,
 N.C., U.S.A. 75 A8
Burlington,
 Vt., U.S.A. . 73 B9
Burlyu-Tyube 29 E8
Burma ■ ... 41 G11
Burnie 62 D4
Burnley 11 E5
Burnside → 70 B9
Bursa 23 D7
Buru 39 E3
Burundi ■ .. 57 E6
Bury St.
 Edmunds . 11 E7
Büshehr ... 44 D2
Busto Arsizio 20 B2
Buton 39 E2
Butte 81 B7
Butterworth . 36 C2
Butuan 38 C3
Buxtehude . 14 B5
Büyük
 Menderes →
 .... 23 F6
Büyükçekmece
 .... 22 D7
Buzău 17 F8
Buzen 32 C2
Byarezina → 17 B10
Bydgoszcz . 16 B3
Byelorussia =
 Belarus ■ . 24 C2
Bykhaw 17 B10
Bylot I. 68 A3
Byrranga,
 Gory 30 B8
Bytom 16 C4

Cabimas ... 90 A4
Cabinda □ .. 56 F2
Cabinet Mts. 81 B6
Cabonga,
 Réservoir . 69 D3
Cabot Str. .. 69 D5
Cabra 18 D3
Cádiz 18 D2
Cádiz, G. de . 18 D2
Caen 12 B3
Cagayan de
 Oro 38 C2
Cágliari 21 E2
Cágliari, G. di 21 E2
Cahors 12 D4
Cahul 17 F9
Caicos Is. .. 87 B5
Cairns 61 D8
Cairo = El
 Qâhira ... 52 B5
Cairo 79 A9
Cajamarca . 91 E3
Calabar 55 H6

Calábria □ .. 21 E6
Calahorra ... 19 A5
Calais 12 A4
Calamian
  Group 38 B1
Calamocha .. 19 B5
Calapan 38 B2
Calatayud ... 19 B5
Calbayog ... 38 B2
Calcutta 41 F7
Caldas da
  Rainha ... 18 C1
Caldwell 80 D5
Caledon 58 E3
Caledon → . 59 E5
Calgary 71 C8
Cali 90 C3
Calicut 43 P9
California □ . 82 B3
California, G.
  de 84 B2
Callao 91 F3
Caltagirone . 21 F5
Caltanissetta 21 F5
Calvi 13 E8
Calviá 19 C7
Calvinia 58 E3
Camagüey .. 86 B4
Camargue .. 13 E6
Cambodia ■ . 36 B3
Cambrai 13 A5
Cambrian Mts. 11 E5
Cambridge,
  U.K. 11 E7
Cambridge,
  U.S.A. ... 73 C10
Cambridge
  Bay =
  Ikaluktutiak 70 B9
Camden, Ark.,
  U.S.A. ... 79 C7
Camden, N.J.,
  U.S.A. ... 73 E8
Cameroon ■ 56 C2
Cameroun,
  Mt. 56 D1
Caminha ... 18 B1
Campánia □ 21 D5
Campbell River 84
Campbellton 63 B4
Campbelltown 10 D4
Campeche .. 85 D6
Campeche, B.
  de 85 D6
Campina
  Grande ... 92 D6
Campinas .. 94 A7
Campo
  Grande ... 93 G3
Campobasso 20 D5
Campos 93 G5
Camrose ... 71 C8
Çan 23 D6
Can Tho ... 36 B3
Canada ■ .. 70 C8
Çanakkale .. 23 D6
Çanakkale
  Boğazı ... 23 D6
Canarias, Is. 54 C1
Canberra .. 63 C4
Cangas de
  Narcea ... 18 A2
Canicatti .. 21 F4
Canigou, Mt. 12 E5
Çankırı 46 B3
Cannes 13 E7
Canora 71 C9
Cantábria □ 18 A4
Cantábrica,
  Cordillera . 18 A3
Cantal, Plomb
  du 13 D5
Canterbury .. 11 F7

Canterbury
  Plains 65 E4
Canton =
  Guangzhou 35 D6
Canton 72 D5
Cape Breton I. 69 D4
Cape Coast . 55 G4
Cape Dorset . 68 B3
Cape Dyer .. 68 B4
Cape
  Girardeau . 79 A9
Cape Town . 58 E3
Cape Verde
  Is. ■ 50 E1
Cape York
  Peninsula . 61 C7
Capraia 20 C2
Capri 21 D5
Caracas ... 90 A5
Caratinga .. 93 F5
Caravaca .. 19 C5
Carballo ... 18 A1
Carbonara, C. 21 E2
Carbondale . 79 A9
Carbonear .. 69 D5
Carbonia ... 21 E2
Carcassonne 12 E5
Carcross ... 70 B6
Cardiff 11 F5
Cardigan B. . 11 E4
Cardston ... 71 D8
Caria 23 F7
Caribbean Sea 86 D5
Cariboo Mts. 71 C7
Carlisle 11 D5
Carlow 11 E3
Carlsbad ... 78 C1
Carmacks .. 70 B6
Carman ... 71 D10
Carmarthen . 11 F4
Carmaux ... 12 D5
Carnarvon,
  Australia . 60 E1
Carnarvon,
  S. Africa . 58 E4
Carnegie, L. 60 F3
Caroline Is. .. 64 J10
Carpathians . 16 D5
Carpații
  Meridionali 17 F7
Carpentaria,
  G. of 60 C6
Carpentras .. 13 D6
Carpi 20 B3
Carrara 20 B3
Carrauntoohill 11 E2
Carrick-on-
  Suir 11 E3
Carşamba .. 46 B4
Carson City . 80 F4
Cartagena,
  Colombia . 90 A3
Cartagena,
  Spain 19 D5
Carthage ... 79 A6
Cartwright .. 68 C5
Caruaru ... 92 D6
Carúpano .. 90 A6
Carvoeiro, C. 18 C1
Casablanca . 54 B3
Cascade Ra. 80 B3
Cascais ... 18 C1
Cáscina ... 20 C3
Caserta 20 D5
Casiquiare → 90 C5
Caspe 19 B5
Casper 81 D10
Caspian Sea 29 E6
Castellammare
  di Stábia . 21 D5

Castellón de
  la Plana ... 19 C5
Castelo
  Branco ... 18 C2
Castelsarrasin 12 D4
Castelvetrano 21 F4
Castilla La
  Mancha □ . 18 C4
Castilla y
  León □ ... 18 A3
Castlebar .. 11 E2
Castleblaney 11 D3
Castlereagh → ... 63 B4
Castres 12 E5
Castries ... 87 D7
Castuera ... 18 C3
Catalca ... 22 D7
Cataluña □ . 19 B6
Catanduanes 38 B2
Catània 21 F5
Catanzaro ... 21 E6
Catskill Mts. . 73 C8
Caucasus
  Mountains 25 E5
Caux, Pays de 12 A4
Cavan 11 D3
Caxias 92 C5
Caxias do Sul 94 B6
Cayenne ... 92 A3
Cayman Is. ■ 67 H11
Ceadâr-Lunga 17 E9
Ceanannus
  Mor 11 E3
Cebu 38 B2
Cedar L. ... 71 C10
Cedar Rapids 77 E9
Cefalù 21 E5
Cegléd 16 E4
Celebes =
  Sulawesi □ 39 E2
Celebes Sea . 39 D2
Celje 20 A5
Celle 14 B6
Central
  African
  Rep. ■ .. 56 C4
Central
  Makran
  Range ... 42 F4
Ceres 58 E3
Cerignola .. 20 D5
Çerkeş 46 B3
Çerkezköy .. 22 D6
Cervera ... 19 B6
Cesena 20 B4
České
  Budějovice 16 D2
Ceskomoravská
  Vrchovina . 16 D2
Çeşme 23 E6
Cessnock ... 63 B5
Cetraro ... 21 E5
Ceuta 18 E3
Cévennes .. 13 D5
Ceyhan 46 C3
Ceylon = Sri
  Lanka ■ .. 43 R12
Chad ■ 53 E2
Chad, L. =
  Tchad, L. .. 53 F1
Chagos Arch. 27 K11
Chakradharpur
  .... 40 F5
Chalisgaon .. 43 J9
Chalon-sur-
  Saône ... 13 C6
Châlons-en-
  Champagne 13 B6
Chamba ... 42 C10
Chambal → . 42 F11
Chambéry .. 13 D6

Chamonix-
  Mont Blanc 13 D7
Champagne . 13 B6
Champaign . 72 D1
Champlain, L. 73 B9
Chandigarh . 42 D10
Chandpur ... 41 F8
Chang
  Jiang → . 35 C7
Changchun . 35 B7
Changde ... 35 D6
Changsha .. 35 D6
Changzhou . 35 C6
Channel Is. .. 11 G5
Chantada .. 18 A2
Chanthaburi . 36 B2
Chantrey Inlet 70 B10
Chanute ... 79 A6
Chao
  Phraya → 36 B2
Charente → . 12 D3
Chärikär ... 42 B6
Chärjew ... 29 F7
Charleroi ... 14 C3
Charles, C. . 73 F8
Charleston,
  S.C., U.S.A. 75 C8
Charleston,
  W. Va.,
  U.S.A. ... 72 E5
Charleville .. 63 A4
Charleville-
  Mézières . 13 B6
Charlotte ... 75 B7
Charlotte
  Amalie ... 87 C7
Charlottesville 73 E6
Charlottetown 69 D4
Charolles ... 13 C6
Charters
  Towers ... 61 E8
Chartres ... 12 B4
Châteaubriant 12 C3
Châteaulin . 12 B1
Châteauroux 12 C4
Châtellerault 12 C4
Chatham,
  N.B.,
  Canada ... 69 D4
Chatham,
  Ont.,
  Canada ... 69 D2
Chatham, U.K. 11 F7
Chattahoochee →
  .... 74 D5
Chattanooga 74 B5
Chaumont .. 13 B6
Chaves 18 B2
Cheb 16 C1
Cheboksary 24 B6
Chechenia □ 25 E6
Chehalis ... 80 B2
Cheju Do ... 35 C7
Chełm 17 C6
Chelmsford . 11 F7
Cheltenham . 11 F5
Chelyabinsk . 29 D7
Chemnitz ... 15 C7
Chenab → . 42 D7
Chengdu ... 35 C5
Chennai ... 43 N12
Cher → ... 12 C4
Cherbourg . 12 B3
Cherepovets 24 B4
Cherkasy .. 24 D3
Chernihiv .. 24 C3
Chernivtsi . 17 D7
Chernobyl =
  Chornobyl 17 C10
Cherven ... 17 B9
Chervonohrad 17 C7
Cherykaw .. 17 B10
Chesapeake . 73 F7

Chesapeake B. 73 E7
Chester, U.K. 11 E5
Chester,
  U.S.A. ... 73 E8
Chesterfield . 11 E6
Chesterfield =
  Igluligaarjuk 70 B10
Cheviot Hills . 10 D5
Cheyenne .. 76 E2
Cheyenne → 76 C4
Chhapra ... 40 E5
Chhatarpur .. 43 G11
Chhindwara . 43 H11
Chiai 20 B2
Chiavari ... 20 B2
Chiavenna .. 20 A2
Chiba 32 B7
Chibougamau 69 D3
Chicago ... 72 D2
Chichagof I. . 71 C6
Chichibu ... 32 A6
Chickasha .. 78 B5
Chiclana de la
  Frontera .. 18 D2
Chiclayo ... 91 E3
Chico 80 F3
Chicoutimi . 69 D3
Chidley, C. . 68 B4
Chiemsee .. 15 E7
Chiese → .. 20 B3
Chieti 20 C5
Chihuahua .. 84 B3
Chile ■ 94 D2
Chilka L. ... 40 H5
Chillán 94 D2
Chiloé, I. de . 95 E2
Chilpancingo 84 D5
Chimborazo . 90 D3
Chimbote .. 91 E3
Chimoio ... 59 B6
China ■ 35 C5
Chincha Alta 91 F3
Chindwin → 41 G10
Chingola ... 59 A5
Chinon 12 C4
Chipata ... 59 A6
Chişinău .. 17 E9
Chita 30 D9
Chitral 42 B7
Chittagong .. 41 F8
Chiusi 20 C3
Civasso ... 20 B1
Cholet 12 C3
Chomutov .. 16 C1
Chŏngjin ... 35 B7
Chongqing .. 35 D5
Chŏnju 35 C7
Chop 17 D6
Chornobyl .. 17 C10
Chortkiv ... 17 D7
Chorzów ... 16 C4
Chōshi 32 B7
Choybalsan . 35 B6
Christchurch 65 E5
Christiana .. 59 D5
Chūgoku-
  Sanchi ... 32 B3
Chula Vista . 82 D4
Chumphon .. 36 B1
Chungking =
  Chongqing 35 D5
Chur 13 C8
Churchill ... 70 C10
Churchill →,
  Man.,
  Canada ... 70 C10
Churchill →,
  Nfld.,
  Canada ... 69 C4
Churchill, C. 70 C10
Churchill Falls 69 C4
Churchill L. . 71 C9
Churu 42 E9
Chushal ... 42 C11

Chuvashia □ . . 24 B6
Cicero 72 D2
Ciechanów . . 16 B5
Ciénaga 90 A4
Cienfuegos . . 86 B3
Cieza 19 C5
Cijara,
  Pantano de 18 C3
Cilician Gates
  P. 46 C3
Cimişlia 17 E9
Cimone, Mte. 20 B3
Cinca → 19 B6
Cincar 20 C6
Cincinnati . . 72 E3
Çine 23 F7
Cinto, Mte. . . 13 E8
Circle 71 B5
Cirebon 37 F3
Citlaltépetl . . 84 D5
Città di
  Castello . . 20 C4
Ciudad Bolívar 90 B6
Ciudad
  Guayana . . 90 B6
Ciudad Juárez 84 A3
Ciudad
  Madero . . 84 C5
Ciudad
  Obregón . . 84 B3
Ciudad Real . 18 C4
Ciudad
  Rodrigo . . 18 B2
Ciudad
  Victoria . . 84 C5
Civitanova
  Marche . . . 20 C4
Civitavécchia 20 C3
Cizre 46 C5
Clanwilliam . 58 E2
Clarksdale . . 79 B8
Clarksville . . 74 A4
Clear, C. 11 F2
Clearwater . . 75 F6
Clearwater
  Mts. 81 B6
Clermont-
  Ferrand . . 13 D5
Cleveland . . 72 D5
Clinton,
  Canada . . 71 C7
Clinton, U.S.A. 77 E9
Clinton
  Colden L. . 70 B9
Clones 11 D3
Clonmel 11 E3
Clovis 78 B2
Cluj-Napoca . 17 E6
Clyde → 10 D4
Clyde, Firth of 10 D4
Clyde River . 68 A4
Coast Mts. . . 70 C7
Coast Ranges 80 F2
Coats I. 68 B2
Coats Land . . 96 B5
Coatzacoalcos 85 D6
Cobalt 69 D3
Cóbh 11 F2
Cobourg 69 D3
Coburg 15 C6
Cochabamba . 91 G5
Cochin 43 Q10
Cochrane . . . 69 D2
Cod, C. . . . 73 C10
Cœur d'Alene 80 B5
Coffeyville . . 79 A6
Coffs Harbour 63 B5
Cognac 12 D3
Coimbatore . 43 P10
Coimbra 18 B1
Coin 18 D3
Colac 62 C3
Colchester . . 11 F7

Coleman 71 D8
Coleraine . . . 11 D3
Colesberg . . 59 E5
Colima 84 D4
Coll 10 C3
Colmar 13 B7
Cologne =
  Köln 14 C4
Colombia ■ . 90 C4
Colombo . . . 43 R11
Colón 85 F9
Colonsay . . . 10 C3
Colorado □ . . 83 A10
Colorado □ . . 82 E5
Colorado
  Plateau . . 83 B7
Colorado
  Springs . . 76 F2
Columbia,
  Mo., U.S.A. 77 F8
Columbia,
  S.C., U.S.A. 75 B7
Columbia,
  Tenn.,
  U.S.A. . . . 74 B4
Columbia → 80 B1
Columbia,
  District of □ 73 E7
Columbia
  Basin 80 B4
Columbretes,
  Is. 19 C6
Columbus,
  Ga., U.S.A. 74 C5
Columbus,
  Miss.,
  U.S.A. . . . 74 C3
Columbus,
  Ohio, U.S.A. 72 E4
Colville → . . 71 A4
Colwyn Bay . 11 E5
Comácchio . . 20 B4
Comilla 41 F8
Comino, C. . . 21 D2
Committee B. 68 B2
Como 20 B2
Como, L. di . 20 B2
Comodoro
  Rivadavia . 95 F3
Comorin, C. . 43 Q10
Comoros ■ . . 51 H8
Comox 71 D7
Compiègne . . 13 B5
Comrat 17 E9
Conakry 55 G2
Concarneau . 12 C2
Concepción . . 94 D2
Conchos → . . 84 B3
Concord, N.C.,
  U.S.A. . . . 75 B7
Concord, N.H.,
  U.S.A. . . 73 C10
Conegliano . . 20 B4
Congo ■ . . . 56 E3
Congo → . . . 56 F2
Congo,
  Democratic
  Republic of
  the ■ 56 E4
Conn, L. 11 D2
Connacht □ . . 11 E2
Connecticut □ 73 D9
Connecticut →
  . . . . 73 D9
Connemara . . 11 E2
Constance, L.
  = Bodensee 13 C8
Constanţa . . 22 B7
Constantine . 54 A6
Cook, Aoraki
  Mt. 65 E4
Cook Inlet . . 71 C4
Cook Is. . . . 65 L14

Cook Strait . . 65 D6
Cootamundra 63 B4
Copenhagen =
  København 9 G10
Copper Center 71 B5
Copper Cliff . 69 D2
Coppermine =
  Kugluktuk . 70 B8
Coppermine →
  . . . . 70 B8
Coral Harbour
  = Salliq . . 68 B2
Coral Sea . . 64 L10
Corato 21 D6
Corby 11 E6
Corcubión . . 18 A1
Córdoba,
  Argentina . 94 C4
Córdoba,
  Spain . . . 18 D3
Córdova 71 B5
Corfu =
  Kérkira . . . 23 E2
Coria 18 C2
Corigliano
  Cálabro . . 21 E6
Cork 11 F2
Cork □ 22 D6
Corner Brook 69 D5
Corneşti . . . 17 E9
Cornwall . . . 69 D3
Coro 90 A5
Coronation
  Gulf 70 B8
Corpus Christi 78 F5
Corrib, L. . . . 11 E2
Corrientes . . 94 B5
Corse 13 E8
Corse, C. . . . 13 E8
Corsica =
  Corse 13 E8
Corsicana . . 79 C5
Corte 13 E8
Çorum 46 B3
Corumbá . . . 91 G7
Corvallis . . . 80 C2
Cosenza . . . 21 E6
Costa Blanca . 19 C5
Costa Brava . 19 B7
Costa del Sol . 18 D3
Costa Dorada 19 B6
Costa Rica ■ . 86 E3
Côte d'Azur . 13 E7
Côte-
  d'Ivoire ■ =
  Ivory
  Coast ■ . . 55 G3
Cotentin . . . 12 B3
Cotonou . . . 55 G5
Cotopaxi . . . 90 D3
Cotswold Hills 11 F5
Cottbus 15 C8
Council 71 B3
Council Bluffs 77 E7
Coventry . . . 11 E6
Covilhã 18 B2
Covington . . 72 E3
Cowra 63 B4
Cox's Bazar . 41 G8
Cradock . . . 59 E5
Craigavon . . 11 D3
Crailsheim . . 14 D6
Craiova 22 B4
Cranbrook . . 71 D8
Crawley 11 F6
Crazy Mts. . . 81 B8
Crema 20 B2
Cremona . . . 20 B3
Cres 20 B5
Crete = Kríti 23 G5
Créteil 12 B5
Creus, C. de . 19 A7

Creuse → . . . 12 C4
Crewe 11 E5
Crimean Pen.
  = Krymskyy
  Pivostriv . . 25 D3
Crişul
  Negru → . . 16 E5
Crna Reka → 22 D3
Croatia ■ . . . 20 B6
Cromer 11 E7
Cross Sound . 71 C6
Crotone 21 E6
Crowsnest
  Pass 71 D8
Cruzeiro do
  Sul 91 E4
Cuba ■ 86 B4
Cubango → . 58 B4
Cúcuta 90 B4
Cuenca,
  Ecuador . . 90 D3
Cuenca, Spain 19 B4
Cuenca,
  Serranía de 19 C5
Cuernavaca . 84 D5
Cuevas del
  Almanzora 19 D5
Cuiabá 93 F2
Culiacán . . . 84 C3
Cullera 19 C5
Cumaná . . . 90 A6
Cumberland,
  Canada . . 71 D7
Cumberland,
  U.S.A. . . . 73 E6
Cumberland
  Pen. 68 B4
Cumberland
  Plateau . . 72 F3
Cumberland
  Sd. 68 B4
Cúneo 20 B1
Curitiba 94 B7
Cuttack 40 G5
Cuxhaven . . 14 B5
Cuzco 91 F4
Cwmbran . . . 11 F5
Cyclades =
  Kikládhes . 23 F5
Cyprus ■ . . . 46 D3
Czech Rep. ■ 16 D2
Częstochowa 16 C4

Da Lat 36 B3
Da Nang 36 A3
Dacca =
  Dhaka . . . 41 F8
Dachau 15 D6
Dadra and
  Nagar
  Haveli □ . . 43 J8
Dadu 42 F5
Dagestan □ . 25 E6
Dagupan . . . 38 A2
Dahod 43 H9
Daió-Misaki . 32 C5
Dakar 55 F1
Dakhla 54 D1
Dalaman → . 23 F7
Dalhousie . . 69 D4
Dalian 35 C7
Dallas 79 C5
Dalmacija . . 20 C6
Daloa 55 G3
Dalton 74 B5
Damaraland . 58 C3
Damascus =
  Dimashq . . 46 D4
Damāvand . . 44 C3
Damiel 18 C4
Dampier 60 E2

Danbury . . . 73 D9
Dandeldhura 40 C3
Dandenong . . 63 C4
Dandong . . . 35 B7
Danger Pt. . . 58 E3
Dannemora . 9 F11
Dannevirke . . 64 D7
Danube =
  Dunărea → 17 F9
Danville 75 A8
Dar es Salaam 57 F7
Darbhanga . . 40 D5
Dardanelles =
  Çanakkale
  Boğazı . . . 23 D6
Dargai 42 B7
Dargaville . . 64 A5
Darıca 22 D7
Darién, G. del 90 B3
Darjiling . . . 40 D7
Darling → . . 62 B3
Darling Ra. . . 60 G2
Darlington . . 11 D6
Darmstadt . . 14 D5
Darnley, C. . 96 A10
Darnley B. . . 70 B7
Dartmoor . . . 11 F5
Dartmouth . . 69 D4
Darwin 60 C5
Dasht → . . . 42 G2
Datça 23 F6
Datong 35 B6
Daugava → . 24 B1
Daugavpils . . 24 B2
Daulpur . . . 42 F10
Dauphin . . . 71 C9
Dauphiné . . . 13 D6
Davao 38 C3
Davao, G. of 38 C3
Davenport . . 77 E9
David 86 E3
Davis Str. . . 68 B5
Davos 13 C8
Davyd
  Haradok . 17 B8
Dawson . . . 70 B6
Dax 12 E3
Dayton 72 E3
Daytona
  Beach . . . 75 E7
Dead Sea . . 47 E3
Death Valley . 82 B4
Debar 22 D3
Debrecen . . 16 E5
Decatur, Ala.,
  U.S.A. . . . 74 B4
Decatur, Ill.,
  U.S.A. . . 77 F10
Deccan . . . 43 L11
Děčín 16 C2
Dee → 10 C5
Deggendorf . 15 D7
Dehra Dun . . 42 D11
Delano 82 C3
Delaware □ . 73 E8
Delaware → . 73 E8
Delhi 42 E10
Delice → . . . 46 C3
Delmenhorst 14 B5
Demanda,
  Sierra de la 18 A4
Demirci 23 E7
Demirköy . . 22 D6
Den Helder . 14 B3
Denia 19 C6
Deniliquin . . 63 C3
Denmark ■ . 9 G9
Denmark Str. 66 C17
Denpasar . . 37 F5
Denton 79 C5
Denver 76 F2
Deoghar . . . 40 E6
Deolali 43 K8

Deosai Mts. . 42 B9
Dera Ghazi
 Khan 42 D7
Dera Ismail
 Khan 42 D7
Derby 11 E6
Derg, L. ... 11 E2
Des Moines . 77 E8
Des
 Moines → 77 E9
Desna → .. 17 C10
Despeñaperros,
 Paso 18 C4
Dessau 14 C5
Detmold 14 C5
Detroit 72 C4
Deutsche
 Bucht ... 14 A5
Deventer ... 14 B4
Devonport .. 64 B6
Dewas 43 H10
Dezhneva,
 Mys 31 C16
Dhaka 41 F8
Dhamtari ... 40 G5
Dhanbad 40 F6
Dhankuta ... 40 E7
Dhar 43 H9
Dharwad ... 43 M9
Dhaulagiri .. 40 C4
Dhenkanal .. 40 G5
Dhíkti Óros .. 23 G5
Dhírfis 23 E4
Dhodhekánisos
 .... 23 F6
Dhuburi ... 41 D7
Dhule 43 J9
Diamantina →
 .... 62 A2
Diefenbaker L. 71 C9
Dieppe 12 B4
Digby 69 D4
Digges Is. .. 68 B3
Digne-les-
 Bains ... 13 D7
Dijlah,
 Nahr → . 47 L6
Dijon 13 C6
Dili 39 F3
Dillingham .. 71 C4
Dimashq ... 46 D4
Dinajpur ... 41 D7
Dinan 12 B2
Dinant 14 C3
Dinar 46 C2
Dinara Planina 20 B7
Dinard 12 B2
Dingle 11 E1
Dingwall ... 10 C4
Dinosaur
 National
 Monument 81 B9
Dir 42 B7
Disteghil Sar 42 A9
Diu 43 J7
Diyarbakır .. 46 C5
Djerid, Chott 54 B6
Djibouti ■ .. 49 E3
Dnepropetrovsk
 =
 Dnipropetrovsk
 .... 25 D3
Dnipro → .. 25 D3
Dniprodzerzhynsk
 .... 25 D3
Dnipropetrovsk
 .... 25 D4
Dnister → .. 17 E10
Dnistrovskyy
 Lyman → 17 E10
Doberai,
 Jazirah .. 39 E4
Doboj 20 B7

Dobreta-
 Turnu-
 Severin .. 22 B4
Dobrich 22 C6
Dobrush ... 17 B10
Dodecanese =
 Dhodhekánisos
 .... 23 F6
Dodge City .. 78 A3
Dodoma 57 F7
Dohazari ... 41 F9
Dolbeau ... 69 D3
Dole 13 C6
Dolomiti ... 20 A3
Dolphin and
 Union Str. . 70 B8
Dominica ■ . 87 C7
Dominican
 Rep. ■ ... 87 C5
Domodóssola 20 A2
Don →,
 Russia ... 25 D4
Don →, U.K. 10 C5
Don Benito . 18 C3
Donau =
 Dunărea → 17 F9
Donauwörth . 14 D6
Doncaster ... 11 E6
Donegal ... 11 D2
Donetsk 25 D4
Dongting Hu 35 D6
Donostia =
 San
 Sebastián . 19 A5
Dora
 Báltea → . 20 B2
Dorchester, C. 68 B3
Dordogne → 12 D3
Dordrecht ... 14 C3
Dornbirn ... 14 E5
Dortmund ... 14 C4
Dos Hermanas 18 D3
Dothan 74 D5
Douai 13 A5
Douala 56 D1
Douarnenez . 12 B1
Doubs → .. 13 C6
Douglas, U.K. 11 D4
Douglas,
 U.S.A. ... 83 E8
Douro → ... 18 B1
Dover 11 F7
Dover, Str. of 11 F9
Dovrefjell .. 8 F9
Dragichyn .. 17 B7
Draguignan . 13 E7
Drakensberg 59 E5
Dráma 22 D5
Drammen ... 9 G10
Drava → ... 20 B7
Dresden ... 15 C7
Dreux 12 B4
Drina → ... 20 B7
Drochia 17 D8
Drogheda .. 11 E3
Drohobych .. 17 D6
Drumheller .. 71 C8
Drut → 17 B10
Drygalski I. . 96 A11
Dubăsari ... 17 E9
Dubăsari
 Vdkhr. ... 17 E9
Dubawnt → 70 B9
Dubawnt, L. . 70 B9
Dubayy 44 E3
Dubbo 63 B4
Dublin, Ireland 11 E3
Dublin, U.S.A. 75 C6
Dubno 17 C7
Dubrovnik .. 20 C7
Dubrovytsya . 17 C8
Dudinka 30 C6
Dugi Otok .. 20 B5

Duisburg ... 14 C4
Duluth 77 B8
Dumfries ... 11 D5
Dun Laoghaire 11 E3
Dunărea → . 17 F9
Dunbar 10 D5
Duncan ... 78 B5
Dundalk 11 D3
Dundee,
 S. Africa . 59 D6
Dundee, U.K. 10 C5
Dunedin ... 65 F4
Dunfermline . 10 C5
Dungarvan .. 11 E3
Dunkerque .. 12 A5
Durance → . 13 E6
Durango,
 Mexico ... 84 C4
Durango,
 Spain ... 19 A4
Durban 59 D6
Düren 14 C4
Durg 40 G3
Durgapur ... 40 F6
Durham, U.K. 11 D6
Durham,
 U.S.A. ... 75 B8
Durrësi 22 D2
Dursunbey .. 23 E7
Dushanbe ... 29 F7
Düsseldorf .. 14 C4
Dutch Harbor 71 C3
Duyun 35 D5
Düzce 46 B2
Dvina,
 Severnaya →
 .... 28 C5
Dwarka ... 43 H6
Dyer, C. ... 68 B4
Dyersburg .. 79 A9
Dymer 17 C10
Dzerzhinsk .. 24 B5
Dzhankoy ... 25 D3
Dzyarzhynsk . 17 B8
Dzyatlava ... 17 B7

East China
 Sea 35 C7
East Kilbride 10 D4
East London 59 E5
East Orange . 73 D6
East St. Louis 77 F9
East Timor =
 Timor
 Timur □ .. 39 F3
Eastbourne . 11 F7
Eastern Ghats 43 N11
Eastmain ... 69 C3
Eastmain → 69 C3
Eau Claire .. 77 C9
Eberswalde-
 Finow ... 15 B7
Ebro → ... 19 B6
Eceabat ... 23 D6
Ech Chéliff .. 54 A5
Echo Bay ... 70 B8
Echuca 63 C3
Ecija 18 D3
Ecuador ■ .. 90 D3
Eder → ... 14 C5
Édhessa ... 23 D4
Edinburg ... 78 F4
Edinburgh .. 10 D5
Ediniţa 17 D8
Edirne 22 D6
Edmonton ... 71 C6
Edmundston 69 C6
Edremit ... 23 E6
Edremit
 Körfezi ... 23 E6
Edson 71 C8
Edward, L. .. 57 E5

Edward VII
 Land 96 C17
Edwards
 Plateau ... 78 D3
Égadi, Ísole . 21 F4
Eger 16 E5
Egersund ... 9 G9
Egmont, Mt. . 64 C6
Eğridir 46 C2
Eğridir Gölü . 46 C2
Egypt ■ ... 52 C5
Eibar 19 A4
Eifel 14 C4
Eigg 10 C3
Eildon, L. ... 63 C4
Eindhoven .. 14 C3
Eire =
 Ireland ■ .. 11 E3
Eisenach ... 14 C6
Eisenerz ... 15 E8
El Aaiún ... 54 C2
El Centro ... 82 D5
El Dorado,
 Ark., U.S.A. 79 C7
El Dorado,
 Kans.,
 U.S.A. ... 78 A5
El Escorial .. 18 B3
El Faiyûm ... 52 C5
El Fâsher ... 53 F4
El Ferrol ... 18 A1
El Gîza 52 C5
El Iskandarîya 52 B4
El Jadida ... 54 B3
El Khartûm .. 53 E5
El Mahalla el
 Kubra ... 52 B5
El Mansûra . 52 B5
El Minyâ ... 52 C5
El Obeid ... 53 F5
El Paso 83 E9
El Prat de
 Llobregat . 19 B7
El Puerto de
 Santa María 18 D2
El Qâhira ... 52 B5
El Reno 78 B5
El Salvador ■ 85 E7
El Suweis ... 52 C5
Elâzığ 46 C4
Elba 20 C3
Elbasani ... 22 D3
Elbe → ... 14 B5
Elbert, Mt. .. 83 A9
Elbeuf 12 B4
Elbidtan ... 46 C4
Elblag 16 A4
Elbrus 25 E5
Elburz Mts. =
 Alborz,
 Reshteh-ye
 Kühhā-ye . 44 B3
Elche 19 C5
Elda 19 C5
Elde → ... 15 B6
Eldoret ... 57 D7
Elephant I. .. 96 A4
Eleuthera ... 86 A4
Elgin, U.K. .. 10 C5
Elgin, U.S.A. 72 C1
Elizabeth,
 Australia . 62 B2
Elizabeth,
 U.S.A. ... 73 D6
Elizabeth City 75 A9
Elizabethton . 75 A6
Elkhart 72 D3
Elko 80 E6
Ellsworth
 Land 96 B1
Elmshorn ... 14 B5
Eluru 40 J3
Elvas 18 C2

Ely 11 E7
Emāmrūd .. 44 B3
Embrun ... 13 D7
Emden 14 B4
Emerson ... 71 D10
Emet 23 E7
Emmen 14 B4
Empangeni . 59 D6
Ems → ... 14 B4
Enderby Land 96 A9
Enez 23 D6
Engadin ... 13 C9
Enggano ... 37 F2
England □ .. 11 E6
Englewood .. 76 F2
English
 Channel .. 11 F5
Enid 78 A5
Enna 21 F5
Ennis 11 E2
Enniskillen .. 11 D3
Enns → ... 15 D8
Enschede ... 14 B4
Ensenada ... 84 A1
Entebbe ... 57 D6
Entroncamento
 .... 18 C1
Enugu 55 G6
Eólie, Ís. ... 21 E5
Épernay ... 13 B5
Ephesus ... 23 F6
Épinal 13 B7
Equatorial
 Guinea ■ . 56 D1
Erciyaş Dağı . 46 C3
Erdek 23 D6
Erebus, Mt. . 96 B15
Ereğli, Konya,
 Turkey ... 46 C3
Ereğli,
 Zonguldak,
 Turkey ... 46 B2
Eresma → .. 18 B3
Erfurt 15 C6
Ergani 46 C4
Érice 21 E4
Erie 73 C5
Erie, L. ... 72 C5
Erimanthos .. 23 F3
Erimo-misaki 32 F12
Eritrea ■ ... 49 E2
Erlangen ... 15 D6
Ermenak ... 46 C3
Erne, Lower L. 11 D3
Erode 43 P10
Erzgebirge .. 15 C7
Erzincan ... 46 C4
Erzurum ... 46 C5
Es Sahrâ' Esh
 Sharqîya . 52 C5
Esbjerg ... 9 J7
Esch-sur-
 Alzette ... 13 B6
Esfahān ... 44 C2
Eskilstuna .. 9 G11
Eskimo Pt. =
 Arviat ... 70 B10
Eskişehir ... 46 C2
Esla → ... 18 B2
Eşme 23 E7
Esmeraldas .. 90 C3
Esperance ... 60 G3
Espichel, C. . 18 C1
Espinhaço,
 Serra do . 93 F5
Essen 14 C4
Esslingen ... 14 D5
Estevan ... 71 D9
Estonia ■ ... 24 B2
Estrêla, Serra
 da 18 B2
Estremoz ... 18 C2
Étampes ... 12 B5

Etawah 42 F11
Ethiopia ■ .. 49 F2
Etna 21 F5
Eufaula 74 D5
Eugene 80 C2
Euphrates =
  Furāt, Nahr
  al → .. 47 E6
Eureka 80 E1
Europa, Picos
  de 18 A3
Evanston .. 72 C2
Evansville .. 72 F2
Everest, Mt. . 40 C6
Everett 80 B2
Everglades
  National
  Park 75 G7
Évora 18 C2
Évreux 12 B4
Évry 12 B5
Évvoia 23 E5
Exeter 11 F5
Exmoor 11 F5
Exmouth ... 11 F5
Extremadura □
  .... 18 C2
Eyre, L. 60 F6
Eyre Cr. → . 62 A2
Eyre Pen. ... 62 B2
Ezine 23 E6

F.Y.R.O.M. =
  Macedonia ■
  .... 22 D3
Fabriano ... 20 C4
Faenza ... 20 B3
Færoe Is. =
  Føroyar ... 6 C4
Fair Isle 10 B6
Fairbanks .. 71 B5
Fairfield, Ala.,
  U.S.A. .. 74 C4
Fairfield,
  Calif., U.S.A. 80 F2
Fairlie 65 F4
Fairweather,
  Mt. 71 C6
Faisalabad .. 42 D8
Faizabad ... 40 D4
Fakfak 39 E4
Falaise ... 12 B3
Falconara
  Marittima . 20 C4
Falcone, C. .. 20 D2
Fălești 17 E8
Falkland Is. □ 95 G5
Fall River .. 73 D10
Falmouth ... 11 F4
False B. 58 E3
Falun 9 F11
Fano 20 C4
Farāh 42 C3
Fareham ... 11 F6
Farghona ... 29 E8
Fargo 76 B6
Faro 18 D2
Fársala ... 23 E4
Farvel, Kap =
  Uummannarsuaq
  .... 68 C6
Fasano 21 D6
Fastiv 17 C9
Fatehgarh .. 42 F11
Fatehpur ... 40 E3
Favara 21 F4
Favignana ... 21 F4
Faya-Largeau 53 E2
Fayetteville,
  Ark., U.S.A. 79 A6
Fayetteville,
  N.C., U.S.A. 75 B8

Fazilka 42 D9
Fdérik 54 D2
Feather → .. 80 F3
Fécamp 12 B4
Fehmarn ... 15 A6
Feilding ... 64 D6
Feira de
  Santana . 93 E6
Feldkirch ... 14 E5
Felixstowe .. 11 F7
Feodosiya .. 25 D4
Fermo 20 C4
Ferrara 20 B3
Ferret, C. ... 12 D3
Fès 54 B4
Fetlar 10 A6
Feuilles → .. 68 C3
Fianarantsoa 59 J9
Ficksburg .. 59 D5
Figeac 12 D5
Figueira da
  Foz 18 B1
Figueras ... 19 A7
Fiji ■ 64 L12
Filiatrá 23 F3
Filyos → ... 46 B3
Finike 46 C2
Finisterre, C. 18 A1
Finland ■ ... 8 F13
Finland, G. of 9 G13
Finlay → ... 70 C7
Fiora → 20 C3
Firenze 20 C3
Firozabad .. 42 F11
Firozpur ... 42 D9
Fish → 58 D3
Fishguard .. 11 E4
Flagstaff ... 83 C7
Flaming
  Gorge
  Reservoir . 81 E9
Flandre ... 14 C2
Flathead L. .. 81 B6
Flattery, C. .. 80 A1
Flensburg .. 14 A5
Flers 12 B3
Flin Flon ... 71 C9
Flinders → .. 61 D7
Flinders Ras. 62 B2
Flint 72 C4
Florence =
  Firenze .. 20 C3
Florence, Ala.,
  U.S.A. .. 74 B4
Florence, S.C.,
  U.S.A. .. 75 B8
Flores 39 F2
Flores Sea .. 39 F2
Florești ... 17 E9
Florianópolis 94 B7
Florida □ ... 75 F6
Florida, Straits
  of 86 B3
Flórina 23 D3
Florø 8 F9
Foça 23 E6
Focșani ... 17 F8
Fóggia 20 D5
Föhr 14 A5
Foix 12 E4
Foligno 20 C4
Folkestone .. 11 F7
Fond du Lac . 77 D10
Fondi 20 D4
Fonsagrada . 18 A2
Fontainebleau 13 B5
Fontenay-le-
  Comte .. 12 C3
Forfar 10 C5
Forli 20 B4
Formentera .. 19 C6
Formentor, C.
  de 19 C7

Fórmia 20 D4
Formosa =
  Taiwan ■ . 35 D7
Føroyar ... 6 C4
Forst 15 C8
Fort Collins . 76 E2
Fort Dodge .. 77 D7
Fort Albany . 69 C2
Fort-de-France 87 D7
Fort Franklin 70 B7
Fort Good-
  Hope 70 B7
Fort
  Lauderdale 75 F7
Fort Liard .. 70 B7
Fort Macleod 71 D8
Fort
  McPherson 70 B6
Fort Myers .. 75 F7
Fort Norman 70 B7
Fort Peck L. . 81 B10
Fort Pierce .. 75 F7
Fort
  Providence 70 B8
Fort
  Resolution 70 B8
Fort
  Sandeman 42 D6
Fort Scott .. 79 A6
Fort Severn . 69 C2
Fort Simpson 70 B7
Fort Smith,
  Canada .. 70 B8
Fort Smith,
  U.S.A. .. 79 B6
Fort Walton
  Beach ... 74 D4
Fort Wayne . 72 D3
Fort William 70 C4
Fort Worth .. 78 C5
Fort Yukon .. 71 B5
Fortaleza .. 92 C6
Foshan 35 D6
Fossano ... 20 B1
Fougères ... 12 B3
Foula 10 A5
Foúrnoi ... 23 F6
Foveaux Str. 65 G3
Foxe Basin .. 68 B3
Foxe Chan. .. 68 B2
Foxe Pen. .. 68 B3
Francavilla
  Fontana . 21 D6
France ■ ... 13 C5
Franche-
  Comté ... 13 C6
Francistown 59 C5
Frankfort,
  Brandenburg,
  Germany . 15 B8
Frankfurt,
  Hessen,
  Germany . 14 C5
Fränkische Alb 15 D6
Franklin B. .. 70 B7
Franklin Mts. 70 B7
Franklin Str. . 70 A10
Frankston ... 63 C4
Frantsa Iosifa,
  Zemlya ... 28 A6
Franz 69 D2
Fraser → ... 71 D7
Fraser I. ... 63 A5
Fraserburgh . 10 C5
Fredericksburg
  .... 73 E7
Fredericton .. 69 D4
Fredrikstad .. 9 G10
Freeport ... 77 D10
Freetown ... 55 G2
Fregenal de la
  Sierra ... 18 C2
Freiburg ... 14 E4

Freising ... 15 D6
Freistadt ... 15 D8
Fréjus 13 E7
Fremont ... 82 B2
French
  Guiana ■ . 92 B3
French
  Polynesia ■ 65 M16
Fresnillo ... 84 C4
Fresno 82 B3
Fribourg ... 13 C7
Friedrichshafen
  .... 14 E5
Frobisher B. . 68 B4
Frome, L. ... 62 B2
Front Range . 81 E11
Frosinone .. 20 D4
Frunze =
  Bishkek .. 29 E8
Frýdek-Mistek 16 D4
Fuengirola .. 18 D3
Fuentes de
  Oñoro ... 18 B2
Fuji-San 32 B6
Fujian □ ... 35 D6
Fujinomiya .. 32 B6
Fujisawa ... 32 B6
Fukuchiyama 32 B4
Fukui 32 A5
Fukuoka ... 32 C2
Fukushima .. 33 G12
Fukuyama .. 32 B3
Fulda 14 C5
Fulda → ... 14 C5
Fullerton ... 82 D4
Funabashi .. 32 B7
Fundão ... 18 B2
Fundy, B. of . 69 D4
Furāt, Nahr
  al → 47 E6
Furneaux
  Group ... 62 D4
Fürstenwalde 15 B8
Fürth 14 D6
Fury and
  Hecla Str. . 68 B2
Fushun 35 B7
Fuxin 35 B7
Fuzhou 35 D6
Fyn 9 G10

Gabès 54 B7
Gabon ■ ... 56 E2
Gaborone .. 59 C5
Gabrovo ... 22 C5
Gadag 43 M9
Gadarwara .. 43 H11
Gadsden ... 74 C4
Gagnon ... 69 C4
Gainesville,
  Fla., U.S.A. 75 E6
Gainesville,
  Ga., U.S.A. 75 B6
Gainesville,
  Tex., U.S.A. 78 C5
Gairdner, L. . 62 B2
Galashiels .. 10 D5
Galați 17 F9
Galatina ... 21 D7
Galdhøpiggen 8 F9
Galesburg .. 77 E9
Galicia □ ... 18 A2
Galilee, Sea of
  = Yam
  Kinneret . 46 D3
Gállego → .. 19 B5
Gallipoli ... 21 D6
Gallivare ... 8 E12
Galloway,
  Mull of .. 11 D4
Galveston .. 79 E6
Galway ... 11 E2

Galway B. .. 11 E2
Gambia ■ .. 55 F1
Gan Jiang → 35 D6
Gäncä 25 E6
Gandak → .. 40 E5
Gander ... 69 D5
Gandhi Sagar 43 G9
Gandia 19 C5
Ganga → ... 41 F8
Ganganagar . 42 E8
Gangdisê
  Shan ... 40 B3
Gangtok ... 41 D7
Gansu □ ... 34 C5
Gap 13 D7
Garabogazköl
  Aylagy ... 29 E6
Garda, L. di . 20 B3
Garden City . 78 A3
Garden Grove 82 D4
Gardēz 42 C6
Gargano, Mte. 20 D5
Garigliano → 20 D4
Garland ... 81 E7
Garmisch-
  Partenkirchen
  .... 14 E6
Garonne → . 12 D3
Garry, L. ... 70 B9
Gary 72 D2
Garzê 34 C5
Gascogne .. 12 E4
Gascogne, G.
  de 12 D2
Gaspé 69 D4
Gaspé, C. de 69 D4
Gaspé, Pén.
  de 69 D4
Gastonia ... 75 B7
Gata, C. de . 19 D4
Gata, Sierra
  de 18 B2
Gateshead .. 11 D6
Gauhati ... 41 D8
Gávdhos ... 23 G5
Gävle 8 F11
Gawilgarh
  Hills 43 J10
Gaya 40 E5
Gaza 47 E3
Gaziantep ... 46 C4
Gdańsk ... 16 A4
Gdańska,
  Zatoka ... 16 A4
Gdynia 16 A4
Gebe 39 D3
Gebze 22 D7
Gediz → ... 23 E6
Gedser 9 H10
Geelong ... 63 C3
Geesthacht .. 14 B6
Gejiu 34 D5
Gela 21 F5
Gelibolu ... 23 D6
Gelsenkirchen 14 C4
Gemerek ... 46 C4
Gemlik 23 D7
Geneva, L. =
  Léman, L. . 13 C7
Genève 13 C7
Genil → ... 18 D3
Gennargentu,
  Mti. del .. 21 D2
Génova ... 20 B2
Génova, G. di 20 C2
Gent 14 C2
George 58 E4
George → ... 68 C4
George Town 36 C2
George V
  Land 96 A14
Georgetown . 90 B7
Georgia □ ... 75 C6

Georgia ■ ... 25 E5
Georgian B. .. 69 D7
Gera 15 C7
Geraldton .. 60 F1
Gerede 14 B5
Germany ■ .. 14 C6
Germiston .. 59 D5
Gerona 19 B7
Getafe 18 B4
Gettysburg . 73 E7
Ghaghara → 40 E5
Ghana ■ ... 55 G4
Ghanzi 58 C4
Ghazâl, Bahr
el → 57 C6
Ghaziabad .. 42 E10
Ghazipur ... 40 E4
Ghazni 42 C6
Ghent = Gent 14 C2
Giarre 21 F5
Gibraltar ■ . 18 D3
Gibraltar, Str.
of 18 E3
Gibson Desert 60 E3
Giessen 14 C5
Gifu 32 B5
Giglio 20 C3
Gijón 18 A3
Gila → 82 D5
Gilgit 42 B9
Gióna, Óros . 23 E4
Giresun 46 B4
Giridih 40 E6
Gironde → .. 12 D3
Girvan 10 F4
Gisborne ... 64 C8
Gjoa Haven . 70 B10
Glace Bay .. 69 D5
Gladstone .. 61 E9
Glasgow ... 10 F4
Glen Canyon
National
Recreation
Area 83 B7
Glendale ... 82 C3
Glenrothes . 10 C5
Glens Falls . 73 C9
Gliwice 16 C4
Głogów 16 C3
Glomma → . 9 G11
Gloucester . 11 F5
Glusk 17 B9
Gmünd 15 D8
Gmunden ... 15 E7
Gniezno ... 16 B3
Go Cong ... 36 B3
Goa 43 M8
Goa □ 43 M8
Gobabis ... 58 C3
Gobi 31 B6
Godavari → . 40 J4
Godhra 43 H8
Gods → 71 C10
Gods L. 71 C10
Godthåb =
Nuuk 68 B5
Goiânia ... 93 F4
Gökçeada .. 23 D5
Gold Coast . 63 A5
Golden Gate . 80 G2
Goldsboro .. 75 B9
Golfo Aranci 20 D3
Golspie 10 C5
Gomel =
Homyel .. 17 B10
Gómez
Palacio .. 84 B4
Gonābād ... 44 C4
Gonda 40 D3
Gonder 53 F6
Gönen 23 D6
Good Hope, C.
of 58 E3

Goondiwindi 63 A5
Göppingen . 14 D5
Gorakhpur .. 40 D4
Goražde ... 20 C7
Gorizia 20 B4
Gorkiy =
Nizhniy
Novgorod . 24 B5
Görlitz 15 C8
Gorontalo .. 39 D2
Gorzów
Wielkopolski 16 B2
Gosford 63 B5
Goslar 14 C6
Gospič 20 B5
Göta kanal . 9 G11
Göteborg .. 9 G10
Gotha 14 C6
Gothenburg =
Göteborg . 9 G10
Gotland ... 9 G11
Göttingen .. 14 C5
Gouda 14 B3
Gouin, Rés. . 69 D3
Goulburn .. 63 B4
Governador
Valadares . 93 F5
Gozo 21 F5
Graaff-Reinet 58 E4
Gračac 20 B5
Grado 18 A2
Grafton 63 A5
Graham Bell,
Os. 28 A7
Graham Land 96 A3
Grahamstown 59 E5
Grampian
Mts. 10 C4
Gran Canaria 54 C1
Gran Chaco . 94 B3
Gran Paradiso 20 B1
Gran Sasso
d'Italia ... 20 C4
Granada 18 D4
Granby 69 D3
Grand
Bahama .. 86 A4
Grand Canyon 83 B6
Grand
Cayman .. 86 C3
Grand Coulee
Dam 80 B4
Grand Forks,
Canada .. 71 D8
Grand Forks,
U.S.A. ... 76 B6
Grand Island 76 E5
Grand Rapids,
Canada .. 71 C10
Grand Rapids,
U.S.A. ... 72 C3
Grand St.-
Bernard, Col
du 13 D7
Grand Teton 81 D8
Grande,
Rio → .. 79 D5
Grande
Baleine, R.
de la → .. 69 C3
Grande de
Santiago → 84 C3
Granite City . 77 F9
Granollers .. 19 B7
Grantham .. 11 E6
Granville ... 12 B3
Gras, L. de . 70 B8
Grasse 13 E7
Graulhet ... 12 E4
's-Gravenhage 14 B3
Graz 15 E8
Great Abaco I. 86 A4

Great
Australian
Bight 60 G4
Great Barrier
Reef 61 D8
Great Basin . 80 F5
Great Bear → 70 B7
Great Bear L. 70 B7
Great Dividing
Ra. 61 E8
Great Falls . 81 B8
Great Inagua
I. 86 B5
Great Karoo . 58 E4
Great
Ouse → .. 11 E7
Great Salt L. 81 E7
Great Salt
Lake Desert 81 E7
Great Sandy
Desert ... 60 E3
Great Slave L. 70 B8
Great Smoky
Mts. Nat.
Pk. 75 B6
Great Victoria
Desert ... 60 F4
Great
Yarmouth . 11 E7
Greater
Antilles ... 86 C5
Gredos, Sierra
de 18 B3
Greece ■ ... 23 E4
Greeley 76 E2
Green → ... 83 A8
Green Bay .. 72 B2
Greenland ■ 66 C9
Greenock ... 10 F4
Greensboro . 75 A8
Greenville,
Ala., U.S.A. 74 D4
Greenville,
Miss.,
U.S.A. ... 79 C8
Greenville,
N.C., U.S.A. 75 B9
Greenville,
S.C., U.S.A. 75 B6
Greenwood,
Miss.,
U.S.A. ... 79 C8
Greenwood,
S.C., U.S.A. 75 B6
Greifswald . 15 A7
Greiz 15 C7
Grenada ■ . 87 D7
Grenoble ... 13 D6
Grey Ra. ... 63 A3
Greymouth . 65 E4
Greytown .. 59 D6
Griffin 75 C5
Griffith 63 B4
Grimsby ... 11 E6
Gris-Nez, C. . 12 A4
Groningen .. 14 B4
Gross
Glockner . 15 E7
Grosser Arber 15 D7
Grosseto ... 20 C3
Groznyy ... 25 E6
Grudziądz .. 16 B4
Guadalajara,
Mexico ... 84 C4
Guadalajara,
Spain ... 18 B4
Guadalete → 18 D2
Guadalquivir →
.... 18 D2
Guadalupe,
Sierra de . 18 C3
Guadarrama,
Sierra de . 18 B4

Guadeloupe ■ 87 C7
Guadiana → 18 D2
Guado 18 D4
Guam ■ ... 64 H9
Guangdong □ 35 D6
Guangxi
Zhuangzu
Zizhiqu □ . 35 D5
Guangzhou . 35 D6
Guantánamo 86 B4
Guaporé → . 91 F5
Guarda 18 B2
Guatemala . 85 E6
Guatemala ■ 85 D6
Guaviare → . 90 C5
Guayaquil .. 90 D3
Guayaquil, G. de 90 D2
Guaymas ... 84 B2
Guecho 19 A4
Guelph 69 D2
Guéret 12 C4
Guernica ... 19 A4
Guernsey ... 11 G5
Guidónia-
Montecélio 20 C4
Guildford ... 11 F6
Guilin 35 D6
Guimarães . 18 B1
Guinea ■ ... 55 F2
Guinea, Gulf
of 51 F3
Guinea-
Bissau ■ .. 55 F1
Guingamp .. 12 B2
Guiyang ... 35 D5
Guizhou □ . 35 D5
Gujarat □ .. 43 H7
Gujranwala . 42 C9
Gujrat 42 C9
Gulbarga ... 43 L10
Gulf, The .. 44 E2
Gümüşhane . 46 B4
Guna 43 G10
Guntur 40 J3
Gurgaon ... 42 E10
Gurkha 40 C5
Güstrow ... 15 B7
Gütersloh .. 14 C5
Guthrie 78 B5
Guyana ■ .. 90 B7
Guyenne ... 12 D4
Gwådar 42 G3
Gwalior ... 42 F11
Gweru 59 B5
Gympie ... 63 A5
Györ 16 E3
Gypsumville 71 C10
Gyumri 25 E5

Haiti ■ 87 C5
Hakken-Zan . 32 B4
Hakodate .. 32 F12
Halab 46 C4
Halberstadt . 15 C6
Halden 9 G10
Haldwani .. 42 E11
Halifax,
Canada .. 69 D4
Halifax, U.K. 11 E6
Hall Beach .. 68 B2
Halle 15 C6
Halmahera . 39 D3
Halmstad .. 9 G10
Hamada ... 32 B3
Hamadán ... 46 C7
Hamah 46 D4
Hamamatsu . 32 B5
Hamar 8 F10
Hamburg .. 14 B6
Hameln ... 14 B5
Hamersley Ra. 60 E2
Hamilton,
Canada .. 69 D3
Hamilton, N.Z. 64 B6
Hamilton, U.K. 10 F4
Hamm 14 C4
Hammerfest . 8 D12
Hammond .. 72 D2
Hampton .. 73 F7
Han Pijesak . 20 B7
Hanamaki .. 33 G12
Hanau 14 C5
Hancock ... 77 C1
Hangzhou .. 35 C7
Hanna 71 C8
Hannibal ... 77 F9
Hannover .. 14 B5
Hanoi 35 D5
Hantsavichy . 17 B8
Haora 40 F7
Haparanda . 8 E12
Happy Valley-
Goose Bay . 69 C4
Hapur 42 E10
Harare 59 B6
Harbin 35 B7
Harbour Grace 69 D5
Hardangerfjorden
.... 9 F9
Hari → 37 E2
Haridwar ... 42 E11
Haringhata → 41 G7
Harlingen .. 78 F5
Harlow ... 11 F7
Harney Basin 80 D4
Härnösand . 8 F11
Harris 10 C3
Harrisburg . 73 D7
Harrison, C. . 68 C5
Harrison Bay 71 A4
Harrogate .. 11 D6
Hartford ... 73 D9
Hartlepool . 11 D6
Harvey 72 D2
Harwich ... 11 F7
Haryana □ .. 42 E10
Haryn → ... 17 B8
Harz 14 C6
Hasa 47 F7
Hastings, N.Z. 64 C7
Hastings, U.K. 11 F7
Hastings,
U.S.A. ... 76 E5
Hathras ... 42 F11
Hatteras, C. . 75 B10
Hattiesburg . 79 D9
Haugesund . 9 G9
Hauraki G. .. 64 B6
Haut Atlas .. 54 B3
Havana = La
Habana .. 86 B3
Havant 11 F6

Havel

Havel → 15 B7
Haverfordwest 11 F4
Havlíčkův
  Brod 16 D2
Havre 81 A9
Havza 46 B3
Hawaii □ .. 82 J12
Hawaiian Is. .. 82 H12
Hawera 64 C6
Hawick 10 D5
Hawke B. .. 64 C7
Hay River .. 70 B8
Hayes → .. 71 C10
Hayrabolu .. 22 D6
Haysyn 17 D9
Hayvoron .. 17 D9
Hazaribag .. 40 F5
Hearst 69 D2
Hebei □ 35 C6
Hebron 68 C4
Hechuan 35 C5
Heerlen 13 A6
Hefa 46 D3
Hefei 35 C6
Hegang 35 B8
Heidelberg .. 14 D5
Heilbron 59 D5
Heilbronn .. 14 D5
Heilongjiang □
  .... 35 B7
Hekimhan .. 46 C4
Helena, Ark.,
  U.S.A. .. 79 B8
Helena, Mont.,
  U.S.A. .. 81 B7
Helgoland .. 14 A4
Hellín 19 C5
Helmand → .. 42 D2
Helmsdale .. 10 B5
Helsingborg .. 9 G10
Helsinki 9 F13
Hemel
  Hempstead 11 F6
Henan □ 35 C6
Henares → .. 18 B4
Henderson .. 75 A8
Hengyang .. 35 D6
Henrietta
  Maria, C. .. 69 C2
Henzada .. 41 J10
Herāt 42 B3
Hereford .. 11 E5
Herford 14 B5
Hermosillo .. 84 B2
Hernád → .. 16 E5
Heron Bay .. 69 D2
's-
  Hertogenbosch
  .... 14 C3
Hessen □ .. 14 C5
Hewett, C. .. 68 A4
Hexham 11 D5
Hibbing 77 B8
Hickory 75 B7
Hida-
  Sammyaku 32 A5
Higashiōsaka 32 B4
High Point .. 75 B8
High River .. 71 C8
High
  Wycombe 11 F6
Hiiumaa 24 B1
Hikone 32 B4
Hildesheim .. 14 B5
Hilo 82 J13
Hilversum .. 14 B3
Himachal
  Pradesh □ 42 D10
Himalaya .. 40 C5
Himeji 32 B4
Himi 32 A5
Ḥimṣ 46 D4
Hindu Kush .. 42 B7

Hingoli 43 K10
Hinojosa del
  Duque .. 18 C3
Hiratsuka .. 32 B6
Hirosaki 33 F12
Hiroshima .. 32 B3
Hisar 42 E9
Hispaniola □ .. 87 C5
Hita 32 C2
Hitachi 32 A7
Hjälmaren .. 9 G11
Hlyboka 17 D7
Hoare B. .. 68 B4
Hobart 62 D4
Hodgson → .. 71 C10
Hódmezővásárhely
  .... 16 E5
Hodonín .. 16 D3
Hoek van
  Holland .. 14 B3
Hof 15 C7
Höfu 32 B2
Hohe Rhön .. 14 C5
Hohhot 35 B6
Hokitika 65 E4
Hokkaidō □ .. 32 F12
Holguín 86 B4
Holman 70 A8
Holy Cross .. 71 B4
Holyhead .. 11 E4
Home B. 68 B4
Homer 71 C4
Homyel 17 B10
Hondeklipbaai 58 E3
Honduras ■ .. 85 E7
Honduras, G.
  de 85 D7
Honfleur .. 12 B4
Hong Kong .. 35 D6
Honiara 64 K10
Honolulu .. 82 H12
Honshū 32 G11
Hood, Mt. .. 80 C3
Hoorn 14 B3
Hoover Dam 82 B5
Hope, Pt. .. 71 B3
Hopedale .. 68 C4
Hopetown .. 58 D4
Hoquiam .. 80 B2
Horlivka 25 D4
Hormuz, Str.
  of 44 E4
Horn 15 D8
Horn, Cape =
  Hornos, C.
  de 95 H3
Hornavan .. 8 E11
Hornos, C. de 95 H3
Hornsby 63 B5
Horodenka .. 17 D7
Horodok,
  Khmelnytskyy,
  Ukraine .. 17 D8
Horodok, Lviv,
  Ukraine .. 17 C7
Horokhiv .. 17 C7
Horsham .. 62 C3
Horton → .. 70 B7
Hospitalet de
  Llobregat . 19 B7
Hot Springs .. 79 B7
Hotan 34 C2
Houlton .. 73 A12
Houma 79 E8
Houston .. 79 E6
Hovd 34 B4
Hövsgöl Nuur 34 A5
Howrah =
  Haora 40 H7
Höxter 14 C5
Høyanger .. 8 F9
Hoyerswerda 15 C8

Hradec
  Králové .. 16 C2
Hrodna 17 B6
Hrodzyanka .. 17 B9
Hron → 16 E4
Hrymayliv .. 17 D8
Hsisha
  Chuntao .. 36 A4
Huainan 35 C6
Huambo 58 A3
Huancayo .. 91 F3
Huang He → 35 C6
Huangshi .. 35 C6
Huánuco .. 91 E3
Hubei □ 35 C6
Huddersfield 11 E6
Hudiksvall .. 8 F11
Hudson → .. 73 D8
Hudson Bay .. 68 B2
Hudson Str. .. 68 B4
Hue 36 A3
Huelva 18 D2
Huesca 19 A5
Hughenden .. 61 E7
Hughli → .. 40 G7
Hull =
  Kingston
  upon Hull . 11 E6
Hull 69 D3
Humber → .. 11 E6
Humboldt .. 71 C9
Humboldt → 80 F4
Hume, L. .. 63 C4
Hunan □ .. 35 D6
Húngaro .. 14 D4
Hüngnam .. 35 C7
Hunsrück .. 14 D4
Huntington .. 72 E4
Huntington
  Beach 82 D3
Huntly 10 C5
Huntsville .. 74 B4
Huron, L. .. 72 B4
Hutchinson .. 78
Hvar 20 C6
Hwang Ho =
  Huang
  He → 35 C6
Hyderabad,
  India 43 L11
Hyderabad,
  Pakistan .. 42 G6
Hyères 13 E7
Hyères, Is. d' 13 E7

Ialomița → .. 22 B6
Iași 17 E8
Ibadan 55 G5
Ibagué 90 C3
Ibiza 19 C6
Icá 91 F3
Iceland ■ .. 8 B4
Ichihara 32 B7
Ichikawa 32 B6
Ichinomiya .. 32 B5
Idaho □ 81 C6
Idaho Falls .. 81 D7
Idar-Oberstein 14 D4
Idhi Óros .. 23 G5
Idhra 23 F4
Ierápetra .. 23 G6
Iesi 20 C4
Ife 55 G5
Igarka 28 C9
Iglésias 21 E2
Igluligaarjuk .. 70 B10
Igneada Burnu 22 D7
Igoumenítsa .. 23 E3
Iguaçu, Cat.
  del 94 B6
Igualada 19 B6

Iida 32 B5
Iisalmi 8 F13
Iizuka 32 C2
IJsselmeer .. 14 B3
Ikaluktutiak .. 70 B9
Ikaría 23 F6
Iki 32 C1
Île-de-France .. 12 B5
Ilhéus 93 E6
Ili → 29 E8
Iller → 14 D5
Iloilo 38 B2
Ilorin 55 G5
Imabari 32 B3
Imari 32 C1
Imola 20 B3
Imperatriz .. 92 D4
Impéria 20 C2
Imperial Dam 82 D5
Imphal 41 E9
Ina 32 B5
Inarijärvi .. 8 E13
Inca 19 C7
İnce-Burnu .. 46 B3
Inchon 35 C7
Íncirliova .. 23 F6
Incomáti → .. 59 D6
Indalsälven → 8 F11
Independence,
  Kans.,
  U.S.A. .. 79 A6
Independence,
  Mo., U.S.A. 77 F7
India ■ 43 J10
Indian → .. 75 F7
Indian
  Harbour .. 68 C5
Indian Head .. 71 C9
Indiana □ .. 72 D3
Indianapolis .. 72 E2
Indigirka → .. 31 B12
Indonesia ■ .. 37 E4
Indore 43 H9
Indre → 12 C4
Indus → 43 G5
İnebolu 15 D6
Ingolstadt .. 15 D6
Ingraj Bazar .. 40 E7
Inhulec 25 D7
Inn → 15 D7
Inner Hebrides 10 C3
Inner
  Mongolia =
  Nei
  Monggol
  Zizhiqu □ . 35 B6
Innisfail 71 C8
Innsbruck .. 15 E6
Inowrocław .. 16 B4
Insein 41 J11
Interlaken .. 13 C7
International
  Falls 77 A8
Inukjuak .. 68 C3
Inuvik 70 B6
Invercargill .. 65 G3
Inverell 63 A5
Invergordon .. 10 C4
Inverness .. 10 C4
Inverurie .. 10 C5
Ioánnina .. 23 E3
Ionian Sea .. 21 F6
Iónioi Nísoi .. 23 E3
Íos 23 F5
Iowa □ 77 D8
Iowa City .. 77 E9
Ipoh 36 D2
Ipsala 22 D6
Ipswich 11 E7
Iqaluit 68 B4
Iquique 91 H4
Iquitos 90 D4

Iráklion 23 G5
Iran ■ 44 C3
Iran, Gunung-
  Gunung .. 37 D4
Irapuato .. 84 C4
Iraq ■ 46 D5
Ireland ■ .. 11 E3
Irian Jaya □ .. 39 E5
Iringa 57 F7
Irish Sea .. 11 E4
Irkutsk 30 D8
Ironwood .. 77 B9
Irpin 17 C10
Irrawaddy → 41 K10
Irtysh → 28 C7
Irún 19 A5
Irunea =
  Pamplona . 19 A5
Irvine 10 D4
Irvine 15 D7
Isar → 15 D7
Íschia 21 D4
Ise 32 B5
Ise-Wan .. 32 B5
Isère → 13 D6
Isérnia 20 D6
Ishikari-Wan .. 32 F12
Ishim → 29 D8
Ishinomaki .. 33 G12
İskenderun .. 46 C4
Islamabad .. 42 C8
Island L. .. 71 C10
Islay 10 D3
Isle → 12 D3
Isle of
  Wight □ .. 11 F6
İsmâ'ilîya .. 47 E3
Isparta 46 C2
Íspica 21 F5
Israel ■ 46 E3
Issoire 13 D5
İstanbul .. 22 D7
Istiaía 23 E4
Istra 20 B4
İstranca
  Dağları .. 22 D6
İstres 13 E6
Itabuna 93 E6
Itaipú,
  Reprêsa de 94 B6
Italy ■ 20 C4
Itháki 23 E3
Ito 32 B6
Itzehoe 14 B5
Ivanava 17 B7
Ivano-
  Frankivsk .. 17 D7
Ivanovo 24 B5
Ivatsevichy .. 17 B7
Ivory Coast ■ 55 G4
Ivrea 20 B1
Ivujivik 68 B3
Iwaki 33 G12
Iwakuni .. 32 B3
Iwata 33 H11
Iwate-San .. 33 G12
Iwo 55 G5
Izhevsk 28 D6
Izmayil 17 F9
İzmir 23 E6
İzmit 25 E2
İznik Gölü .. 23 D7
Izumi-sano .. 32 B4
Izumo 32 B3
Izyaslav .. 17 C8

Jabalpur 43 H11
Jablanica .. 22 D3
Jablonec .. 16 C2
Jaca 19 A5
Jackson,
  Mich.,
  U.S.A. .. 72 C3

Jackson, Miss., U.S.A. 79 C8
Jackson, Tenn., U.S.A. 74 B3
Jacksonville, Fla., U.S.A. 75 D7
Jacksonville, Ill., U.S.A. .. 77 F9
Jacksonville, N.C., U.S.A. 75 B9
Jacobabad ... 42 E6
Jaén 18 D4
Jaffna 43 Q12
Jahrom 44 D3
Jaipur 42 F9
Jakarta 37 F3
Jalalabad 42 B7
Jalgaon 43 J9
Jalna 43 K9
Jalón → 19 A5
Jalpaiguri ... 41 D7
Jamaica ■ ... 86 C4
Jamalpur, Bangla. 41 E7
Jamalpur, India 40 E6
Jambi 37 E2
James → 76 D6
James B. 69 C2
Jamestown, N. Dak., U.S.A. 76 B5
Jamestown, N.Y., U.S.A. 73 C6
Jammu 42 C9
Jammu & Kashmir □ 42 B10
Jamnagar ... 43 H7
Jamshedpur . 40 F6
Janesville ... 77 D10
Jaora 43 H9
Japan ■ 33 G11
Japan, Sea of 33 G11
Japurá → 90 D5
Jarama → 18 B4
Jāsk 44 E4
Jasper 74 C4
Játiva 19 C5
Jaunpur 40 E4
Java = Jawa 37 F3
Java Sea 37 E3
Jawa 37 F3
Jean Marie River 70 B7
Jedburgh ... 10 D5
Jedda = Jiddah 47 G4
Jefferson City 77 F8
Jelenia Góra 16 C4
Jelgava 24 B1
Jena 15 C6
Jequié 93 E5
Jerez de la Frontera .. 18 D2
Jerez de los Caballeros 18 C2
Jersey 11 G5
Jersey City . 73 D8
Jerusalem ... 47 E3
Jessore 41 F7
Jhang Maghiana . 42 D8
Jhansi 43 G11
Jhelum 42 C8
Jhelum → ... 42 D8
Jiamusi 35 B8
Ji'an 35 D6
Jiangsu □ ... 35 C6
Jiangxi □ ... 35 D6
Jiddah 47 G4
Jihlava 16 D2

Jihlava → .. 16 D3
Jilin 35 B7
Jima 53 G6
Jinan 35 C6
Jindrichuv Hradeç .. 16 D2
Jinja 57 D6
Jinzhou 35 B7
Jixi 35 B8
João Pessoa 92 D7
Jodhpur 42 F8
Johannesburg 59 D5
Johnson City 75 A6
Johnstown .. 73 D6
Johor Baharu 37 D2
Joliet 72 D1
Joliette 69 D3
Jolo 38 C2
Jonesboro .. 79 B8
Jönköping .. 9 G10
Jonquière .. 69 D3
Joplin 79 A6
Jordan ■ ... 47 E4
Jos 55 G6
Juan de Fuca Str. 80 A1
Juan Fernández, Arch. de . 89 G3
Juàzeiro do Norte ... 92 D6
Júcar → 19 C5
Juiz de Fora . 93 G5
Juliaca 91 G4
Jullundur ... 42 D9
Jumilla 19 C5
Junagadh ... 43 J7
Juneau 71 C6
Jungfrau ... 13 C7
Junggar Pendi 34 B3
Jura 10 D4
Jura, Mts. du 13 C7
Juruá → 90 D5
Jutland = Jylland .. 9 G9
Jylland 9 G9
Jyväskylä .. 8 F13

K

K2 .... 42 B10
Kabardino Balkaria □ 25 E5
Kābul 42 B6
Kabwe 59 A5
Kachchh, Gulf of 43 H6
Kachchh, Rann of .. 43 G6
Kachin □ ... 41 D11
Kaçkar 46 B5
Kadirli 46 C4
Kaduna 55 F6
Kaesŏng ... 35 C7
Kafirévs, Ákra 23 E5
Kağizman .. 46 B5
Kagoshima . 33 D2
Kagoshima-Wan 33 D2
Kahoolawe .. 82 H12
Kahramanmaras 46 C4
Kai, Kepulauan 39 F4
Kaifeng 35 C6
Kaiserslautern 14 D4
Kaitaia 64 A5
Kajaani 8 F13
Kakamas ... 58 D4
Kakhovka .. 25 D3
Kakhovka Vdskh. .. 25 D3
Kakinada ... 40 J4

Kalaallit Nunaat = Greenland ■ 66 C9
Kalahari ... 58 C4
Kalámai 23 F4
Kalamazoo . 72 C3
Kalan 46 C4
Kalce 20 B5
Kale 23 F7
Kalemie 57 F5
Kalgoorlie-Boulder .. 60 G3
Kalimantan . 37 E4
Kálimnos ... 23 F6
Kaliningrad . 24 C1
Kalinkavichy 17 B9
Kalisz 16 C4
Kalispell ... 81 A6
Kalmar 9 G11
Kalmykia □ . 25 D6
Kaluga 24 C4
Kalush 17 D7
Kama → 29 D6
Kamaishi ... 33 G12
Kamchatka, P-ov. 31 D13
Kamenjak, Rt. 20 B4
Kamensk Uralskiy .. 29 D7
Kamin-Kashyrskyy 17 C7
Kamina 57 F5
Kamloops .. 71 C7
Kampala 57 D6
Kampen 14 B3
Kampuchea = Cambodia ■ 36 B3
Kamsack ... 71 C9
Kamyanets-Podilskyy . 17 D8
Kamyanka-Buzka ... 17 C7
Kanaaupscow 69 C3
Kananga ... 56 F4
Kanazawa .. 32 A5
Kanchanjunga 40 D7
Kanchipuram 43 N11
Kandahar = Qandahār . 42 D4
Kandalaksha 8 C4
Kandi 55 F5
Kandy 43 R12
Kangean, Kepulauan 37 F5
Kangerlussuaq 66 C5
Kangiqsualujjuaq 68 C4
Kangiqsujuaq 68 B3
Kangirsuk .. 68 C4
Kaniapiskau → 68 C4
Kaniapiskau L. 69 C4
Kanin, Poluostrov 28 C5
Kankakee .. 72 D2
Kankan 55 F3
Kannapolis . 75 B7
Kano 55 F6
Kanoya 33 D2
Kanpur 40 D3
Kansas □ ... 76 F5
Kansas City, Kans., U.S.A. .. 77 F7
Kansas City, Mo., U.S.A. 77 F7
Kansk 30 D7
Kanuma 32 A6
Kanye 59 C5
Kaolack ... 55 F1
Kapan 25 F6
Kapfenberg 15 E8
Kaposvár .. 16 E3
Kapuas → .. 37 E3

Kapuas Hulu, Pegunungan 37 D4
Kara Kum .. 29 F6
Kara Sea ... 28 B8
Karabiğa ... 23 D6
Karabük ... 46 B3
Karaburun . 23 E6
Karacabey . 23 D6
Karacasu .. 23 F7
Karachi ... 43 G5
Karadeniz Boğazı .. 22 D7
Karaganda = Qaraghandy 29 E8
Karakalpakstan □ 29 E6
Karaman ... 46 C3
Karasburg . 58 D3
Karbalā 47 D6
Kardhitsa .. 23 E3
Karelia □ ... 28 C4
Karimata, Kepulauan 37 E3
Karimunjawa, Kepulauan 37 F4
Karkinitska Zatoka ... 25 D3
Karlovac ... 20 B5
Karlovy Vary 16 C1
Karlskrona . 9 G11
Karlsruhe .. 14 D5
Karlstad ... 9 G10
Karnal 42 E10
Karnataka □ 43 N10
Kärnten □ .. 15 E7
Kárpathos .. 23 G6
Kars 46 B5
Karsakpay . 29 E7
Karviná 16 D4
Kasai → 56 E3
Kasba L. ... 70 B9
Käshän 44 C2
Kashi 34 C2
Kásos 23 G6
Kassalâ 53 E6
Kassel 14 C5
Kastamonu . 46 B3
Kastoria ... 23 D3
Kasur 42 D9
Katanga = Shaba □ .. 57 F4
Katerini ... 23 D4
Katha 41 E11
Katihar 40 E6
Katmandu .. 40 D5
Katoomba .. 63 B5
Katowice ... 16 C4
Katsina ... 55 F6
Kattegat ... 9 G10
Kauai 82 G11
Kaunas 24 C1
Kaválla 22 D5
Kawagoe ... 32 B6
Kawaguchi . 32 B6
Kawardha .. 40 G3
Kawasaki .. 32 B6
Kawthule □ . 41 H11
Kayes 55 F2
Kayseri 46 C3
Kazakstan ■ 29 E7
Kazan 24 D2
Kazerun ... 44 D2
Kéa 23 F5
Kebnekaise . 8 E11
Kecskemét . 16 E4
Kediri 37 F4
Keetmanshoop 58 D3
Kefallinía .. 23 E3
Keighley ... 11 E6
Keith Arm .. 70 B7
Kelang 37 D2
Kelowna ... 71 D8

Kemah 46 C4
Kemerovo .. 29 D9
Kemi 8 E12
Kemijoki → . 8 E12
Kemp Land . 96 A9
Kempten ... 14 E6
Kendari ... 39 E2
Kenhardt .. 58 D4
Kenitra ... 54 B3
Kennedy ... 75 A6
Kennewick . 80 B4
Kenogami → 69 C2
Kenosha ... 72 C2
Kent Pen. .. 70 B9
Kentucky □ 72 F3
Kentville .. 69 D4
Kenya ■ ... 57 D7
Kenya, Mt. . 57 E7
Kerala □ ... 43 P10
Kerch 25 D4
Kerinci ... 37 E2
Kérkira ... 23 E2
Kermadec Trench .. 65 N13
Kermān ... 44 D4
Kerme Körfezi 23 F6
Kerrobert .. 71 C9
Keşan 22 D6
Ketchikan .. 71 C6
Keweenaw B. 69 D2
Key West .. 86 B3
Khabarovsk . 31 E11
Khairpur ... 42 F6
Khalkís ... 23 E4
Khambat, G. of 43 J8
Khandwa .. 43 J10
Khanewal .. 42 D7
Khaniá 23 G5
Khanion, Kólpos ... 23 G4
Kharagpur . 40 F6
Khargon ... 43 J9
Kharkiv ... 24 D4
Kharta 22 D7
Khartoum = El Khartûm 53 E5
Khaskovo .. 22 D5
Khatanga .. 30 B8
Khemelnik . 17 D8
Kherson ... 25 D3
Khíos 23 E6
Khmelnytskyy 17 D8
Khodoriv .. 17 D7
Khóra Sfakíon 23 G5
Khorrâmshahr 47 E7
Khotyn 17 D8
Khouribga . 54 B3
Khoyniki .. 17 C9
Khulna 41 F7
Khulna □ .. 41 F7
Khushab ... 42 C8
Khust 17 D6
Khuzdar ... 42 F5
Kicking Horse Pass ... 71 C8
Kiel 14 A6
Kiel Canal = Nord-Ostsee-Kanal → . 14 A5
Kielce 16 C5
Kieler Bucht . 14 A6
Kiev = Kyyiv 17 C10
Kigali 57 E6
Kigoma-Ujiji 57 E5
Kii-Suidō .. 32 C4
Kikládhes .. 23 F5
Kikwit 56 E3
Kilimanjaro . 57 E7
Kilis 46 C4
Kiliya 17 F9
Kilkenny .. 11 E3
Kilkís 23 D4

Killarney

Killarney 11 E2
Killeen 78 D5
Killini 23 F4
Kilmarnock . 10 D4
Kilrush 11 E2
Kimberley . 58 D4
Kimberley
  Plateau . . 60 B4
Kimmirut .. 68 B4
Kindu 57 E5
King George I. 96 A4
King George
  Is. 69 C2
King William I. 70 B10
King William's
  Town 59 E5
Kings Canyon
  National
  Park 82 B3
King's Lynn .. 11 E7
Kingsport .. 75 A6
Kingston,
  Canada .. 69 D2
Kingston,
  Jamaica . 86 C4
Kingston upon
  Hull 11 E6
Kingstown .. 87 D7
Kingsville .. 78 F5
Kinik 23 E6
Kinsale 11 F2
Kinshasa .. 56 E3
Kinston 75 B9
Kiparissia .. 23 F3
Kiparissiakós
  Kólpos .. 23 F3
Kirghizstan =
  Kyrgyzstan ■
  .... 29 E8
Kiribati ■ .. 64 K12
Kırıkkale .. 46 C3
Kirkcaldy .. 10 C5
Kirkcudbright 11 D4
Kirkenes .. 8 E14
Kirkland Lake 69 D2
Kırklareli .. 22 D6
Kirkük 46 D6
Kirkwall .. 10 B5
Kirov 28 D5
Kirovohrad .. 25 C3
Kırşehir 46 C3
Kirthar Range 42 F5
Kiruna 8 E12
Kiryū 32 A6
Kisangani .. 57 D5
Kishanganj .. 40 D7
Kishinev =
  Chişinău .. 17 E9
Kishiwada . 32 B4
Kiska I. 71 C1
Kiso-
  Sammyaku 32 B5
Kisumu 57 E6
Kitakami-
  Gawa → . 33 G12
Kitakyūshū .. 32 C2
Kitchener .. 69 D2
Kíthira 23 F4
Kíthnos 23 F5
Kitwe 59 A5
Kivertsi 17 C7
Kivu, L. 57 E5
Kızıl Irmak → 25 E4
Kladno 16 C2
Klagenfurt .. 15 E8
Klaipėda .. 24 B1
Klamath Falls 80 E2
Klamath Mts. 80 E2
Klarälven → . 9 G10
Klatovy 16 D1
Klawer 58 E3
Klerksdorp . 59 D5
Klondike .. 70 B6

Kluane L. .. 70 B6
Klyetsk 17 B8
Knossós .. 23 G5
Knoxville .. 75 B6
Kobarid 20 A4
Kōbe 32 B4
København .. 9 G10
Koblenz .. 14 C4
Kobroor,
  Kepulauan 37 F4
Kobryn 17 B7
Kočani 22 D4
Koch Bihar .. 41 D7
Kōchi 32 C3
Kodiak 71 C4
Kodiak I. 71 C4
Koforidua .. 55 G4
Kōfu 32 B6
Koh-i-Bābā .. 42 B5
Kohat 42 C7
Kokomo .. 72 D2
Kökshetaū .. 29 D7
Koksoak → . 68 C4
Kokstad 59 E5
Kolar 43 N11
Kolkata =
  Calcutta .. 41 F7
Kolguyev,
  Ostrov .. 28 C5
Kolhapur .. 43 L9
Kolín 16 C2
Köln 14 C4
Kolomna .. 24 B4
Kolomyya .. 17 D7
Kolskiy
  Poluostrov 28 C4
Kolwezi 57 G5
Kolyma → . 31 C13
Komatsu .. 32 A5
Komi □ 28 C6
Kommunizma,
  Pik 29 F8
Komotini .. 22 D5
Kompong
  Cham .. 36 B3
Kompong
  Chhnang .. 36 B2
Kompong
  Som 36 B2
Komsomolets,
  Ostrov .. 30 A7
Konin 16 B4
Konjic 20 C6
Konotop .. 24 C3
Konstanz .. 14 E5
Konya 46 C3
Konya Ovası . 46 C3
Kootenay L. . 71 D8
Koper 20 B4
Koprivnica .. 20 A6
Kopychyntsi . 17 D7
Korab 22 D3
Korça 23 D3
Korčula 20 C6
Korea,
  North ■ . 35 C7
Korea,
  South ■ . 35 C7
Korea Strait . 35 C7
Korets 17 C8
Korinthiakós
  Kólpos .. 23 E4
Kórinthos .. 23 F4
Kóriyama .. 33 G12
Körös → . 16 E5
Korosten .. 17 C9
Korostyshev . 17 C9
Kortrijk 14 C2
Kos 23 F6
Košice .. 16 D5
Kosovo □ .. 22 C3
Kôstî 53 F5
Kostopil .. 17 C8

Kostroma .. 24 B5
Koszalin .. 16 A3
Kota 43 G9
Kota Baharu . 36 C2
Kota Kinabalu 36 C5
Kotka 9 F13
Kotovsk 17 E9
Kotri 42 G6
Kotuy → . 30 B8
Kotzebue .. 71 B3
Kounradskiy . 29 E8
Kovel 17 C7
Köyceğiz .. 23 F7
Koyuk 71 B3
Koyukuk → . 71 B4
Kozan 46 C3
Kozáni 23 D3
Kozyatyn .. 17 D9
Kra, Kho Khot 36 B1
Kragujevac .. 22 B3
Krajina 20 B6
Krakatau =
  Rakata,
  Pulau 37 F3
Kraków 16 C4
Kramatorsk . 25 D4
Kranj 20 A5
Krasnodar .. 25 D4
Krasnoperekopsk
  .... 25 D3
Krasnoturinsk 28 D7
Krasnovodsk 29 E6
Krasnoyarsk . 30 D7
Krasnyy Luch 25 D4
Kratie 36 B3
Krefeld 14 C4
Kremen 20 B5
Kremenchuk . 24 D3
Kremenchuksk
  Vdskh. .. 24 D3
Kremenets .. 17 C7
Krems 15 D8
Krishna → . 40 K3
Krishnanagar 41 F7
Kristiansand . 9 G9
Kristiansund . 8 F9
Kríti 23 G5
Krivoy Rog =
  Kryvyy Rih . 25 D3
Krk 20 B5
Kronstad .. 59 D5
Krosno 16 D5
Krugersdorp . 59 D5
Krupki 17 A9
Kruševac .. 22 C3
Krychaw .. 17 B10
Krymskyy
  Pivostriv . 25 D3
Kryvyy Rih .. 25 D3
Kuala Lumpur 36 D2
Kuala
  Terengganu 36 C2
Kualakapuas 37 E4
Kuantan .. 37 D2
Kucing 37 D4
Kudat 36 C5
Kufstein .. 15 E7
Kuglaktuk .. 70 B8
Kujū-San .. 32 C2
Kula 23 E7
Kumagaya .. 32 A6
Kumamoto .. 32 C2
Kumanovo .. 22 C3
Kumasi 55 G4
Kumbakonam 43 P11
Kunlun Shan 34 C3
Kunming .. 34 D5
Kuopio 8 F13
Kupa → . 20 B6
Kupyansk .. 24 D3
Kür →. .. 25 E6
Kurashiki .. 25 B3
Kurayoshi .. 32 B3

Kure 32 B3
Kurgan 29 D7
Kurilskiye
  Ostrova .. 31 E12
Kurnool 43 L11
Kurri Kurri .. 63 B5
Kursk 24 C4
Kuruman .. 58 D4
Kurume 32 C2
Kuşadası .. 23 F6
Kushiro 32 F12
Kushtia 41 F7
Kuskokwim → 71 B3
Kuskokwim B. 71 C3
Kütahya 46 C2
Kutaisi 25 E5
Kuujjuaq .. 68 C4
Kuwait = Al
  Kuwayt .. 47 E7
Kuwait ■ .. 47 E6
Kuwana .. 32 B5
Kuybyshev =
  Samara .. 24 C7
Kuzey
  Anadolu
  Dağları .. 46 B3
Kvarner 20 B5
Kvarnerič .. 20 B5
Kwangju .. 35 C7
Kyō-ga-Saki . 32 B4
Kyōto 32 B4
Kyrgyzstan ■ 29 E8
Kyūshū 32 C2
Kyūshū-
  Sanchi .. 32 C2
Kyyiv 17 C10
Kyyivske
  Vdskh. .. 17 C10
Kyzyl Kum .. 29 E7

La Albufera . 19 C5
La Alcarria . 19 B4
La Chaux de
  Fonds .. 13 C7
La Coruña .. 18 A1
La Crosse .. 77 D9
La Estrada .. 18 A1
La Grange .. 74 C5
La Habana .. 86 B3
La Línea de la
  Concepción 18 D3
La Mancha .. 19 C4
La Palma del
  Condado . 18 D2
La Paz 91 G5
La Plata 94 D5
La Rioja □ .. 19 A4
La Robla .. 18 A3
La Roche-sur-
  Yon 12 C3
La Rochelle . 12 C3
La Roda .. 19 C4
La Seyne-sur-
  Mer 13 E6
La Spézia .. 20 B2
La Tuque .. 69 D3
Labé 55 F2
Labrador,
  Coast of .. 69 C4
Labuk, Telok 36 C5
Lac La Biche 71 C8
Lac la Martre 70 B8
Lacanau .. 12 D3
Lachine 69 D3
Lachlan → . 63 B3
Lackawanna . 73 C6
Lacombe .. 71 C8
Ladakh Ra. .. 42 B10
Ladozhskoye
  Ozero .. 28 C4

Ladysmith,
  Canada .. 71 D7
Ladysmith,
  S. Africa .. 59 D5
Lae 61 B8
Lafayette .. 79 D7
Lagos, Nigeria 55 G5
Lagos,
  Portugal .. 18 D1
Lahn → . 14 C4
Lahore 42 D9
Lahti 8 F13
Lairg 10 B4
Lake Charles 79 D7
Lake City .. 75 D6
Lake Harbour
  = Kimmirut 68 B4
Lake Worth . 75 F7
Lakeland .. 75 E7
Lakewood . 72 D5
Lakonikós
  Kólpos .. 23 F4
Lakshadweep
  Is. 26 H11
Lalín 18 A1
Lamego .. 18 B2
Lamia 23 E4
Lamon Bay . 38 B2
Lanai I. 82 H12
Lancaster,
  U.K. 11 D5
Lancaster,
  U.S.A. .. 73 D7
Lancaster Sd. 68 A2
Lanciano .. 20 C5
Landeck .. 14 E6
Landes 12 D3
Land's End . 11 F4
Landshut .. 15 D7
Langres .. 13 C6
Langres,
  Plateau de 13 C6
Languedoc .. 13 E5
Lannion .. 12 B2
Lansing .. 72 C3
Lanusei .. 21 E2
Lanzhou .. 35 C5
Laoag 38 A2
Laon 13 B5
Laos ■ 36 A3
Lappland .. 8 E12
Lapseki .. 23 D6
Laptev Sea .. 30 B10
L'Áquila .. 20 C4
Laramie .. 76 E2
Laredo 78 F4
Lárisa 23 E4
Larne 11 D4
Larvik 9 G9
Las Cruces . 83 D9
Las Palmas . 54 C1
Las Vegas .. 82 B5
Lashio 41 F11
Lassen Pk. .. 80 E3
Lastovo .. 20 C6
Latina 20 D4
Latvia ■ 24 B1
Lauchhammer 15 C7
Launceston . 62 D4
Laun 21 D5
Laurel 79 D9
Lauria 21 D5
Laurium .. 69 D2
Lausanne .. 13 C7
Laut 37 E5
Laut Kecil,
  Kepulauan 37 E5
Laval 12 B3
Lávrion 23 F5
Lawrence .. 77 F7
Lawton 78 B4
Laylá 47 G6
Lazio □ 20 C4
Le Creusot .. 13 C6

Le Havre	12 B4	Lexington, N.C., U.S.A. 75 B7	Livingstone . 59 B5	Lublin	17 C6	Mâcon, France 13 C6
Le Mans	12 C4	Leyte 38 B2	Livorno 20 C4	Lubumbashi . 59 A5	Macon, U.S.A. 75 C6
Le Mont-St.-Michel	12 B3	Lhasa 34 D4	Ljubljana .. 20 A5	Lucca 20 C3	Madagascar ■ 59 J9
Le Puy-en-Velay	13 D5	Liaoning □ .. 35 B7	Ljungan → . 8 F11	Lucena 18 D3	Madaripur . 41 F8
Le Touquet-Paris-Plage	12 A4	Liaoyuan .. 35 B7	Ljusnan → . 8 F11	Luckenwalde 15 B7	Maddalena . 20 D2
Le Tréport	12 A4	Liard → 70 B7	Llanelli 11 F4	Lucknow .. 40 D3	Madeira 54 B1
Le Verdon-sur-Mer	12 B4	Liberal 78 A3	Llanes 18 A3	Lüderitz .. 58 D3	Madeira → . 90 D7
Leavenworth	77 F7	Liberec 16 C2	Llano Estacado . 78 C2	Ludhiana .. 42 D9	Madhya Pradesh □ 43 H10
Lebanon ■	46 D3	Liberia ■ .. 55 G3	Llanos 90 C4	Ludwigsburg 14 D5	Madînat ash Sha'b .. 49 E3
Lebrija	18 D2	Libîya, Sahrâ' 52 C4	Llobregat → 19 B7	Ludwigshafen 14 D5	Madison .. 77 D10
Lecce	23 D2	Libourne .. 12 D3	Lloret de Mar 19 B7	Lufkin 79 D6	Madiun 37 F4
Lecco	20 B2	Libreville .. 56 D1	Lluchmayor . 19 C7	Lugano 13 C8	Madras = Chennai . 43 N12
Lech →	14 D6	Libya ■ 52 C2	Lobatse 59 D5	Lugo, Italy .. 20 B3	Madre, Laguna . 78 F5
Leduc	71 C8	Licata 21 F4	Lobito 58 A2	Lugo, Spain . 18 A2	Madre, Sierra 38 A2
Leeds	11 E6	Lichinga .. 59 A7	Locarno 13 C8	Luhansk 25 D4	Madrid 18 B4
Leer	14 B4	Lichtenburg . 59 D5	Loches 12 C4	Lule älv → . 8 E12	Madurai 43 Q11
Leeton	63 B4	Lida 17 C8	Lodi, Italy .. 20 B2	Luleå 8 E12	Maebashi .. 32 A6
Leeuwarden	14 B3	Liechtenstein ■ 14 E5	Lodi, U.S.A. . 80 F3	Lüleburgaz . 22 D6	Maestrazgo, Mts. del .. 19 B5
Leeuwin, C.	60 G2	Liège 14 C3	Łódź 16 C4	Lüneburg .. 14 B6	Mafeking .. 59 D5
Leeward Is.	87 C7	Lienz 15 E7	Lofoten 8 E10	Lüneburger Heide 14 B6	Mafra 18 C1
Leganés	18 C4	Liepāja 24 B1	Logan 15 E7	Lunéville .. 13 B7	Magadan .. 31 D13
Legnago	20 B3	Liffey → 11 E3	Logan, Mt. .. 70 B5	Luni → 43 G7	Magallanes, Estrecho de 95 G2
Legnica	16 C3	Lifford 11 D3	Logroño 19 A4	Luninyets .. 17 B8	Magdalena → 90 A4
Leh	42 B10	Liguria □ .. 20 B2	Lohardaga . 40 F5	Luoyang .. 35 C6	Magdeburg . 15 B6
Leicester	11 E6	Ligurian Sea 20 C3	Loir → 12 C3	Lurgan 11 D3	Magelang .. 37 F4
Leiden	14 B3	Likasi 57 G5	Loire → 12 C2	Lusaka 59 B5	Maggiore, L. 20 B2
Leie →	14 C2	Lille 13 A5	Loja 18 D3	Luta = Dalian 35 C7	Magnitogorsk 29 D6
Leine →	14 B5	Lillehammer . 8 F10	Lombárdia □ 20 B2	Luton 11 F6	Mahakam → 37 E5
Leinster □	11 E3	Lilongwe .. 59 A6	Lomblen 39 F2	Lutsk 17 C7	Mahalapye . 59 C5
Leipzig	15 C7	Lim → 20 C7	Lombok 37 F5	Luxembourg ■ 13 B7	Mahanadi → 40 G6
Leiria	18 C1	Lima, Peru . 91 F3	Lomé 55 G5	Luxembourg ■ 14 D4	Maharashtra □ 43 J9
Leitrim	11 D2	Lima, U.S.A. 72 D3	Lomond, L. .. 10 C4	Luzern 13 C8	Mahesana .. 43 H8
Lékva Ori	23 G5	Lima → 18 B1	Łomza 16 B6	Luzhou 35 D5	Mahilyow .. 17 B10
Léman, L.	13 C7	Limburg .. 14 C5	London 11 F6	Luzon 38 A2	Mahón 19 C8
Lemhi Ra.	81 C7	Limerick .. 11 E2	Londonderry 11 D3	Lviv 17 D7	Maidstone . 11 F7
Lena →	30 B10	Limfjorden . 9 G9	Londrina .. 94 A6	Lyakhavichy . 17 B8	Maiduguri . 53 F1
Leningrad = St. Peterburg	24 B3	Límnos 23 E5	Long Beach . 82 D3	Lyakhovskiye, Ostrova . 31 B12	Maijdi 41 F8
Leninsk-Kuznetskiy	29 D9	Limoges .. 12 D4	Long I., Bahamas . 86 B4	Lydenburg .. 59 D6	Maikala Ra. . 40 G3
Lens	13 A5	Limousin .. 12 D4	Long I., U.S.A. 73 D9	Lydia 23 E7	Main → 14 D5
Lentini	21 F5	Limoux 12 E5	Long Xuyen . 36 B3	Lyepyel 24 B3	Maine 12 C3
Leoben	15 E8	Limpopo → . 59 D6	Longford .. 11 E3	Lynchburg .. 73 F6	Mainland, Orkney, U.K. 10 B5
León, Mexico	84 C4	Linares 18 C4	Longlac 69 D2	Lynn Lake .. 71 C9	Mainland, Shet., U.K. 10 A6
León, Spain	18 A3	Lincoln, U.K. . 11 E6	Longview, Tex., U.S.A. 79 C6	Lyon 13 D6	Mainz 14 C5
León, Montañas de	18 A2	Lincoln, U.S.A. 77 E6	Longview, Wash., U.S.A. 80 B2	Lyonnais .. 13 D6	Maitland .. 63 B5
Leova	17 E9	Lindhos .. 23 F7	Lons-le-Saunier ... 13 C6	Lysychansk . 25 D4	Maizuru .. 32 B4
Lérida	19 B6	Lingen 14 B4	Lop Nur 34 B4	Lyuboml ... 17 C7	Majorca = Mallorca . 19 C7
Lerwick	10 A6	Lingga, Kepulauan 37 E2	Lora del Río . 18 D3	Ma'ān 47 E3	Makasar, Selat 39 E1
Les Sables-d'Olonne	12 C3	Linköping .. 9 G11	Lorain 72 D4	Maas → 14 C3	Makedhonía □ 23 D4
Leskovac	22 C3	Linxia 34 C5	Loralai 42 D6	Maastricht . 13 A6	Makgadikgadi Salt Pans . 59 C5
Lesotho ■	59 D5	Linz 15 D8	Lorca 19 D5	McAllen 78 H4	Makhachkala 25 E6
Lésvos	23 E6	Lion, G. du .. 13 E6	Lorient 12 C2	Macapá 93 B8	Makiyivka .. 25 D4
Leszno	16 C3	Lipari 21 E5	Lorraine .. 13 B7	Macau □ .. 35 D6	Makkah 47 G4
Lethbridge	71 D8	Lipcani 17 D8	Los Alamos . 83 C9	M'Clintock Chan. .. 70 A9	Makran Coast Range 42 G4
Leti, Kepulauan	39 F3	Lipetsk 24 C4	Los Angeles, Chile .. 94 D2	McComb .. 79 D8	Makurazaki . 33 D2
Letterkenny	11 D3	Lipovets .. 17 D9	Los Angeles, U.S.A. .. 82 C3	MacDonnell Ras. 60 E5	Malabar Coast 43 P9
Leuven	14 C3	Lippe → 14 C4	Los Mochis . 84 B3	Macdougall L. 70 B10	Malacca, Str. of 36 D1
Levádhia	23 E4	Liria 19 C5	Lošinj 20 B5	Macedonia ■ 22 D3	Maladzyechna 17 A8
Lévis	69 D3	Lisboa 18 C1	Lot → 12 D4	Maceió 93 D6	Málaga 18 D3
Levkás	23 E3	Lisburn 11 D3	Louis Trichardt . 59 C5	Macerata .. 20 C4	Malang 37 F4
Levkôsia = Nicosia	46 D3	Lisburne, C. . 71 B3	Louis XIV, Pte 69 C3	Macgillycuddy's Reeks 11 F2	Malanje .. 56 F3
Lewis	10 C3	Lisieux 12 B4	Louisiana □ . 79 D8	Mach 42 E5	Mälaren .. 9 G11
Lewisporte	69 D5	Lismore 63 A5	Louisville .. 72 F3	Machakos .. 57 E7	Malartya .. 17 C7
Lewiston, Idaho, U.S.A.	80 B5	Listowel .. 11 E2	Loulé 18 D1	Machala .. 90 D3	Malatya .. 46 C4
Lewiston, Maine, U.S.A.	73 B10	Lithgow 63 B5	Lourdes .. 12 E3	Machilipatnam 40 J3	Malawi ■ .. 59 A6
Lexington, Ky., U.S.A.	72 E3	Lithinon, Ákra 23 G5	Louth 11 E6	Macintyre → 63 A5	Malawi, L. .. 59 A6
		Lithuania ■ . 24 B1	Lowell 73 C10	Mackay 61 E8	Malaysia ■ . 36 D4
		Litoměřice . 16 C2	Lower Hutt . 65 D6	Mackay, L. .. 60 E4	Malazgirt .. 46 C5
		Little Missouri → 76 B3	Lowestoft .. 11 E7	Mackenzie → 70 B6	Maldives ■ . 26 J11
		Little Rock . 79 B7	Loyew 17 C10	Mackenzie Mts. 70 B6	Maléa, Ákra . 23 F4
		Liuzhou .. 35 D5	Luanda 56 F2	McKinley, Mt. 71 B4	
			Luanshya .. 59 A5	McKinney .. 79 C5	
			Luarca 18 A2	Maclear 59 E5	
			Lubbock .. 78 C4	McMurdo Sd. 96 B15	
			Lübeck 15 B6		

Maléa, Ákra

Malegaon

Malegaon 43 J9
Mali ■ 55 E4
Malin Hd. .. 10 D3
Malkara 22 D6
Mallaig 10 C4
Mallorca 19 C7
Mallow 11 E2
Malmö 9 G10
Malta ■ 21 G5
Maluku 39 E3
Malyn 17 C9
Mamahatun .. 46 C5
Man, I. of .. 11 D4
Manacor 19 C7
Manado 39 D2
Managua .. 85 E7
Manaus 90 D7
Manchester,
 U.K. 11 E5
Manchester,
 U.S.A. .. 73 C10
Mandal 9 G9
Mandalay .. 41 F11
Mandi 42 D10
Mandla 40 F3
Mandsaur .. 43 G5
Mandvi 43 H6
Manfredónia 20 D5
Mangalore .. 43 N9
Manggar .. 37 E3
Mangole 39 E3
Manicouagan →
 .... 69 D7
Manila 38 B2
Manila B. .. 38 B2
Manipur □ .. 41 E9
Manisa 23 E6
Manitoba □ .. 71 C10
Manitoba, L. 71 C10
Manitowoc .. 72 B2
Manizales .. 90 B3
Manly 63 B5
Mannar 43 Q11
Mannar, G. of 43 Q11
Mannheim .. 14 D5
Manokwari .. 39 E4
Manosque .. 13 E6
Manresa 19 B6
Mansel I. .. 68 B2
Mansfield,
 U.K. 11 E6
Mansfield,
 U.S.A. .. 72 D4
Mantes-la-
 Jolie .. 12 B4
Mántova 20 B3
Manzai 42 C7
Manzanares 18 C4
Manzhouli .. 35 B6
Maoming .. 35 D6
Mapam
 Yumco .. 40 B3
Maputo 59 D5
Mar del Plata 94 D5
Mar Menor . 19 D5
Marabá 92 D4
Maracaibo .. 90 A4
Maracaibo, L.
 de 90 B4
Maracay 90 A5
Marajó, I. de 92 C4
Marañón → .. 90 D4
Marbella .. 18 D3
Marburg .. 14 C5
Marche 12 C4
Marchena .. 18 D3
Mardan 42 B8
Mardin 46 C4
Margarita, I.
 de 90 A6
Margate .. 11 F7
Mari El □ .. 24 C8
Maribor 20 A5

Marie Byrd
 Land 96 B18
Marie-Galante 87 C7
Mariental .. 58 C3
Marília 93 G3
Marin 18 A1
Marion 79 A9
Maritimes,
 Alpes 13 D7
Mariupol .. 25 D3
Markham, Mt. 96 C15
Marmara .. 23 D6
Marmara,
 Denizi .. 22 D7
Marmaris .. 23 F7
Marmolada,
 Mte. 20 A3
Marne → .. 12 B5
Maroua 53 F1
Marquette .. 69 D2
Marquises, Is. 65 K17
Marrakech .. 54 B3
Marsala 21 F4
Marseille .. 13 E6
Marshall .. 79 C6
Marshall Is. ■ 64 J12
Marshalltown 77 D8
Martaban, G.
 of 41 J11
Martigny .. 13 C7
Martigues .. 13 E6
Martina
 Franca .. 21 D6
Martinique ■ 87 D7
Martinsville . 75 A8
Martos 18 D4
Marugame .. 32 B3
Marwar 42 G8
Maryborough 62 C3
Masan 35 C7
Maseru 59 D5
Mashhad .. 44 B4
Mashike 32 F12
Mask, L. .. 11 E2
Mason City . 77 D8
Masqat 45 F4
Massa 20 B3
Massachusetts □
 .... 73 C9
Massena .. 73 B8
Massif Central 13 D5
Masterton .. 65 D6
Masty 17 B7
Masuda 32 B2
Masvingo .. 59 C6
Matadi 56 F2
Matagami, L. 69 D3
Matamoros . 84 B5
Matane 69 D4
Mataró 19 B7
Matera 21 D6
Mathura .. 42 F10
Mato
 Grosso □ . 93 E3
Mato Grosso,
 Planalto do 93 F3
Matosinhos . 18 B1
Matsue 32 B3
Matsumoto . 32 A6
Matsusaka . 32 C5
Matsuyama . 32 C3
Mattagami → 69 C2
Matterhorn . 13 D7
Maturín 90 B6
Maubeuge .. 13 A5
Maudin Sun . 41 K10
Maui 82 H12
Maumere .. 39 F2
Maun 58 B4
Mauritania ■ 55 D2
Mauritius ■ . 51 H9
Mawlaik .. 41 F10

Mayenne → .. 12 C3
Mayo 70 B6
Mayo L. .. 70 B6
Mazar-e Sharîf 45 B6
Mazara del
 Vallo .. 21 F4
Mazarrón .. 19 D5
Mazatlán .. 84 C3
Mazurski,
 Pojezierze . 16 B5
Mazyr 17 C9
Mbabane .. 59 D6
Mbandaka .. 56 D3
Mbanza
 Ngungu .. 56 F2
Mbeya 57 F6
Mbini □ .. 56 D2
Mbuji-Mayi . 56 F4
Mead, L. .. 82 B5
Meaux 13 B5
Mecca =
 Makkah .. 47 G4
Mechelen .. 14 C3
Mecklenburg 15 B6
Mecklenburger
 Bucht .. 15 A6
Medan 37 D1
Medellín .. 90 B3
Medford 80 D2
Medicine Bow
 Ra. 81 E10
Medicine Hat 71 C8
Medina = Al
 Madînah .. 47 F4
Medina del
 Campo .. 18 B3
Medina-
 Sidonia .. 18 D3
Mediterranean
 Sea 50 C5
Médoc 12 D3
Meekatharra 60 F2
Meerut 42 E10
Mégara 23 F4
Meghalaya □ 41 E8
Mei Xian .. 35 D6
Meissen 15 C7
Mekhtar .. 42 D6
Meknès 54 B3
Mekong → .. 36 C3
Melaka 37 D2
Melanesia .. 64 K10
Melbourne,
 Australia . 63 C3
Melbourne,
 U.S.A. .. 75 E7
Mélèzes → .. 68 C3
Melfort 71 C9
Melitopol .. 25 D4
Melk 15 D8
Melun 13 B5
Melville 71 C9
Melville I. .. 60 C5
Melville Pen. 68 B2
Memmingen 14 E6
Memphis,
 Tenn.,
 U.S.A. .. 74 B3
Memphis,
 Tex., U.S.A. 78 B3
Mende 13 D5
Mendocino, C. 80 E1
Mendoza .. 94 C3
Menemen .. 23 E6
Menindee .. 62 B3
Menominee . 72 C2
Menorca .. 19 C7
Mentawai,
 Kepulauan 37 E1
Menton 13 E7
Meppel 14 B4
Merabéllou,
 Kólpos .. 23 G5

Merano 20 A3
Merced 82 B2
Mercy C. .. 68 B4
Mérida,
 Mexico .. 85 C7
Mérida, Spain 18 C2
Mérida,
 Venezuela . 90 B4
Mérida, Cord.
 de 87 E5
Meriden .. 74 C3
Merseburg . 15 C6
Mersin 46 C3
Merthyr Tydfil 11 F5
Mértola 18 D2
Mesa 83 D7
Mesolóngion 23 E3
Mesopotamia
 = Al Jazirah 46 D5
Messina, Italy 21 E5
Messina,
 S. Africa . 59 C6
Messina, Str.
 di 21 E5
Messíni 23 F4
Messiniakós
 Kólpos .. 23 F4
Metairie .. 79 E8
Metlakatla .. 71 C6
Metz 13 B7
Meuse → .. 13 A6
Mexicali .. 84 A1
México 84 D5
Mexico ■ .. 84 C4
Mexico, G. of 85 B7
Meymaneh .. 42 B4
Mézène 13 D6
Mhow 43 H9
Miami 75 G7
Miami Beach 75 G7
Mianwali .. 42 C7
Michigan □ . 72 C3
Michigan, L. . 72 C2
Michipicoten 69 D2
Micronesia,
 Federated
 States of ■ 64 J10
Middelburg . 58 E5
Middlesbrough
 .... 11 D6
Midi, Canal
 du — 12 E4
Midland .. 78 D3
Midyat 46 C5
Mieres 18 A3
Mihara 32 B3
Mikkeli 9 F13
Míkonos .. 23 F5
Mikura-Jima 32 C6
Milano 20 B2
Milâs 23 F6
Milazzo 21 E5
Mildura .. 62 B3
Miletus 23 F6
Milford Haven 11 F4
Millau 13 D5
Millinocket . 73 B11
Milne Inlet . 68 A2
Milos 23 F5
Milton Keynes 11 E6
Milwaukee .. 72 C2
Minamata .. 32 C2
Minas 94 C5
 Gerais □ . 93 F4
Mindanao .. 38 C2
Minden 14 B5
Mindoro .. 38 B2
Mindoro Str. 38 B2
Mingan 69 C4
Minho 18 B1
Minneapolis . 77 C8
Minnedosa . 71 C10
Minnesota □ 77 B8
Miño → 18 B1

Minorca =
 Menorca .. 19 C7
Minot 76 A4
Minsk 24 C2
Minto 71 B5
Mira 20 B4
Miranda de
 Ebro .. 19 A4
Miranda do
 Douro .. 18 B2
Mirpur Khas . 42 G6
Mirzapur .. 40 E4
Miskolc 16 D5
Misool 39 E4
Misrātah .. 52 B2
Misriç 46 C5
Missinaibi → 69 C2
Mississippi □ 79 C9
Mississippi →
 .... 79 E9
Mississippi
 River Delta 79 E9
Missoula .. 81 B6
Missouri □ . 77 F8
Missouri → . 77 F9
Mistassini L. 69 C3
Mitchell 76 D5
Mitchell → . 61 D7
Mitilíni 23 E6
Mito 32 A7
Mitumba,
 Chaîne des 57 F5
Miyake-Jima 32 B6
Miyako 33 G12
Miyakonojô . 32 D2
Miyazaki .. 32 D2
Mizoram □ . 41 F9
Mjøsa 8 F10
Mladá
 Boleslav . 16 C2
Mljet 20 C6
Mmabatho .. 59 D5
Mobile 74 D3
Mochudi .. 59 C5
Modane 13 D7
Módena 20 B3
Modesto .. 82 B2
Módica 21 F5
Moe 63 C4
Mogadishu =
 Muqdisho . 49 G4
Mogami → .. 33 G12
Mohyliv-
 Podilskyy . 17 D8
Moisie 69 C4
Moisie → .. 69 C4
Mojave Desert 82 C4
Moldavia ■ =
 Moldova ■ 17 E9
Molde 8 F9
Moldova ■ . 17 E9
Molepolole . 59 C5
Molfetta .. 20 D6
Moline 77 E9
Mollendo .. 91 G4
Molokai .. 82 H12
Molucca Sea 39 E2
Moluccas =
 Maluku .. 39 E3
Mombasa .. 57 E7
Mona, Canal
 de la 87 C6
Monaco ■ . 13 E7
Monahans .. 78 D2
Moncayo,
 Sierra del . 19 B5
Mönchengladbach
 .... 14 C4
Monchique . 18 D1
Monclova .. 84 B4
Mondego → . 18 B1
Mondovì .. 20 B1

Monforte de
Lemos 18 A2
Mongolia ■ . 35 B5
Mongu 58 B4
Monópoli .. 21 D6
Monroe, La.,
U.S.A. .. 79 C7
Monroe, N.C.,
U.S.A. .. 75 B7
Monrovia .. 55 G2
Mons 14 C2
Mont-de-
Marsan .. 12 E3
Montalbán . 19 B5
Montana □ . 81 B9
Montargis . 13 C5
Montauban . 12 D4
Montbéliard . 13 C7
Montceau-les-
Mines ... 13 C6
Monte-Carlo . 20 C1
Monte Santu,
C. di 21 D2
Montecristo . 20 C3
Montego Bay 86 C4
Montélimar . 13 D6
Montenegro □ 22 C2
Monterey .. 82 B2
Montería .. 90 B3
Monterrey .. 84 B4
Montes Claros 93 F5
Montesilvano
Marina .. 20 C5
Montevideo 94 C5
Montgomery 74 C4
Montijo 18 C2
Montilla ... 18 D3
Montluçon . 13 C5
Montmorillon 12 C4
Montoro ... 18 C3
Montpellier . 13 E5
Montréal .. 69 D3
Montreux .. 13 C7
Montrose,
U.K. 10 C5
Montrose,
U.S.A. ... 83 A9
Montserrat ■ 87 C7
Monza 20 B2
Monzón ... 19 B6
Moonie → . 63 A4
Moose Jaw . 71 C9
Moosomin . 71 C9
Moosonee .. 69 C2
Mopti 55 F4
Mora 8 F10
Moradabad . 42 E11
Morava →,
Serbia, Yug. 22 B3
Morava →,
Slovak Rep. 16 D4
Moray Firth . 10 C5
Morden ... 71 D10
Mordvinia □ . 24 C5
Morelia 84 D4
Morella ... 19 B5
Morena,
Sierra .. 18 C3
Morgan City 79 E8
Morioka .. 33 G12
Morlaix ... 12 B2
Moro G. ... 38 C2
Morocco ■ . 54 B3
Morogoro .. 57 F7
Morón de la
Frontera . 18 D3
Morotai ... 39 D3
Morristown 75 A6
Morvan →, . 13 C6
Morwell .. 63 C4
Moscow =
Moskva .. 24 B4
Moscow ... 80 B5

Mosel → .. 13 A7
Moshi 57 E7
Moskva .. 24 B4
Mosselbaai . 58 E4
Mossoró .. 92 D6
Most 16 C1
Mostaganem 54 A4
Mostar ... 20 C6
Mostyska .. 17 D6
Mosul = Al
Mawsil .. 46 C5
Motihari .. 40 D5
Motril ... 18 D4
Moúdhros .. 23 E5
Moulins ... 13 C5
Moulmein .. 41 J11
Mount
Gambier .. 62 C3
Mount Isa .. 61 E6
Mount Lofty
Ra. 62 B3
Mount
McKinley
National
Park 71 B4
Mount Vernon 73 D9
Mountain
View ... 82 B1
Moura 18 C2
Mozambique ■
.... 59 B7
Mozambique
Chan. ... 59 H8
Mu Us Shamo 35 C5
Muar 37 D2
Mudanjiang . 33 B7
Mudanya .. 23 D7
Mudgee ... 63 B4
Mufulira ... 59 A5
Muğla 23 F7
Mühlhausen . 14 C6
Mukacheve . 17 D6
Muktsar .. 42 D9
Mukur 42 C5
Mula 19 C5
Mulde → .. 15 C7
Mulgrave .. 69 D4
Mulhacén .. 18 D4
Mulhouse .. 13 C7
Mull 10 C4
Muller,
Pegunungan 37 D4
Mullingar .. 11 E3
Multan ... 42 D7
Mumbai .. 43 K8
Muna 39 F2
München .. 15 D6
Muncie ... 72 D3
Münden ... 14 C5
Munger ... 40 E6
Munich =
München . 15 D6
Münster .. 14 C4
Munster □ .. 11 E2
Muqdisho .. 49 G4
Muratlı ... 22 D6
Murchison → 60 F1
Murcia ... 19 C5
Murcia □ .. 19 D5
Mureş → .. 16 E5
Murfreesboro 74 B4
Müritz-see . 15 B7
Murmansk .. 24 A4
Muroran .. 32 F12
Muroto-Misaki 32 C4
Murray → .. 62 B2
Murrumbidgee →
.... 62 B3
Murtar → .. 20 C4
Murwara .. 40 F3
Murwillumbah 63 A5
Mürzzuschlag 15 E8
Muş 46 C5
Mûsa, G. .. 47 E3

Muscat =
Masqat .. 45 F4
Muscatine .. 77 E9
Musgrave
Ras. 60 F5
Musi → ... 37 E2
Muskogee .. 79 B6
Mustafakemalpaşa
.... 23 D7
Mustang .. 40 C4
Muswellbrook 63 B5
Mut 46 C3
Mutare ... 59 B6
Muzaffarnagar 42 E10
Muzaffarpur . 40 D5
Mwanza ... 57 E6
Mweru, L. .. 57 F5
My Tho ... 36 B3
Myanmar =
Burma ■ . 41 G11
Mycenae .. 23 F4
Myingyan .. 41 G10
Myitkyina .. 41 E11
Mykolayiv .. 25 D3
Mymensingh 41 E8
Mysia 23 E6
Mysore ... 43 N10

Naab → ... 15 D7
Naberezhnyye
Chelny .. 29 D6
Nâbulus ... 46 D3
Nacogdoches 79 D6
Nadiad ... 43 H8
Nadvirna .. 17 D7
Nagaland □ . 41 E10
Nagano ... 32 A6
Nagaoka .. 33 G11
Nagasaki .. 32 C1
Nagaur ... 42 F8
Nagercoil .. 43 Q10
Nagoya ... 32 B5
Nagpur ... 43 J11
Nahannin Butte 70
Nain 68 C4
Nairn 10 C5
Nairobi ... 57 E7
Najd 47 F5
Najibabad .. 42 E11
Nakamura .. 32 C3
Nakhodka .. 31 E11
Nakhon
Ratchasima 36 B2
Nakhon Si
Thammarat 36 C1
Nakina ... 69 C2
Nakuru ... 57 E7
Nalchik .. 25 E5
Nam Co ... 34 C4
Namland .. 58 C2
Namangan .. 29 E8
Namibe ... 58 B2
Namibia ■ .. 58 C2
Namibwoestyn
.... 58 C2
Namlea ... 39 E3
Nampa ... 80 D5
Nampula .. 59 B7
Namur ... 14 C2
Namwala .. 59 B5
Nanaimo .. 71 D7
Nanao ... 32 A5
Nanchang .. 35 D6
Nanchong .. 35 C5
Nancy ... 13 B7
Nanda Devi . 42 D11
Nandan ... 35 D5
Nandurbar .. 43 J9
Nanga Parbat 42 B9
Nanjing ... 35 C6
Nanning .. 35 D5
Nanping .. 35 D6
Nantes ... 12 C3

Nao, C. de la 19 C6
Naoetsu ... 32 A6
Napa 80 F2
Napier 64 C7
Naples 75 F7
Nápoli ... 21 D5
Nara 32 B4
Narayanganj 41 F8
Narbonne .. 13 E5
Nardò 23 D2
Narmada → . 43 J8
Narrandera . 63 B4
Narromine .. 63 B4
Narva 24 B2
Narvik 8 E11
Naser,
Buheirat en 52 D5
Nashville .. 74 A4
Nasik 43 K8
Nasirabad .. 42 F9
Nassau ... 86 A4
Nata 59 C5
Natal 92 D6
Natashquan . 69 C4
Natashquan →
.... 69 C4
Natchez ... 79 D8
Nathdwara .. 43 G8
Natuna Besar,
Kepulauan 37 D3
Natuna
Selatan,
Kepulauan 37 D3
Naumburg .. 15 C6
Nauru ■ ... 64 K11
Navahrudak . 17 B7
Navalmoral de
la Mata .. 18 C3
Navarra □ .. 19 A5
Navápaktos . 23 E3
Návplion ... 23 F4
Navsari ... 43 J8
Nawabshah .. 42 F6
Naxçıvan .. 25 F6
Náxos 23 F5
Nazilli ... 23 F7
Ndjamena .. 53 F1
Ndola 59 A5
Neagh, Lough 11 D3
Near Is. ... 71 C1
Neath 11 F5
Nebraska □ . 76 E5
Nébrodi,
Monti ... 21 F5
Neckar → .. 14 D5
Neepawa .. 71 C10
Negro →,
Argentina . 95 E4
Negro →,
Brazil ... 90 D6
Negros ... 38 C2
Nei Monggol
Zizhiqu □ . 35 B6
Neijiang ... 35 D5
Neiva 90 C3
Nellore ... 43 M11
Nelson,
Canada .. 71 D8
Nelson, N.Z. . 64 D5
Nelson → .. 71 C10
Nelspruit .. 59 D6
Neman → .. 9 J19
Nemuro ... 32 F13
Nemuro-
Kaikyō .. 32 F13
Nenagh ... 11 E2
Nenana ... 71 B5
Nepal ■ ... 40 D5
Neretva → .. 20 C6
Ness, L. ... 10 C4
Nesterov ■ . 17 C6
Netherlands ■ 14 B3

Netherlands
Antilles ■ . 87 D6
Nettilling L. . 68 B3
Neubrandenburg
.... 15 B7
Neuchâtel .. 13 C7
Neuchâtel, Lac
de 13 C7
Neumünster . 14 A5
Neunkirchen . 14 D4
Neuquén .. 95 D3
Neuruppin .. 15 B7
Neustrelitz .. 15 B7
Nevada □ .. 80 F5
Nevada,
Sierra,
Spain .. 18 D4
Nevada,
Sierra,
U.S.A. .. 80 F3
Nevers 13 C5
Nevşehir .. 46 C3
New
Amsterdam 90 B7
New Bedford 73 D10
New Bern .. 75 B9
New Brighton 65 E5
New Britain,
Papua N. G. 64 K10
New Britain,
U.S.A. ... 73 D9
New
Brunswick □
.... 69 D4
New
Caledonia ■ 64 M11
New Glasgow 69 D4
New Guinea . 64
New
Hampshire □
.... 73 C10
New Haven . 73 D9
New Jersey □ 73 E9
New London . 73 D9
New
Mexico □ .. 83 C9
New Orleans 79 E8
New
Plymouth . 64 C6
New South
Wales □ .. 63 B4
New
Westminster 71 D7
New York □ . 73 C8
New York City 73 D9
New
Zealand ■ . 64 D7
Newark ... 73 D8
Newburgh .. 73 D8
Newbury ... 11 F6
Newcastle,
Australia . 63 B5
Newcastle,
S. Africa . 59 D5
Newcastle-
upon-Tyne . 11 D6
Newfoundland □
.... 69 C5
Newman ... 60 E2
Newport,
Gwent, U.K. 11 F5
Newport,
I. of W.,
U.K. 11 F6
Newport,
U.S.A. .. 73 D10
Newport
News .. 73 F7
Newquay .. 11 F4
Newry ... 11 D3
Nha Trang .. 36 B3
Niagara Falls,
Canada .. 69 D3

Niagara Falls

Niagara Falls, U.S.A. . . 73 C6
Niamey . . 55 F5
Nias . . 37 D1
Nicaragua ■ 85 E7
Nicaragua, L. de . . 85 E7
Nicastro . . 21 E6
Nice . . 13 E7
Nichinan . . 33 D2
Nicobar Is. . . 27 J13
Nicosia . . 46 D3
Nicoya, Pen. de . . 85 F7
Niedersachsen □ . . 14 B5
Nienburg . . 14 B5
Niğde . . 46 C3
Niger ■ . . 55 E6
Niger → . . 55 G6
Nigeria ■ . . 55 G6
Nii-Jima . . 32 B6
Niigata . . 33 G11
Niihama . . 32 C3
Niihau . . 82
Nijmegen . . 14 C2
Nikopol . . 25 D3
Nil, Nahr en → . . 52 B5
Nil el Abyad → . 53 E5
Nil el Azraq → . 53 E5
Nile = Nil, Nahr en → . 52 B5
Nimach . . 43 G9
Nîmes . . 13 E6
Ningbo . . 35 D7
Ningxia Huizu Zizhiqu □ . 35 C5
Niobrara → . 76 D5
Niort . . 12 C3
Nipawin . . 71 C9
Nipigon, L. . 69 D2
Niš . . 22 C3
Nishinomiya 32 B4
Niterói . . 93 G5
Nitra . . 16 D4
Nitra → . . 16 E4
Niue . . 65 L14
Nivernais . . 13 C5
Nizamabad . 43 K11
Nizhniy Novgorod . 24 B6
Nizhniy Tagil 29 D6
Nizhyn . . 24 C3
Nizip . . 46 C4
Nizké Tatry . 16 D4
Nkongsamba 56 D1
Noatak . . 71 B3
Nobeoka . . 32 C2
Nocera Inferiore . 21 D5
Nogales, Mexico . 84 A2
Nogales, U.S.A. . . 83 E7
Nōgata . . 32 C2
Noire, Mts. . 12 E2
Noirmoutier, I. de . . 12 C2
Nokomis . . 71 C9
Nome . . 71 B3
Noranda . . 69 D3
Nord-Ostsee-Kanal → . 14 A5
Nordegg . . 71 C8
Norderney . . 14 B4
Norderstedt . 14 B6
Nordfriesische Inseln . . 14 A5
Nordhausen . 14 C6
Nordkapp . . 8 D13

Nordrhein-Westfalen □ 14 C4
Nordvik . . 30 B9
Norfolk . . 73 F7
Norfolk I. . . 64 M11
Norilsk . . 30 C6
Norman . . 78 B5
Norman Wells 70 B7
Normandie . 12 B4
Norrköping . 9 G11
Norrland . . 8 F11
Norseman . . 60 G3
North Battleford . 71 C9
North Bay . . 69 D3
North Bend . 80 D1
North Carolina □ . 75 B7
North Channel, Canada . . 69 D2
North Channel, U.K. . . 11 D4
North Dakota □ . 76 B4
North I. . . 64 B6
North Minch 10 B5
North Ossetia □ . 25 E5
North Platte . 76 E4
North Platte → . 76 E4
North Saskatchewan → . 71 C8
North Sea . . 10 D8
North Thompson → . 71 C7
North Uist . 10 C3
North West Frontier □ 42 B8
North West Highlands . 10 C4
North West River . . 69 C4
North West Territories □ . 70 B9
Northampton 11 E6
Northern Ireland □ . 11 D3
Northern Marianas ■ 64 H9
Northern Territory □ 60 D5
Northland □ . 64 A5
Northumberland Str. . . 69 D4
Norton Sd. . . 71 B3
Norway ■ . . 8 F10
Norway House . . 71 C10
Norwegian Sea . . 6 B5
Norwich . . 11 E7
Nossob → . . 58 D4
Noto-Hantō . 33 G11
Notre Dame B. . . 69 D5
Nottaway → 69 C3
Nottingham . 11 E6
Nouâdhibou . 54 D1
Nouakchott . 55 E1
Nouméa . . 64 M11
Noupoort . . 58 E4
Nova Iguaçu . 93 G5
Nova Scotia □ 69 D4
Novara . . 20 B2
Novaya Zemlya . . 28 B6
Novgorod . . 24 B3

Novhorod-Siverskyy . 24 C3
Novi Lígure . 20 B2
Novi Sad . . 22 B2
Novo Mesto . 20 B5
Novocherkassk . . . 25 D5
Novohrad-Volynskyy . 17 C8
Novokuznetsk 29 D9
Novomoskovsk . . . 24 C4
Novorossiysk 25 E4
Novoselytsya . 17 D8
Novoshakhtinsk . . . 25 D4
Novosibirsk . 29 D9
Novosibirskiye Ostrova . . 31 B12
Novotroitsk . 29 D6
Novovolynsk 17 C7
Novska . . 20 B6
Nowy Sącz . 16 D5
Noyon . . 13 B5
Nûbîya, Es Sahrâ En . . 52 D5
Nueltin L. . . 70 B10
Nuevo Laredo 84 B5
Nulato . . 71 B4
Nullarbor Plain . . 60 G4
Numazu . . 32 B6
Nunavut □ . . 68 B2
Nuneaton . . 11 E6
Nunivak I. . . 71 B3
Núoro . . 21 D2
Nuremberg = Nürnberg . 15 D6
Nürnberg . . 15 D6
Nutak . . 68 C4
Nuuk . . 68 B5
Nuweveldberge . . . 58 E3
Nyasa, L. = Malawi, L. 59 A6
Nyasvizh . . 17 B8
Nyíregyháza . 17 E5
Nylstroom . . 59 C5
Nysa . . 16 C3
Nysa → . . 16 B2

Ō-Shima . . 32 B6
Oahe, L. . . 76 C4
Oahu . . 82 H12
Oak Ridge . . 75 A5
Oakland . . 82 B1
Oamaru . . 65 F4
Oates Land . 96 A15
Oaxaca . . 84 D5
Ob → . . 28 C7
Oba . . 69 D2
Oban . . 10 C4
Oberhausen . 14 C4
Obi, Kepulauan 39 E3
Obihiro . . 32 F12
Obskaya Guba 28 C8
Ocala . . 75 E6
Ocaña . . 18 C4
Oceanside . . 82 D4
Ocnița . . 17 D8
Odate . . 33 F12
Odawara . . 32 B6
Ödemiş . . 23 E6
Odense . . 9 G10
Oder → . . 15 B8
Odesa . . 25 D3
Odessa . . 78 D3
Odra → . . 16 B2
Ofanto → . . 20 D6
Offa . . 55 G5
Offenbach . . 14 C5

Offenburg . . 14 D4
Oga-Hantō . 33 G11
Ōgaki . . 32 B5
Ogbomosho . 55 G5
Ogden . . 81 E8
Ogdensburg . 73 B8
Oglio → . . 20 B3
Ohio □ . . 72 D4
Ohio → . . 72 F1
Ohre → . . 16 C2
Ohrid . . 22 D3
Ohridsko Jezero . . 23 D3
Oise → . . 12 B5
Ōita . . 32 C2
Ojos del Salado, Cerro . . 94 B3
Okahandja . 58 C3
Okanogan → 80 A4
Okara . . 42 D8
Okavango Swamps . . 58 B4
Okaya . . 32 A6
Okayama . . 32 B3
Okazaki . . 32 B5
Okeechobee, L. . . 75 F7
Okefenokee Swamp . . 75 D6
Okhotsk, Sea of . . 31 D12
Oki-Shotō . . 32 A3
Okiep . . 58 D3
Okinawa-Jima 35 D7
Oklahoma □ . 78 B5
Oklahoma City 78 B5
Okmulgee . . 79 B6
Oktyabrskoy Revolyutsii, Os. . . 30 B7
Okushiri-Tō . 32 F11
Öland . . 9 G11
Ólbia . . 20 D2
Old Crow . . 70 B6
Oldenburg . 14 B5
Oldham . . 11 E5
Olekminsk . 31 C10
Oleksandriya 17 C8
Olenek → . . 30 B10
Oléron, I. d' . 12 D3
Olevsk . . 17 C8
Olhão . . 19 D2
Ólimbos, Óros 23 D4
Olinda . . 92 D7
Olivenza . . 18 C2
Olomouc . . 16 D3
Olot . . 19 A7
Olsztyn . . 16 B5
Olt → . . 22 C5
Oltu . . 46 B5
Olympia, Greece . . 23 F3
Olympia, U.S.A. . . 80 B2
Olympic Mts. 80 B2
Omagh . . 11 D3
Omaha . . 77 E7
Oman ■ . . 48 C6
Oman, G. of . 45 E4
Omaruru . . 58 C3
Ombai, Selat 39 F2
Ombrone → . 20 C3
Omdurmân . 53 E5
Ōmiya . . 32 B6
Omsk . . 29 D8
Ōmura . . 32 C1
Ōmuta . . 32 C2
Onda . . 19 C5
Ondo . . 55 G5
Onega → . . 8 F15
Onehunga . . 64 B6

Onezhskaya Guba . . 28 C4
Onezhskoye Ozero . . 28 C4
Onitsha . . 55 G6
Onoda . . 32 B2
Ontario □ . 69 D2
Ontario, L. . 73 C7
Oostende . . 14 C2
Opava . . 16 D3
Opole . . 16 C3
Oradea . . 17 E5
Orai . . 42 G11
Oral . . 24 C7
Oran . . 54 A4
Orange, Australia . . 63 B4
Orange, France . . 13 D6
Orange, U.S.A. . . 79 D7
Orangeburg . 75 C7
Oranienburg 15 B7
Oranje → . . 58 D3
Oranjemund . 58 D3
Orbetello . . 20 C3
Ordu . . 46 B4
Örebro . . 9 G11
Oregon □ . . 80 C3
Orekhovo-Zuyevo . . 24 B4
Orel . . 24 C4
Ören . . 23 F6
Orenburg . . 29 D6
Orense . . 18 A2
Orgaz . . 18 C4
Orhaneli . . 23 E7
Orhangazi . 23 D7
Orhei . . 17 E9
Orihuela . . 19 C5
Orinoco → . . 90 B6
Orissa □ . . 40 G5
Oristano . . 21 E2
Oristano, G. di 21 E2
Orizaba . . 84 D5
Orkney Is. . . 10 B5
Orlando . . 75 E7
Orléanais . . 12 C5
Orléans . . 12 C4
Ormara . . 42 G4
Ormoc . . 38 B2
Örnsköldsvik 8 F11
Orsha . . 24 C3
Orsk . . 29 D6
Ortaca . . 23 F7
Ortegal, C. . 18 A2
Orthez . . 12 E3
Ortigueira . 18 A2
Ortles . . 20 A3
Orümiyeh, Daryācheh-ye . . . 46 C6
Oruro . . 91 G5
Orvieto . . 20 C4
Ōsaka . . 32 B4
Osh . . 29 E8
Oshawa . . 69 D3
Oshkosh . . 76 B1
Oshogbo . . 55 G5
Osijek . . 20 B7
Oskarshamn 9 G11
Öskemen . . 29 E9
Oslo . . 9 G10
Oslofjorden . 9 G10
Osmaniye . . 46 C4
Osnabrück . 14 B5
Osorno . . 95 E2
Óssa, Óros . 23 E4
Ostend = Oostende . 14 C2
Öster . . 17 C10
Österdalälven 8 F10
Östersund . . 8 F10

Ostfriesische
 Inseln 14 B4
Ostrava 16 D4
Ostroh 17 C8
Ostrołęka .. 16 B5
Ostrów
 Wielkopolski 16 C3
Ostrowiec-
Świętokrzyski
 .... 16 C5
Ostuni 21 D6
Ōsumi-Kaikyō 33 D2
Osuna 18 D3
Oswego 73 C7
Otago □ ... 65 F3
Ōtake 32 B3
Otaru 32 F12
Otjiwarongo . 58 C2
Otranto ... 23 D2
Otranto, C. d' 23 D2
Otranto, Str.
 of 23 D2
Ōtsu 32 B4
Ottawa 69 D3
Ottawa Is. .. 68 C2
Ottumwa ... 77 E8
Ouachita Mts. 79 B6
Ouagadougou 55 F4
Oubangi → .. 56 E3
Oudtshoorn . 58 E4
Ouessant, I. d' 12 B1
Oujda 54 B4
Oulu 8 E13
Oulujärvi ... 8 E13
Oulujoki → .. 8 E13
Outer
 Hebrides .. 10 C3
Outjo 58 C3
Oviedo 18 A3
Ovruch 17 C9
Owase 32 B5
Owen Sound 69 D2
Owo 55 G6
Owyhee → .. 80 D5
Oxford 11 F6
Oxnard 82 C3
Oxus =
Amudarya →
 .... 29 E6
Oyama 32 A6
Oyo 55 G5
Ozamiz 38 C2
Ozark Plateau 79 A8

Paarl 58 E3
Pab Hills .. 42 F5
Pabna 41 E7
Pacaraima,
 Sierra ... 90 C6
Pachuca ... 84 C5
Padang 37 E2
Paderborn .. 14 C5
Padloping
 Island ... 68 B4
Pádova 20 B3
Paducah ... 72 F1
Pag 20 B5
Pagastikós
 Kólpos ... 23 E4
Painted Desert 83 C7
País Vasco □ 19 A4
Paisley 10 D4
Pajares,
 Puerto de . 18 A3
Pakistan ■ .. 42 E7
Pakse 36 A3
Palagruža .. 20 C6
Palanpur ... 43 G8
Palapye ... 59 C5
Palau ■ 36 C4
Palembang . 37 E2
Palencia ... 18 A3

Palermo ... 21 E4
Palestine .. 79 D6
Palghat ... 43 P10
Pali 42 G8
Paliouríon,
 Ákra 23 E4
Palk Strait .. 43 Q11
Palm Springs 82 D4
Palma, B. de 19 C7
Palma de
 Mallorca . 19 C7
Pálmas, G. di 21 E2
Palmer 71 B5
Palmer Land 96 B3
Palmerston
 North ... 64 D6
Palmi 21 E5
Palmira ... 90 C3
Palos, C. de . 19 D5
Palu 46 C5
Pamiers ... 12 E4
Pamirs 29 F8
Pamlico Sd. . 75 B10
Pampa 78 B3
Pampas ... 94 D4
Pamplona .. 19 A5
Panaji 43 M8
Panamá 85 F9
Panamá ■ .. 86 E4
Panamá, G. de 86 E4
Panama City 74 D5
Panay 38 B2
Pančevo ... 22 B3
Pandan 38 B2
Panevežys .. 24 B1
Pangkalpinang 37 E3
Pangnirtung 68 B4
Pantar 39 F2
Pantelleria . 21 F4
Papua New
 Guinea ■ . 61 B8
Pará □ 92 C3
Paracel Is. =
 Hsisha
 Chuntao . 36 A4
Paraguay ■ . 94 A5
Paraguay → . 94 B5
Paramaribo . 92 A4
Paraná 94 C4
Paraná → .. 94 C5
Parbhani ... 43 K10
Parchim ... 15 B6
Pardubice .. 16 C2
Parecis, Serra
 dos 91 F7
Parepare ... 39 E1
Párga 23 E3
Paris, France 12 B5
Paris, U.S.A. 79 C6
Park Range . 81 F10
Parkersburg . 72 E5
Parkes 63 B4
Parla 18 B4
Parma 20 B3
Parnaíba → . 92 C5
Parnassós .. 23 E4
Pärnu 24 B1
Páros 23 F5
Parramatta . 63 B5
Parry Sound 69 D3
Partinico ... 21 E4
Pasadena,
 Calif., U.S.A. 82 C3
Pasadena,
 Tex., U.S.A. 79 E6
Pascagoula . 79 D9
Pasco 80 B4
Pašman ... 20 C5
Pasni 42 G3
Passau 15 D7
Passero, C. .. 21 F5
Pasto 90 C3
Patagonia .. 95 F3

Patan, India . 43 H8
Patan, Nepal 40 D5
Paternò 21 F5
Paterson ... 73 D8
Pathankot .. 42 C9
Patiala 42 D10
Pátmos 23 F6
Patna 40 E5
Patos, L. dos 94 C6
Pátrai 23 E3
Patrakós
 Kólpos ... 23 E3
Patuakhali . 41 F8
Pau 12 E3
Pavia 20 B2
Pavlodar ... 29 D8
Pavlohrad .. 25 D4
Pawtucket .. 73 D10
Paxoí 23 E3
Pazar 46 B5
Pazardzhik . 22 C5
Peace → ... 70 C8
Peary Land . 4 A6
Pebane 59 B7
Pechenizhyn 17 D7
Pechora ... 28 C6
Pecos → ... 78 E3
Pécs 16 E4
Peebles ... 10 D5
Peel → 70 B6
Pegasus Bay 65 E5
Pegu 41 J11
Pegu Yoma . 41 H10
Peine 14 B6
Pekalongan . 37 F3
Pekanbaru . 37 D2
Pekin 77 E10
Peking =
 Beijing .. 35 C6
Pelagie, Is. .. 21 G4
Peleng 39 E2
Peljesac ... 20 C6
Pelly → 70 B6
Pelly Bay .. 68 B2
Pelly L. 70 B9
Pelopónnisos □
 .... 23 F4
Peloro, C. .. 21 E5
Pelotas 94 C6
Pelvoux,
 Massif du . 13 D7
Pematangsiantar
 .... 37 D1
Pemba I. ... 57 F7
Pembroke,
 Canada .. 69 D3
Pembroke,
 U.K. 11 F4
Peñarroya-
Pueblonuevo
 .... 18 C3
Peñas, C. de . 18 A3
Pend Oreille L. 80 A5
Pendleton .. 80 C4
Peniche ... 18 C1
Peninsular
 Malaysia □ 37 D2
Penmarch,
 Pte. de .. 12 C1
Pennines ... 11 D5
Pennsylvania □
 .... 73 D7
Penrith ... 63 B5
Pensacola .. 74 D4
Pensacola
 Mts. 96 C4
Penticton .. 71 D8
Pentland Firth 10 B5
Penza 24 C6
Penzance .. 11 F4
Peoria 77 E10
Perche,
 Collines du 12 B4
Perdido, Mte. 19 A6
Pereira 90 C3

Pereyaslav-
Khmelnytskyy
 .... 24 C3
Péribonca → 69 D3
Périgueux .. 12 D4
Perm 29 D6
Perpignan .. 13 E5
Pershotravensk
 .... 17 C8
Persian Gulf =
 Gulf, The . 44 E2
Perth,
 Australia . 60 G2
Perth, U.K. . 10 C5
Perth Amboy 73 D8
Peru ■ 90 C3
Perúgia 20 C4
Pervomaysk . 25 D3
Pésaro 20 C4
Pescara ... 20 C5
Peshawar .. 42 B7
Peterborough,
 Canada .. 69 D3
Peterborough,
 U.K. 11 E6
Peterhead .. 10 C6
Petersburg,
 Alaska,
 U.S.A. ... 71 C6
Petersburg,
 Va., U.S.A. 73 F7
Petitsikapau,
 L. 69 C4
Petropavl .. 29 D7
Petropavlovsk-
Kamchatskiy 31 D13
Petrópolis .. 93 G5
Petrozavodsk 28 C4
Pforzheim .. 14 D5
Phalodi 42 F8
Phan Rang . 36 B3
Phanh Bho Ho
 Chi Minh . 36 B3
Philadelphia 73 E8
Philippines ■ 38 B2
Phitsanulok . 36 A2
Phnom Penh 36 B2
Phoenix ... 83 D6
Phuket 36 C1
Piacenza ... 20 B2
Pianosa ... 20 C3
Piatra Neamţ 17 E8
Piave → 20 B4
Picardie ... 13 B5
Pictou 69 D4
Piedras
 Negras .. 84 B4
Piemonte □ . 20 B1
Piet Retief . 59 D6
Pietermaritzburg
 .... 59 D6
Pietersburg . 59 C5
Piketberg .. 58 E3
Pilcomayo → 94 B5
Pilibhit ... 42 E11
Pilica → ... 16 C5
Pílos 23 F3
Pinang 36 C2
Pínaros → .. 22 D6
Pindos Óros . 23 E3
Pine Bluff .. 79 B7
Pine Point .. 70 B8
Pinerolo ... 20 B1
Pinetown ... 59 D6
Píngxiang .. 35 D5
Pinhel 18 B2
Piniós → ... 23 E4
Pinnes, Ákra 23 D5
Pinsk 17 B8
Piombino .. 20 C3
Piotrków
 Trybunalski 16 C4
Piraiévs ... 23 F4

Pírgos 23 F3
Pirmasens . 14 D4
Pisa 20 C3
Pisciotta .. 21 D5
Písek 16 D2
Pishan 34 C2
Pistóia 20 C3
Pisuerga → . 18 B3
Pitcairn I. .. 65 M17
Piteå 8 E12
Piteşti 22 B5
Pitlochry .. 10 C5
Pittsburg .. 79 A6
Pittsburgh . 73 D5
Piura 90 E2
Placentia .. 69 D5
Placentia B. . 69 D5
Plainview .. 78 B3
Pláka, Ákra . 23 G6
Plasencia .. 18 B2
Plata, Río de
 la 94 C5
Platani → .. 21 F4
Platte → ... 77 F7
Plauen 15 C7
Plenty, B. of . 64 B7
Pleven 22 C5
Płock 16 B4
Plöckenstein 15 D7
Ploieşti ... 22 B6
Plovdiv 22 C5
Plymouth .. 11 F4
Plzeň 16 D1
Po → 20 B4
Pocatello .. 81 D7
Podgorica .. 22 C2
Podilska
 Vysochyna 17 D8
Podolsk ... 24 B4
Pofadder ... 58 D3
Pointe-à-Pitre 87 C7
Pointe Noire 56 E2
Poitiers ... 12 C4
Poitou 12 C3
Poland ■ ... 16 B5
Polatsk ... 24 B3
Polillo Is. .. 38 B2
Políyiros .. 23 D4
Polonne ... 17 C8
Poltava 24 D3
Polynesia .. 65 L15
Pombal 18 C1
Pomézia ... 20 D4
Ponca City . 78 A5
Ponce 87 C6
Pond Inlet . 68 A3
Pondicherry . 43 P11
Ponferrada . 18 A2
Ponta Grossa 94 B6
Pontarlier .. 13 C7
Pontchartrain
 L. 79 D8
Pontevedra . 18 A1
Pontiac ... 72 C4
Pontianak .. 37 E3
Pontivy ... 12 B2
Pontoise .. 12 B5
Ponziane,
 Ísole 21 D4
Poole 11 F6
Poona = Pune 43 K8
Poopó, L. de 91 G5
Popayán ... 90 C3
Poplar Bluff . 79 A8
Popocatépetl,
 Volcán ... 84 D5
Porbandar .. 43 J6
Porcupine → 71 B5
Pordenone . 20 B4
Pori 8 F12
Porkkala .. 9 G12
Poroshiri-Dake 32 F12
Porretta,
 Passo di .. 20 B3
Port Alberni . 71 D7

Port Alfred

Port Alfred . . 59 E5
Port Angeles . 80 A2
Port Antonio . 86 C4
Port Arthur . . 79 E7
Port-au-Prince 87 C5
Port Augusta . 62 B2
Port Bou 19 A7
Port-Cartier . . 69 C4
Port Elizabeth 59 E5
Port-Gentil . . 56 E1
Port Harcourt 55 H6
Port
  Hawkesbury 69 C4
Port Hedland 60 D2
Port Huron . . 72 C4
Port Laoise . . 11 E3
Port
  Macquarie . 63 B5
Port Moresby . 61 B8
Port Nelson . . 71 C10
Port Nolloth . 58 D3
Port of Spain 87 D7
Port Phillip B. 63 C3
Port Pirie . . . 62 B2
Port Said =
  Bûr Sa'îd . 52 B5
Port
  Shepstone . 59 E6
Port Talbot . . 11 F5
Port-Vendres . 11 D3
Portadown . . 11 D3
Portage La
  Prairie . . . 71 D10
Portalegre . . 18 C2
Portile de Fier 22 B4
Portimão . . . 18 D1
Portland,
  Australia . . 62 C2
Portland,
  Maine,
  U.S.A. . . . 73 C10
Portland,
  Oreg.,
  U.S.A. . . . 80 C2
Portland
  Prom. . . . 68 C3
Porto 18 B1
Pôrto Alegre 94 C6
Porto
  Empédocle . 21 F4
Porto Novo . . 55 G5
Porto Tórres . 20 D2
Porto-Vecchio 13 F8
Pôrto Velho . 91 E6
Portoferráio . 20 C3
Portoscuso . . 21 E2
Portoviejo . . 90 D2
Portree 10 C3
Portsmouth,
  U.K. 11 F6
Portsmouth,
  U.S.A. . . . 73 F7
Porttipahtan
  tekojärvi . 8 E13
Portugal ■ . . 18 C1
Posadas . . . 94 B5
Postojna . . . 20 B5
Potchefstroom 59 D5
Potenza . . . 21 D5
Potgietersrus 59 C5
Poti 25 E5
Potomac → . 73 F7
Potosí 91 G5
Potsdam . . . 15 B7
Poughkeepsie 73 D9
Póvoa de
  Varzim . . . 18 B1
Powder → . . 76 B2
Powell L. . . . 83 B7
Poyang Hu . . 35 D6
Poznań 16 B3
Pozoblanco . 18 C3
Pozzuoli . . . 21 D5

Prague =
  Praha . . . 16 C2
Praha 16 C2
Prairies . . . 71 C9
Prato 20 C3
Pravia 18 A2
Přerov 16 D3
Presidente
  Prudente . 93 G3
Prespansko
  Jezero . . . 23 D3
Presque Isle . 73 A11
Preston . . . 11 E5
Pretoria . . . 59 D5
Préveza . . . 23 E3
Příbram . . . 16 D2
Prichard . . . 74 D3
Prieska 58 D4
Prilep 22 D3
Prince Albert 71 C9
Prince Albert
  Pen. 70 A8
Prince Albert
  Sd. 70 A8
Prince Charles
  I. 68 B3
Prince Charles
  Mts. 96 B10
Prince Edward
  I. □ 69 D4
Prince of
  Wales I.,
  Canada . . 70 A10
Prince of
  Wales I.,
  U.S.A. . . . 71 C6
Pripet
  Marshes . . 17 B9
Priština . . . 22 C3
Privas 13 D6
Privolzhskaya
  Vozvyshennost
  . . . . . . 24 C6
Prizren 22 C3
Prokopyevsk 29 D9
Prostějov . . 16 D3
Provence . . . 13 E6
Providence . . 73 D10
Provins 13 B5
Provo 81 E8
Prut → 17 F9
Pruzhany . . . 17 B7
Pryluky 24 C3
Prypyat → . . 17 C10
Przemyśl . . . 17 D6
Psará 23 E5
Pskov 24 B2
Ptich → . . . 17 B9
Puebla 84 D5
Pueblo 76 F2
Puente-Genil . 18 D3
Puerto La Cruz 90 A6
Puerto Montt 95 E2
Puerto Rico ■ 87 C6
Puertollano . 18 C3
Puget Sound 80 B2
Puigcerdá . . 19 A6
Pula 20 B4
Pullman . . . 80 B5
Punakha . . . 41 D7
Pune 43 K8
Punjab □,
  India . . . 42 D9
Punjab □,
  Pakistan . 42 D8
Punta Arenas 95 G2
Punto Fijo . . 90 A4
Puri 40 H5
Purnia 40 E6
Puruliya . . . 40 F6
Purus → . . . 90 D6
Pusan 35 C7

Putignano . . 21 D6
Puttalam . . . 43 Q11
Puttgarden . . 15 A6
Putumayo → 90 D5
Puy-de-Dôme 13 D5
Pwllheli . . . 11 E4
Pyè 41 H10
Pyetrikaw . . 17 B9
P'yongyang . 35 C7
Pyrénées . . . 19 A6

Qandahär . . 42 D4
Qaraghandy . 29 E8
Qarshi 29 F7
Qatar ■ . . . 44 E2
Qattâra,
  Munkhafed
  el 52 C4
Qazvin 46 C7
Qena 52 C5
Qiqiqtarjuaq 68 B4
Qilian Shan . 34 C4
Qingdao . . . 35 C7
Qinghai □ . . 34 C4
Qinghai Hu . 34 C5
Qiqihar 35 B7
Qom 44 C2
Qostanay . . 29 D7
Quang Ngai . 38 A3
Quartu
  Sant'Elena 21 E2
Quatsino . . . 71 C7
Queanbeyan . 63 C4
Québec 69 D3
Québec □ . . 69 D3
Queen
  Charlotte Is. 70 C6
Queen
  Charlotte
  Str. 71 C7
Queen
  Elizabeth Is. 66 B9
Queen Maud
  G. 70 B9
Queen Maud
  Land . . . 96 B7
Queensland □ 61 E7
Queenstown,
  N.Z. 65 F3
Queenstown,
  S. Africa . 59 E5
Querétaro . . 84 C4
Quetta 42 D5
Quezon City . 38 B2
Qui Nhon . . 36 B3
Quiberon . . . 12 C2
Quimper . . . 12 B1
Quimperlé . . 12 C2
Quincy 77 F9
Quintana de
  la Orden . 18 C4
Quito 90 D3
Qüqon 29 E8
Qyzylorda . . 29 E7

Raahe 8 F12
Raba 39 F1
Rabat 54 B3
Rābigh 47 G4
Race, C. . . . 69 D5
Racine 72 D2
Radekhiv . . . 17 C7
Radom 16 C5
Radomyśl . . 17 C9
Radstock, C. . 62 B1
Rae 70 B8
Rae Bareli . . 40 E3
Rae Isthmus 68 B2
Ragachow . . 17 B10
Ragusa 21 F5
Rahimyar
  Khan . . . 42 E7
Raigarh 40 G4
Rainier, Mt. . 80 B3
Raipur 40 G3
Raj Nandgaon 40 G3
Rajahmundry 40 J3
Rajasthan □ . 42 F8
Rajasthan
  Canal . . . 42 F8
Rajkot 43 H7
Rajshahi . . . 41 E7
Rakaposhi . . 42 A9
Rakata, Pulau 37 F3
Rakhiv 17 D7
Raleigh 75 B8
Ramgarh . . . 40 F5
Rampur 42 E11
Ramree Kyun 41 H9
Rancagua . . 94 C2
Ranchi 40 F5
Randers . . . 9 G10
Rangoon . . . 41 J11
Rangpur . . . 41 E7
Rankin Inlet . 70 B10
Rapallo 20 B2
Rapid City . . 76 C3
Rasht 46 C7
Rat Islands . 71 C1
Ratangarh . . 42 E9
Rathenow . . 15 B7
Ratlam 43 H9
Raukumara
  Ra. 64 C7
Raurkela . . . 40 F5
Rava-Ruska . 17 C6
Ravenna . . . 20 B4
Ravensburg . 14 E5
Ravi → 42 D7
Rawalpindi . . 42 C8
Rawlins 81 E10
Ray, C. 69 D5
Raymond . . . 71 D8
Raz, Pte. du . 12 B1
Ré, I. de . . . 12 C3
Reading, U.K. 11 F6
Reading,
  U.S.A. . . . 73 D8
Rebun-Tô . . 32 E12
Rechytsa . . . 17 B10
Recife 92 D7
Red → , La.,
  U.S.A. . . . 79 D8
Red →,
  N. Dak.,
  U.S.A. . . . 76 A6
Red Deer . . . 71 C8
Red Sea . . . 48 C2
Redcar 11 D6
Redding . . . 80 E2
Redditch . . . 11 E6
Redon 12 C2
Redondela . . 18 A1
Redwood City 82 B1
Ree, L. 11 E3
Regensburg . 15 D7
Réggio di
  Calábria . . 21 E5
Réggio
  nell'Emília 20 B3
Regina 71 C9
Rehoboth . . 58 C3
Reichenbach 15 C7
Reidsville . . 75 A8
Reigate 11 F6
Reims 13 B6
Reindeer L. . 71 C9
Reinosa . . . 18 A3
Reliance . . . 70 B9
Rendsburg . . 14 A5
Reni 17 F9
Renmark . . . 62 B3
Rennes 12 B3
Reno 80 F4

Reno → . . . 20 B4
Renteria . . . 19 A5
Republican →
  . . . . . . 76 F6
Repulse Bay . 68 B2
Requena . . . 19 C5
Resistencia . 94 B5
Resolution I. . 68 B4
Rethimnon . . 23 G5
Réunion ■ . . 51 J9
Reus 19 B6
Reutlingen . . 14 D5
Revelstoke . . 71 C8
Rewa 40 E3
Rewari 42 E10
Reykjavík . . . 8 D2
Reynosa . . . 84 B5
Rhein → . . . 14 C4
Rhein-Main-
  Donau-
  Kanal → . 15 D6
Rheine 14 B4
Rheinland-
  Pfalz □ . . 14 C4
Rhine =
  Rhein → . 14 C4
Rhode
  Island □ . . 73 D10
Rhodes =
  Ródhos . . 23 F7
Rhodopi
  Planina . . 22 D5
Rhondda . . . 11 F5
Rhône → . . 13 E6
Rhum 10 C3
Riau,
  Kepulauan 37 D2
Ribadeo . . . 18 A2
Ribeirão Prêto 93 G4
Ribnița 17 E9
Riccarton . . . 65 E5
Richland . . . 80 B4
Richmond,
  Calif., U.S.A. 80 G2
Richmond,
  Va., U.S.A. 73 F7
Ridder 29 D9
Ried 15 D7
Riesa 15 C7
Rieti 20 C4
Riga 24 B1
Riga, G. of . . 24 B1
Rigolet 68 C5
Rijeka 20 B5
Rímini 20 B4
Rîmnicu
  Vîlcea . . . 17 F7
Rimouski . . . 69 D4
Rio Branco . . 91 E5
Rio de Janeiro 93 G5
Rio Gallegos 95 G3
Rio
  Grande → . 78
Rio Grande do
  Norte □ . . 92 D7
Riobamba . . 90 D3
Rishiri-Tô . . . 32 E12
Riva del
  Garda . . . 20 B3
Riversdale . . 58 E4
Riverside . . . 82 D4
Riverton . . . 71 C10
Riviera di
  Levante . . 20 B2
Riviera di
  Ponente . . 20 B2
Rivière-du-
  Loup 69 D4
Rivne 17 C8
Rívoli 20 B1
Riyadh = Ar
  Riyâḍ . . . 47 F6

Rize 46 B5
Rizzuto, C. .. 21 E6
Roanne 13 C6
Roanoke ... 73 F6
Robertson .. 58 E3
Robson, Mt. . 71 C8
Roca, C. da .. 18 C1
Rochefort ... 12 D3
Rochester,
  Minn.,
  U.S.A. 77 C8
Rochester,
  N.Y., U.S.A. 73 C7
Rock Hill ... 75 B7
Rock Island . 77 E9
Rock Springs 81 E9
Rockford ... 77 D10
Rockhampton 61 E9
Rocky Mount 75 B9
Rocky Mts. .. 70 C7
Rodez 13 D5
Ródhos 23 F7
Roes
  Welcome
  Sd. 68 B2
Rogatyn ... 17 D7
Rohtak 42 E10
Roma,
  Australia . 63 A4
Roma, Italy . 20 D4
Romania ■ . 22 B5
Romans-sur-
  Isère 13 D6
Rome 74 B5
Romorantin-
  Lanthenay 12 C4
Ronda 18 D3
Rondônia □ . 91 F6
Ronge, L. la . 71 C9
Ronne Ice
  Shelf 96 B3
Roodepoort . 59 D5
Roosevelt I. 96 B16
Roquetas de
  Mar 19 D4
Roraima □ . 90 C6
Roraima, Mt. 90 B6
Rosario 94 C4
Rosas, G. de 19 A7
Roscommon . 11 E2
Roseau,
  Domin. .. 87 C7
Roseau,
  U.S.A. 77 A7
Roseburg .. 80 D2
Rosenheim .. 15 E7
Rosetown .. 71 C9
Roseville .. 80 F3
Rosignano
  Maríttimo . 20 C3
Ross Ice Shelf 96 C16
Ross Sea .. 96 B15
Rossano
  Cálabro .. 21 E6
Rossland .. 71 D8
Rosslare ... 11 E3
Rosthern ... 71 C9
Rostock 15 A7
Rostov 25 D4
Roswell ... 78 C1
Rotherham .. 11 E6
Rotondo Mte. 13 E8
Rotorua ... 64 C7
Rotorua, L. .. 64 C7
Rotterdam .. 14 C3
Rottweil ... 14 D5
Roubaix ... 13 A5
Rouen 12 B4
Roussillon . 13 E5
Rouyn 69 D3
Rovaniemi .. 8 E13
Roveretto .. 20 B3

Rovigo 20 B3
Rovinj 20 B4
Royal
  Leamington
  Spa ... 11 E6
Royan 12 D3
Rozdilna ... 17 E10
Rozhyshche .. 17 C7
Ruahine Ra. . 64 C7
Rub' al Khali 48 D4
Rugby 11 E6
Rügen 15 A7
Ruhr → 14 C4
Rumania =
  Romania ■ 22 B5
Rumoi 32 F12
Rupat 37 D2
Rupert → .. 69 C3
Ruse 22 C5
Rustavi ... 25 E6
Rustenburg . 59 D5
Ruteng 39 F2
Ruwenzori .. 57 D5
Rwanda ■ . 57 E6
Ryazan 24 C4
Rybinsk ... 24 B4
Rybinskoye
  Vdkhr. ... 24 B4
Ryūkyū-rettō 35 D7
Rzeszów ... 16 C5

Saale → .. 15 C6
Saalfeld ... 15 C6
Saar → 13 B7
Saarbrücken 14 D4
Saaremaa .. 9 B7
Sabadell ... 19 B7
Sabah □ ... 36 C5
Sabhah ... 52 C1
Sable, C.,
  Canada ... 69 D4
Sable, C.,
  U.S.A. 86 A3
Sable I. 69 D5
Sachsen □ . 15 C7
Sachsen-
  Anhalt □ .. 15 C7
Sacramento 80 F3
Sacramento →
  .... 80 F3
Sacramento
  Mts. 83 D10
Sado 33 G11
Safi 54 B3
Saga 32 C2
Saginaw ... 72 C4
Saguenay → 69 D3
Sagunto ... 19 C5
Sahagún ... 18 A3
Sahara 54 D6
Saharanpur . 42 E10
Sahel 54 B5
Sahiwal ... 42 D8
Saïdabad ... 44 D3
Saidpur ... 41 E7
Saigon =
  Phanh Bho
  Ho Chi Minh 36 B3
Saijō 32 C3
Saiki 32 C2
St. Andrews . 11 C5
St-Augustin-
  Saguenay . 69 C5
St. Augustine 75 E7
St. Austell .. 11 F4
St. Boniface . 71 D10
St-Brieuc .. 12 B2
St. Catharines 69 D3
St.-Chamond 13 D6

St.
  Christopher-
  Nevis = St.
  Kitts-
  Nevis ■ .. 87 C7
St. Cloud .. 77 C7
St.-Denis .. 12 B5
St.-Dizier ... 13 B6
St. Elias, Mt. 70 B5
St.-Étienne .. 13 D6
St.-Flour ... 13 D5
St. Francis, C. 58 E4
St.-Gaudens . 12 E4
St. George's 87 D7
St. George's
  Channel .. 11 F3
St. Helena ■ 51 H3
St. Helena B. 58 E3
St. Helier ... 11 G5
St-Hyacinthe 69 D3
St. John 69 D4
St. John's,
  Antigua .. 87 C7
St. John's,
  Canada .. 69 D5
St. Johns → 75 D7
St. Joseph .. 77 F7
St. Joseph, L. 69 C1
St. Kilda ... 10 C2
St. Kitts-
  Nevis ■ .. 87 C7
St.
  Lawrence
  → 69 D4
St. Lawrence,
  Gulf of ... 69 D4
St. Lawrence
  I. 71 B2
St. Leonard . 69 C5
St.-Lô 12 B3
St-Louis ... 55 E1
St. Louis ... 77 F9
St. Lucia ■ . 87 D7
St. Lucia, L. . 59 D6
St.-Malo ... 12 B2
St.-Mathieu,
  Pte. 12 B1
St.-Nazaire . 12 C2
St.-Omer ... 12 A5
St. Paul ... 77 C8
St. Peter Port 11 G5
St. Petersburg 24 B3
St. Petersburg 75 F6
St-Pierre et
  Miquelon □ 69 D5
St.-Quentin . 13 B5
St.-Tropez .. 13 E7
St. Vincent &
  the
  Grenadines ■
  .... 87 D7
Saintes 12 D3
Saintonge .. 12 D3
Sakai 32 C4
Sakakawea, L. 76 B4
Sakarya → . 25 E3
Sakata 33 G11
Sakhalin ... 31 D12
Sala 9 G11
Sala Consilina 21 D5
Salado → .. 94 C4
Salamanca .. 18 B3
Salamis ... 23 F4
Salayar 39 F2
Saldanha ... 58 E3
Sale 63 C4
Salekhard .. 28 C7
Salem, India 43 P11
Salem, U.S.A. 80 D2
Salerno 21 D5
Salihli 23 E7
Salihorsk ... 17 B8
Salina, Italy . 21 E5

Salina, U.S.A. 76 F6
Salinas 82 B2
Salisbury,
  U.K. 11 F6
Salisbury,
  U.S.A. 75 B7
Salliq 68 B2
Salluit 68 B3
Salmon → . 80 C5
Salmon River
  Mts. 81 C6
Salon-de-
  Provence . 13 E6
Salso → ... 21 F4
Salt Lake City 81 E8
Salta 94 A3
Saltillo 84 B4
Salto 94 C5
Salto → ... 20 C4
Salton Sea .. 82 D5
Salvador ... 93 E6
Salween → . 41 J11
Salzach → . 15 D7
Salzburg ... 15 E7
Salzgitter ... 14 B6
Salzwedel .. 15 B6
Sama de
  Langreo . 18 A3
Samar 38 B3
Samara ... 24 C7
Samarinda .. 37 E5
Samarqand . 29 F7
Sambalpur .. 40 G5
Sambhal ... 42 E11
Sambhar ... 42 F9
Sambiase .. 21 E6
Sambir 17 D6
Samoa ■ .. 65 L13
Sámos 23 F6
Samothráki,
  Évros,
  Greece .. 23 D3
Samothráki,
  Kérkira,
  Greece .. 23 E1
Samsun ... 25 F5
San → 16 C5
San Agustin,
  C. 38 C3
San Angelo . 78 D3
San Antonio,
  Spain ... 19 C6
San Antonio,
  U.S.A. 78 E4
San Benedetto
  del Tronto 20 C4
San
  Bernardino 82 C4
San
  Bernardino
  Str. 38 B2
San Diego .. 82 D4
San Felíu de
  Guíxols .. 19 B7
San Fernando,
  Spain ... 18 D2
San Fernando,
  U.S.A. 82 C3
San Francisco 82 B1
San Gottardo,
  P. del ... 13 C8
San
  Joaquin → 82 A2
San Jorge, B. 84 B2
San Jorge, G.
  de 19 B6
San José,
  Costa Rica 86 E3
San Jose,
  U.S.A. 82 B2
San Juan,
  Argentina . 94 C3

San Juan,
  Puerto Rico 87 C6
San Juan Mts. 83 B9
San Leandro 82 B1
San Lucas, C. 84 C2
San Luis
  Obispo ... 82 C3
San Luis
  Potosí ... 84 C4
San Marino ■ 20 C4
San Matías, G. 95 E4
San Miguel de
  Tucumán . 94 B3
San Pedro
  Sula 85 D7
San Pieto ... 21 E2
San Rafael .. 80 G2
San Remo .. 20 C1
San Roque .. 18 D3
San Salvador 85 E7
San Salvador
  de Jujuy .. 94 A4
San Sebastián 19 A5
San Severo .. 20 D5
San Vicente
  de la
  Barquera . 18 A3
Sana' 49 D3
Sana → 20 B6
Sancy, Puy de 13 D5
Sandakan .. 36 C5
Sanday ... 10 B5
Sandıklı ... 46 C2
Sandusky .. 72 D4
Sandy, L. .. 71 C10
Sanford, Fla.,
  U.S.A. 75 E7
Sanford, N.C.,
  U.S.A. 75 B8
Sanford, Mt. 71 B5
Sangerhausen 15 C6
Sangihe, P. . 39 D3
Sangli 43 L9
Sangre de
  Cristo Mts. 78 A1
Sankt Gallen 13 C8
Sankt Moritz 13 C8
Sankt-
  Peterburg 24 B3
Sankt Pölten 15 D8
Sanliurfa ... 46 C4
Sanlúcar de
  Barrameda 18 D2
Sannicandro
  Gargánico . 20 D4
Santa Ana .. 82 D4
Santa Barbara 82 C3
Santa Catalina
  I. 82 D3
Santa Clara . 86 B4
Santa Coloma
  de
  Gramanet . 19 B7
Santa Cruz,
  Bolivia ... 91 G6
Santa Cruz,
  U.S.A. 82 B1
Santa Cruz de
  Tenerife .. 54 C1
Santa Fe,
  Argentina . 94 C4
Santa Fe,
  U.S.A. 83 C10
Santa Lucia
  Range ... 82 C2
Santa Maria,
  Brazil ... 94 B6
Santa Maria,
  U.S.A. 82 C2
Santa Maria di
  Leuca, C. . 23 E2
Santa Marta . 90 A4

Santa Marta, Sierra Nevada de

Name		
Santa Marta, Sierra Nevada de	90	A4
Santa Rosa	80	F2
Santander	18	A4
Sant'Antíoco	21	E2
Santarém, Brazil	92	C3
Santarém, Portugal	18	C1
Santiago □	94	C2
Santiago de Compostela	18	A1
Santiago de Cuba	86	C4
Santiago de los Cabelleros	87	C5
Santo Domingo	87	C6
Santoña	18	A4
Santorini = Thíra	23	F5
Santos	94	A7
São Francisco →	93	E6
São João da Madeira	18	B1
São José do Rio Preto	94	A7
São Luís	92	C5
São Paulo	94	A7
São Roque, C. de	92	D6
São Tomé & Príncipe ■	51	F4
São Vicente, C. de	18	D1
Saône →	13	D6
Sapporo	32	F12
Sapulpa	79	B5
Sar Planina	22	C3
Sarada →	40	D3
Sarajevo	22	C3
Sarangani B.	38	C3
Saransk	24	C6
Sarasota	75	F6
Saratov	24	C6
Sarawak □	37	D4
Saray	22	D6
Sarayköy	23	F7
Sardegna □	21	D2
Sardinia = Sardegna □	21	D2
Sardis	23	E7
Sargodha	42	C8
Sarh	53	G2
Sangöl	23	E7
Sarikamiş	46	B5
Sark	11	G5
Şarköy	23	D6
Sarlat-la-Canéda	12	D4
Sarnia	69	D2
Sarny	24	C2
Saronikós Kólpos	23	F4
Sarreguemines	13	B7
Sarthe →	12	C3
Sasebo	32	C1
Saser	42	B10
Saskatchewan □	71	C9
Saskatchewan →	71	C9
Saskatoon	71	C9
Sássari	21	D2
Sassnitz	15	A7
Sassuolo	20	B3
Sasyk, Ozero	17	F9
Sata-Misaki	33	D2
Satmala Hills	43	J9
Satna	40	E3
Satpura Ra.	43	J10
Satu Mare	17	E6
Saudi Arabia ■	47	F5
Sauerland	14	C4
Sault Ste. Marie, Canada	69	D2
Sault Ste. Marie, U.S.A.	72	A3
Saumur	12	C3
Sava →	22	B3
Savanna la Mar	86	C4
Savannah □	75	C7
Savannah	75	C7
Savoie □	13	D7
Savona	20	B2
Sawahlunto	37	E2
Sawara	32	B7
Sawatch Mts.	83	A9
Sawu	39	F2
Sawu Sea	39	F2
Saxony, Lower = Niedersachsen □	14	B5
Sayan, Zapadnyy	30	D7
Saydā	46	D3
Sãzava →	16	D2
Scandicci	20	C3
Scandinavia	8	F10
Scarborough	11	D6
Schaffhausen	13	C8
Schefferville	69	C4
Schelde →	14	C3
Schenectady	73	C9
Schiermonnikoog	14	B4
Schio	20	B3
Schleswig	14	A5
Schleswig-Holstein □	14	A5
Schwäbische Alb	14	D5
Schwaner, Pegunungan	37	E4
Schwarzwald	14	D5
Schwedt	15	B8
Schweinfurt	14	C6
Schwerin	15	B6
Schwyz	13	C8
Sciacca	21	F4
Scilla	21	E5
Scilly, Isles of	11	G3
Scotland □	10	C4
Scott Inlet	68	A3
Scottsbluff	76	E3
Scranton	73	D8
Scunthorpe	11	E6
Seattle	80	B2
Şebinkarahisar	46	B4
Sedalia	77	F8
Sedan	13	B6
Seeheim	58	D3
Seferihisar	23	E6
Segesta	21	F4
Segovia	18	B3
Segre →	19	B6
Segura →	19	C5
Sehore	43	H10
Seine →	12	B4
Sekondi-Takoradi	55	H4
Selaru	39	F4
Selçuk	23	F6
Sele →	21	D5
Selkirk	71	C10
Selkirk Mts.	71	C8
Selma	75	B8
Selvas	91	E5
Semarang	37	F4
Semey	29	D9
Semisopochnoi I.	71	C1
Semmering P.	15	E8
Sendai, Kagoshima, Japan	32	D2
Sendai, Miyagi, Japan	33	G12
Senegal ■	55	F2
Senegal →	55	E1
Senigállia	20	C4
Senj	20	B5
Senja	8	E11
Senlis	13	B5
Senneterre	69	D3
Sens	13	B5
Seo de Urgel	19	A6
Seoul = Sôul	35	C7
Sept-Îles	69	C4
Sequoia National Park	82	B3
Seram	39	E3
Seram Sea	39	E3
Serbia □	22	C3
Seremban	37	D2
Sergiyev Posad	24	B4
Sérifos	23	F5
Serowe	59	C5
Serpukhov	24	C4
Sérrai	22	D4
Sète	13	E5
Sétif	54	A6
Seto	32	B5
Settat	54	B3
Setúbal	18	C1
Setúbal, B. de	18	C1
Sevana Lich	25	E6
Sevastopol	25	E3
Severn →, Canada	69	C2
Severn →, U.K.	11	F5
Severnaya Zemlya	30	B7
Sevilla	18	D2
Seward	71	B5
Seward Pen.	71	B3
Seychelles ■	26	K9
Sfax	52	B1
Sfîntu Gheorghe	17	F7
Shaanxi □	35	C5
Shaba □	57	F4
Shache	34	C2
Shahjahanpur	42	F11
Shajapur	43	H10
Shakhty	25	D5
Shaki	55	G5
Shan □	41	G12
Shandong □	35	C6
Shanghai	35	C7
Shangrao	35	D6
Shannon →	11	E2
Shantou	35	D6
Shanxi □	35	C6
Shaoguan	35	D6
Shaoyang	35	D6
Sharon	72	D5
Shasta, Mt.	80	E2
Shatt al'Arab →	47	E7
Shaunavon	71	D9
Shawinigan	69	D3
Sheboygan	72	C2
Sheffield	11	E6
Shelburne	69	D4
Shelby	75	B7
Shelbyville	74	B4
Shellharbour	63	B5
Shenandoah →	73	E7
Shenyang	35	B7
Shepetivka	17	C8
Shepparton	63	C4
Sherbrooke	69	D3
Sheridan	81	C10
Sherman	79	C5
Sherridon	71	C9
Shetland Is.	10	A6
Shijiazhuang	35	C6
Shikarpur	42	F6
Shikoku	32	C3
Shikoku □	33	H10
Shikoku-Sanchi	32	C3
Shiliguri	40	D7
Shillong	41	E8
Shimada	32	B6
Shimizu	32	B6
Shimoga	43	N9
Shimonoseki	32	C2
Shinano →	32	A6
Shingū	32	C4
Shirane-San	32	A6
Shiráz	44	D3
Shire →	59	B7
Shiretoko-Misaki	32	F13
Shiriya-Zaki	32	F12
Shivpuri	43	G10
Shizuoka	32	B6
Shklov	17	A10
Shkodra	22	C2
Shoshone Mts.	80	F5
Shoshong	59	C5
Shreveport	79	C7
Shrewsbury	11	E5
Shuangyashan	35	B8
Shumagin Is.	71	C4
Shungnak	71	B4
Shwebo	41	F10
Shymkent	29	E7
Sialkot	42	C9
Šiauliai	24	B1
Šibenik	20	C5
Siberut	37	E1
Sibi	42	E5
Sibiu	17	F7
Sibolga	37	D1
Sibu	37	D4
Sibuyan	38	B2
Sichuan □	34	C5
Sicilia	21	F5
Siedlce	17	B6
Sieg →	14	C4
Siegen	14	C5
Siena	20	C3
Sierra Leone ■	55	G2
Sifnos	23	F5
Sigüenza	19	B4
Siirt	46	C5
Sikar	42	F9
Sikhote Alin, Khrebet	31	E11
Sikkim □	40	D7
Sil →	18	A2
Silesia = Śląsk	16	C3
Silifke	46	C3
Silivri	22	D7
Simav	23	E7
Simbirsk	24	C6
Simeulue	37	D1
Simferopol	25	E3
Simi	23	F6
Simla	42	D10
Simplon P.	13	C8
Simpson Desert	60	F6
Sinai, Mt. = Mûsa, G.	47	E3
Sind □	42	F6
Sind Sagar Doab	42	D7
Sines	18	D1
Sines, C. de	18	D1
Singapore ■	37	D2
Singitikós Kólpos	23	D5
Sinni →	21	D6
Sinop	46	B3
Sintra	18	C1
Sion	13	C7
Sioux City	77	D6
Sioux Falls	76	D6
Sioux Lookout	71	C10
Siping	35	B7
Sípura	37	E1
Siracusa	21	F5
Sirajganj	41	E7
Sirohi	43	G8
Síros	23	F5
Sirsa	42	E9
Sisak	20	B6
Sitapur	40	D3
Sitges	19	B6
Sitia	23	G6
Sitka	71	C6
Sittwe	41	G9
Sivas	46	C4
Siverek	46	C4
Sivrihisar	46	C2
Siwan	40	D5
Sjælland	9	G10
Skagerrak	9	G9
Skagway	71	C6
Skala-Podilska	17	D8
Skalat	17	D7
Skardu	42	B9
Skeena →	70	C6
Skegness	11	E7
Skellefte älv →	8	F12
Skellefteå	8	F12
Skíathos	23	E4
Skien	9	G9
Skikda	54	A6
Skíros	23	E5
Skole	17	D6
Skópelos	23	E4
Skopje	22	C3
Skvyra	17	D9
Skye	10	C3
Slamet	37	F3
Śląsk	16	C3
Slatina	22	B5
Slave →	70	B8
Slavonski Brod	20	B7
Slavuta	17	B10
Slawharad	17	B10
Sleeper Is.	68	C2
Sligo	11	D2
Sliven	22	C6
Slobozia	22	B6
Slonim	17	B7
Slough	11	F6
Slovak Rep. ■	16	D5
Slovenia ■	20	B5
Slovenské Rudohorie	16	D4
Slovyansk	25	D4
Sluch →	17	C8
Slutsk	17	B8
Smarhon	17	A8
Smederevo	22	B3
Smith Arm	70	B7
Smolensk	24	C3
Smolikas, Óros	23	D3

Smyrna =
İzmir 23 E6
Snake → .. 80 B4
Snake River
 Plain . 81 B4
Sneek ... 14 B3
Snøhetta .. 8 F9
Snowdon .. 11 E4
Snowdrift . 70 B6
Snowy Mts. . 63 C4
Snyatyn .. 17 D7
Snyder ... 78 C3
Sobral ... 92 C5
Sochi ... 25 E4
Société, Is. de
 la 65 L15
Socotra ... 49 E5
Söderhamn . 8 F11
Sofiya 22 C4
Sognefjorden . 8 F9
Sohâg 52 C5
Soissons .. 13 B5
Sokal ... 17 C7
Söke 23 F6
Sokhumi .. 25 E5
Sokoto ... 55 F6
Solapur ... 43 L9
Solingen .. 14 C4
Sóller ... 19 C7
Sologne .. 12 C4
Solomon Is. ■ 64 K10
Solothurn .. 13 C7
Sólta 20 C6
Solunska
 Glava .. 22 D3
Soma 23 E6
Somali Rep. ■ 49 F4
Somerset East 59 E5
Somerset I. . 70 A10
Somme → .. 12 A4
Somosierra,
 Puerto de . 18 B4
Somport,
 Puerto de . 12 C3
Søndre
 Strømfjord
 =
 Kangerlussuaq
 ...... 68 B5
Sóndrio ... 20 A2
Songkhla .. 36 C2
Sopot ... 16 A4
Sorel ... 69 D3
Sorgono .. 21 D2
Soria 19 B4
Soroca ... 17 D9
Sorong ... 39 E4
Sørøya ■ 8 D12
Sorsogon .. 38 B2
Sosnowiec . 16 C4
Soûdhas,
 Kólpos .. 23 G5
Sôul 35 C7
Souris ... 71 D9
Souris → .. 71 D10
Sousse ... 52 A1
South
 Africa ■ . 58 E4
South
 Australia □ 62 B2
South Bend . 72 D2
South
 Carolina □ 75 C7
South China
 Sea ... 36 C4
South
 Dakota □ . 76 C4
South I. ... 65 F3
South
 Magnetic
 Pole ... A13
South
 Nahanni → . 70 B7

South Orkney
 Is. 96 A4
South
 Platte → . 76 E4
South Pole . 96 C
South
 Ronaldsay 10 B5
South
 Saskatchewan →
 ...... 71 C9
South
 Shetland Is. 96 A4
South Shields 11 D6
South Uist . 10 C3
Southampton 11 F6
Southampton
 I. 68 B2
Southend-on-
 Sea 11 F7
Southern Alps 65 F3
Southern
 Indian L. . 71 C10
Southern
 Uplands . 10 D5
Soutpansberg 59 C5
Sôya-Misaki 32 E12
Sozh → ... 17 C10
Spain ■ ... 18 C4
Spanish Town 86 C4
Spartanburg 75 B7
Spárti 23 F4
Spartivento,
 C., Calabria,
 Italy 21 F6
Spartivento,
 C., Sard.,
 Italy 21 E2
Spátha, Ákra 23 G4
Spence Bay =
 Taloyoak . 70 B10
Spencer G. . 62 B2
Spey → ... 10 C5
Speyer ... 14 D5
Split 20 C6
Spokane .. 80 B5
Spoleto ... 20 C4
Spree → ... 15 B7
Springbok . 58 D3
Springfield,
 Ill., U.S.A. 77 F10
Springfield,
 Mass.,
 U.S.A. .. 73 C9
Springfield,
 Mo., U.S.A. 79 A8
Springfield,
 Ohio, U.S.A. 72 E4
Springfield,
 Oreg.,
 U.S.A. .. 80 C2
Springfontein 59 E5
Springhill . 69 D4
Springs ... 59 D5
Squamish .. 71 D7
Srebrnica . 20 B7
Sredinnyy
 Khrebet .. 31 D14
Sri Lanka ■ . 43 R12
Srikakulam . 40 H4
Srinagar .. 42 B9
Stade 14 B5
Stadlandet . 8 F9
Stafford ... 11 E5
Stakhanov . 25 D4
Stamford .. 73 D9
Stanley,
 Canada .. 71 C8
Stanley,
 Falk. Is. . 95 G5
Stanovoy
 Khrebet .. 31 D10
Stara Planina 22 C4
Stara Zagora 22 C5

Starokonstyantyniv
 ...... 17 D8
Staryy
 Chartoriysk 17 C7
State College 73 D7
Statesville . 75 B7
Stavanger . 9 G9
Stavropol .. 25 D5
Steiermark □ 15 E8
Steinkjer .. 8 F10
Stellenbosch 58 E3
Stendal ... 15 B6
Sterlitamak . 29 D6
Stettiner Haff 15 B8
Stettler ... 71 C8
Steubenville . 72 D5
Stevenage . 11 F7
Stewart ... 70 B6
Stewart I. .. 65 G2
Steyr 15 D8
Stillwater .. 78 A5
Ştip 22 D4
Stirling ... 10 C5
Stockerau .. 15 D9
Stockholm . 9 G11
Stockport .. 11 E5
Stockton .. 82 B2
Stockton-on-
 Tees 11 D6
Stoke on
 Trent ... 11 E5
Stolac ... 20 C6
Stolin ... 17 C8
Stonehaven . 10 C5
Stonewall . 71 C10
Stora
 Lulevatten . 8 E11
Storavan ■ 8 E11
Store Bælt . 9 G10
Storm B. ... 62 D4
Stormberge . 59 E5
Stornoway . 10 B3
Storozhynets 17 D7
Storsjön ■ 8 F10
Storuman . 8 E11
Stowbtsy .. 17 B8
Stralsund .. 15 A7
Strand ... 58 E2
Stranraer .. 11 D4
Strasbourg . 13 B7
Stratford .. 69 D2
Straubing .. 15 D7
Strimón → .. 23 D4
Strimonikós
 Kólpos .. 23 D5
Strómboli .. 21 E5
Stronsay ■ 10 B5
Strumica .. 22 D4
Stryy ... 17 D6
Stutterheim . 59 E5
Stuttgart .. 14 D5
Subotica .. 16 E4
Suceava ... 17 E8
Sucre ■ ... 91 G5
Sudan ■ ... 53 E5
Sudbury ... 69 D2
Sudety ... 16 C3
Sueca ... 19 C5
Suez = El
 Suweis ... 52 C5
Suhl 14 C6
Sukkur ... 42 F6
Sulaiman
 Range ... 42 D6
Sulawesi □ . 39 E2
Sulitjelma ■ 8 E11
Sulu Arch. . 38 C2
Sulu Sea .. 38 C2
Sumatera □ . 37 D2
Sumba ... 39 F1
Sumbawa .. 37 F5
Summerside 69 D4
Sumperk .. 16 D3
Sumter ... 75 C7

Sumy 24 C3
Sunda, Selat 37 F3
Sundarbans,
 The 41 G7
Sunderland . 11 D6
Sundsvall .. 8 F11
Sungurlu .. 46 B3
Sunnyvale . 82 B1
Superior ... 77 B8
Superior, L. 69 D2
Suphan Daği 46 C5
Supiori ... 39 E5
Sür 46 D3
Surabaya .. 37 F4
Surakarta .. 37 F4
Surat 43 J8
Surgut ... 29 C8
Surinam ■ . 92 B3
Suruga-Wan 32 B6
Susanville .. 80 E3
Susquehanna →
 ...... 73 E7
Susurluk .. 23 E7
Suva 64 L12
Suwałki ... 17 A6
Suwannee → 17 D4
Suzhou ... 35 C7
Suzu-Misaki . 32 A6
Svealand □ . 9 G10
Sverdlovsk =
 Yekaterinburg
 ...... 29 D7
Svislach .. 17 B7
Svyetlahorsk 17 B9
Swakopmund 58 C2
Swan Hill .. 62 C3
Swansea .. 11 F5
Swaziland ■ 59 D6
Sweden ■ . 9 G10
Sweetwater . 78 C3
Swellendam . 58 E3
Swift Current 71 C9
Swindon ... 11 F6
Switzerland ■ 13 C8
Sydney,
 Australia . 63 B5
Sydney,
 Canada . 69 D4
Syktyvkar . 28 C6
Sylhet ... 41 E8
Sylt 14 A5
Syracuse .. 73 C7
Syrdarya → 29 E7
Syria ■ ... 46 D4
Syzran ... 24 C6
Szczecin .. 16 B2
Szechwan =
 Sichuan □ 34 C5
Szeged ... 16 E5
Székesfehérvár
 ...... 16 E4
Szekszárd .. 16 E4
Szolnok ... 16 E5
Szombathely 16 E3

Tabas 44 C4
Tablas ... 38 B2
Table Mt. .. 58 E3
Tábor ... 16 D2
Tabora ... 57 F6
Tabriz 46 C6
Tacloban .. 38 B2
Tacna 91 G4
Tacoma ... 80 B2
Tacuarembó . 94 C5
Tadoussac . 69 D4
Tadzhikistan =
 Tajikistan ■ 29 F8
Taegu ... 35 C7
Taejŏn ... 35 C7
Tafalla ... 19 A5
Tafelbaai .. 58 E3

Taganrog .. 25 D4
Tagish ... 70 B6
Tagish L. .. 70 B6
Tagliamento →
 ...... 20 B4
Tagus =
 Tejo → .. 18 C1
Tahiti 65 L16
Tahoe, L. .. 80 F3
Taibei ... 35 D7
Tain 10 C4
Tainan ... 35 D7
Tainaron, Ákra 23 F4
T'aipei =
 Taibei ... 35 D7
Taiping ... 36 D2
Taiwan ■ . 35 D7
Taïyetos Óros 23 F4
Taiyuan ... 35 C6
Taizhong .. 35 D7
Ta'izz ... 49 E3
Tajikistan ■ . 29 F8
Tak 36 A1
Takada ... 32 A6
Takamatsu . 32 B4
Takaoka ... 32 A5
Takapuna .. 64 B6
Takasaki .. 32 A6
Takatsuki .. 32 B4
Takayama .. 32 A5
Takefu ... 32 B5
Takaud,
 Kepulauan . 38 D3
Talavera de la
 Reina ... 18 C3
Talca 94 D2
Talcahuano . 94 D2
Talladega .. 74 C4
Tallahassee . 75 D5
Tallinn ... 24 B7
Taloyoak .. 70 B10
Talue 55 G4
Tambov ... 24 C5
Tampa → .. 18 B1
Tamil Nadu □ 43 P10
Tamo Abu,
 Pegunungan 37 D5
Tampa ... 75 F6
Tampere .. 8 F12
Tampico ... 84 C5
Tamworth . 63 B5
Tana → .. 8 D13
Tana, L. ... 53 F6
Tanami Desert 60 D5
Tanana ... 71 B4
Tanana → . 71 B4
Tánaro → .. 20 B2
Tando Adam 42 G6
Tane-ga-
 Shima ... 33 D2
Tanga ... 57 F7
Tanganyika, L. 57 F5
Tanger ... 54 A3
Tangshan .. 35 C6
Tanimbar,
 Kepulauan 39 F4
Tanjungbalai 37 D1
Tanjungkarang
 Telukbetung 37 F3
Tanzania ■ . 57 F6
Tapajós → . 92 C3
Tapi → ... 43 J8
Tarabagatay,
 Khrebet .. 29 E9
Tarâbulus,
 Lebanon . 46 D3
Tarâbulus,
 Libya .. 52 B1
Tarakan .. 37 D5
Taranaki □ . 64 C6
Tarancón .. 19 B4
Táranto ... 21 D6
Táranto, G. di 21 D6
Tarashcha .. 17 D10

Taraz

Name	Ref		Name	Ref		Name	Ref		Name	Ref		Name	Ref
Taraz	29 E8		Térmoli	20 C5		Tilburg	14 C3		Toroníios			Trollhättan	9 G10
Tarazona	19 B5		Ternate	39 D3		Tilos	23 F6		Kólpos	23 D4		Trondheim	8 F10
Tarbes	12 E4		Terni	20 C4		Timaru	65 F4		Toronto	69 D3		Trondheimsfjorden	
Taree	63 B5		Ternopil	17 D7		Timbuktu =			Toros Dağları	46 C3			8 F10
Tarifa	18 D3		Terracina	20 D4		Tombouctou			Tôrre de			Trout L.	70 B7
Tarim Pendi	34 C3		Terralba	21 E2			55 E4		Moncorvo	18 B2		Trouville-sur-	
Tarkhankut,			Terre Haute	72 E2		Timișoara	16 F5		Torre del			Mer	12 B4
Mys	25 D3		Terschelling	14 B3		Timmins	69 D2		Greco	21 D5		Troy, Turkey	23 E6
Tarn →	12 D4		Teruel	19 B5		Timor	39 F2		Torrejón de			Troy, Ala.,	
Tarnów	16 C5		Teshio-			Timor			Ardoz	18 B4		U.S.A.	74 D5
Tarragona	19 B6		Gawa →	32 F12		Timur □	39 F3		Torrelavega	18 A3		Troy, N.Y.,	
Tarrasa	19 B7		Teslin	70 B6		Tinaca Pt.	38 C3		Torremolinos	18 D3		U.S.A.	73 C9
Tarsus	46 C3		Teterev →	17 C10		Tinos	23 F5		Torrens, L.	62 B2		Troyes	13 B6
Tartu	24 B2		Tetiyev	17 D9		Tipperary	11 E2		Torrente	19 C5		Trujillo, Peru	91 E3
Taschereau	69 D3		Tétouan	54 A3		Tirana	22 D2		Torreón	84 B4		Trujillo, Spain	18 C3
Táshkent =			Tetovo	22 C3		Tiraspol	17 E9		Torres Vedras	18 C1		Truk	64 J10
Toshkent	29 E7		Teutoburger			Tire	23 E6		Torrevieja	19 D5		Truro, Canada	69 D4
Tasman B.	65 D5		Wald	14 B5		Tirebolu	46 B4		Tortosa	19 B6		Truro, U.K.	11 F4
Tasmania □	62 D4		Tévere →	20 D4		Tiree	10 C3		Tortosa, C. de	19 B6		Truskavets	17 D6
Tatarbunary	17 F9		Texarkana	79 C6		Tirgoviște	22 B5		Toruń	16 B4		Trutnov	16 C2
Tatarsk	29 D8		Texas □	78 D4		Tirgu-Jiu	17 F6		Tosa-Wan	32 C3		Tsau	58 C4
Tatarstan □	29 D9		Texas City	79 E6		Tirgu Mureș	17 E7		Toscana □	20 C3		Tshabong	58 D4
Tateyama	32 B6		Texel	14 B3		Tirich Mir	42 A7		Toshkent	29 E7		Tshane	58 C4
Tatry	16 D4		Tezpur	41 D9		Tirnavos	23 E4		Tosya	46 B3		Tshwane	58 C4
Tatta	43 G5		Thabana			Tirol □	14 E6		Toteng	58 C4		Tsimlyanskoye	
Tatvan	46 C5		Ntlenyana	59 D5		Tirso →	21 E2		Tottori	32 B4		Vdkhr.	25 D5
Tauern	15 E7		Thabazimbi	59 C5		Tiruchchirappalli			Toul	13 B6		Tskhinvali	25 E5
Taunton	11 F5		Thailand ■	36 A2			43 P11		Toulon	13 E6		Tsu	32 B5
Taunus	14 C5		Thailand, G.			Tirunelveli	43 Q10		Toulouse	12 E4		Tsuchiura	32 A7
Taupo	64 C7		of	36 B2		Tisa →	22 B3		Touraine	12 C4		Tsugaru-	
Taupo, L.	64 C6		Thal	42 C7		Tisdale	71 C9		Tourcoing	13 A5		Kaikyō	32 F12
Tauranga	64 B7		Thames →	11 F7		Titicaca, L.	91 G5		Touriñán, C.	18 A1		Tsumis	58 C3
Taurianova	21 E6		Thane	43 K8		Titov Veles	22 D3		Tournai	14 C2		Tsuruga	32 B5
Taurus Mts. =			Thar Desert	42 F7		Tívoli	20 D4		Tournon	13 D6		Tsurugi-San	32 C4
Toros			Thásos	23 D5		Tizi-Ouzou	54 A5		Tours	12 C4		Tsuruoka	33 G11
Dağları	46 C3		The Pas	71 C9		Toamasina	59 H9		Townsville	61 D8		Tsyelyakhany	17 B7
Tavira	18 D2		Thermaïkós			Toba	32 B5		Toyama	32 A5		Tuamotu Is.	65 L16
Tavoy	36 B1		Kólpos	23 D4		Toba Kakar	42 D6		Toyohashi	32 B5		Tübingen	14 D5
Tawau	36 D5		Thermopylae			Tobago	87 D7		Toyonaka	32 B4		Tubuai Is.	65 M16
Tay →	10 C5		P.	23 D4		Tobermory	10 C3		Toyooka	32 B4		Tucson	83 D7
Taymyr,			Thessaloníki	23 D4		Tobol →	29 D7		Toyota	32 B5		Tucumcari	78 B2
Poluostrov	30 B7		Thetford	11 E7		Tocantins →	92 C4		Trabzon	46 B4		Tudela	19 A5
Tbilisi	25 E5		Thetford			Tochigi	32 A6		Trafalgar, C.	18 D2		Tuktoyaktuk	70 B6
Tchad =			Mines	69 D3		Togliatti	24 C6		Trail	71 D8		Tula	24 C4
Chad ■	53 E2		Thiers	13 D5		Togo ■	55 G5		Tralee	11 E2		Tulare	82 B3
Tchad, L.	53 F1		Thies	55 F1		Tōkamachi	32 A6		Trang	36 C1		Tulcán	90 C3
Te Anau, L.	65 F2		Thimphu	41 D7		Tokat	46 B4		Trangan	39 F4		Tulcea	17 F9
Te Aroha	64 B6		Thionville	13 B7		Tokelau Is.	65 K13		Trani	20 D6		Tulchyn	17 D9
Tebingtinggi	37 D1		Thira	23 F5		Tokushima	32 B4		Transantarctic			Tullamore	11 E3
Tegal	37 F3		Thívai	23 E4		Tokuyama	32 B2		Mts.	96 C3		Tulle	12 D4
Tegucigalpa	85 E7		Thomasville,			Tōkyō	32 B6		Transilvania	17 F7		Tulsa	79 A6
Tehachapi	82 C3		Ga., U.S.A.	75 D6		Toledo, Spain	18 C3		Trápani	21 E4		Tulua	90 C3
Tehrān	44 C2		Thomasville,			Toledo, U.S.A.	72 D4		Traralgon	63 C4		Tumaco	90 C3
Tehuantepec,			N.C., U.S.A.	75 B7		Toledo,			Trasimeno, L.	20 C4		Tunguska,	
G. de	85 D5		Thompson →	71 C10		Montes de	18 C3		Traun	15 D8		Nizhnyaya →	
Tehuantepec,			Thrace	22 D6		Toliara	59 J8		Travemünde	15 B6			30 C6
Istmo de	85 D6		Thun	13 C7		Toluca	84 D5		Travnik	20 B6		Tunis	54 A7
Tejo →	18 C1		Thunder Bay	69 D2		Tomakomai	32 F12		Trébbia →	20 B2		Tunisia ■	54 B6
Tekirdağ	22 D6		Thüringer			Tomar	18 C1		Trebič	16 D2		Tunja	90 B4
Tel Aviv-Yafo	46 D3		Wald	14 C6		Tomaszów			Trebinje	20 C7		Tupelo	74 B3
Telavi	25 E6		Thurles	11 E3		Mazowiecki	16 C4		Tremp	19 A6		Turabah	47 E5
Telford	11 E5		Thurso	10 B5		Tombouctou	55 E4		Trent →	11 E6		Turgutlu	23 E6
Telukbutun	37 D3		Tian Shan	34 B3		Tomelloso	18 C4		Trento	20 A3		Turhal	46 B4
Tema	55 G4		Tianjin	35 C6		Tomini, Teluk	39 E2		Trenton	73 D8		Turia →	19 C5
Temirtau	29 D8		Tianshui	35 C5		Tomsk	29 D9		Trepassey	69 D5		Turin =	
Temora	63 B4		Tiber =			Tonawanda	73 C6		Treviso	20 B4		Torino	20 B1
Tempe	83 D7		Tévere →	20 D4		Tonga ■	65 L13		Trier	14 D4		Turkana, L.	57 D7
Temple	78 D5		Tibesti	52 D2		Tonga Trench	65 L13		Trieste	20 B4		Turkey ■	46 C3
Tenali	40 J3		Tibet =			Tongue →	76 B2		Triglav	20 A4		Turkmenistan ■	
Tenda, Col di	20 B1		Xizang □	34 C3		Tonk	42 F9		Trikkala	23 E3			29 F6
Tenerife	54 C1		Ticino →	20 B2		Tonkin, G. of	35 D5		Trinidad	78 A1		Turks &	
Tennessee □	74 B4		Tierra de			Tonlé Sap	36 B2		Trinidad &			Caicos Is. ■	87 B5
Tennessee →	72 F1		Campos	18 A3		Toowoomba	63 A5		Tobago ■	87 D7		Turku	9 F12
Tenryū-			Tierra del			Topeka	77 F7		Trinity →	79 E6		Turnhout	14 C3
Gawa →	32 B6		Fuego, I. Gr.			Torbalı	23 E6		Trinity B.	69 D5		Tuscaloosa	74 C4
Teófilo Otoni	93 F5		de	95 G3		Torbay	11 F5		Trinity Range	80 F4		Tuscany =	
Tepic	84 C4		Tiétar →	18 C2		Tordesillas	18 B2		Tripoli =			Toscana □	20 C3
Teplice	16 C1		Tighina	17 E9		Torgau	15 C7		Tarābulus	52 B1		Tuticorin	43 Q11
Ter →	19 A7		Tignish	69 D4		Torino	20 B1		Tripolis	23 F4		Tuttlingen	14 E5
Téramo	20 C4		Tigris =			Torne älv →	8 E11		Tripura □	41 F8		Tuxtla	
Terebovlya	17 D7		Dijlah,			Torneträsk	8 E11		Trivandrum	43 Q10		Gutiérrez	85 D6
Teresina	92 D5		Nahr →	47 E6		Tornio	8 E12		Trnava	16 D3		Tuy	18 A1
Términi			Tijuana	84 A1					Troglav	20 C6		Tuz Gölü	46 C3
Imerese	21 F4		Tiksi	30 B10					Trois-Rivières	69 D3			

Tuzla 20 B7
Tver 24 B4
Twillingate .. 69 D5
Twin Falls .. 81 D6
Tyachiv ... 17 D6
Tychy ... 16 C4
Tyler 79 C6
Tyrrhenian
  Sea 21 E4
Tyumen ... 29 D7
Tzaneen ... 59 C6

Ube 32 C2
Ubeda 18 C4
Uberaba .. 93 F4
Uberlândia . 93 F4
Ubort → .. 17 B9
Ucayali → .. 90 D4
Uchiura-Wan 32 F12
Udaipur ... 43 G8
Udaipur Garhi 40 D6
Údine 20 A4
Udmurtia □ . 28 D6
Udon Thani . 36 A2
Ueda 32 A6
Uelzen 14 B6
Ufa 29 D6
Uganda ■ .. 57 D6
Ugljane ... 20 B5
Uinta Mts. .. 81 E8
Uitenhage .. 59 E5
Ujjain 43 H9
Ujung
  Pandang . 39 F1
Ukraine ■ .. 25 D3
Ulaanbaatar . 35 B5
Ulan Ude .. 30 D8
Ulhasnagar . 43 K8
Ullapool ... 10 C4
Ulm 14 D5
Ulster □ ... 11 D3
Ulubat Gölü . 23 D7
Uludağ 23 D7
Ulyasutay .. 34 B4
Uman 17 D10
Ume älv → . 8 F12
Umeå 8 F12
Umnak I. ... 71 C4
Umtata 59 E5
Una → 20 B6
Unalaska ... 71 C3
Ungava B. .. 68 C4
Ungava Pen. . 68 C3
Ungheni ... 17 E8
Unimak I. ... 71 C3
United Arab
  Emirates ■ 44 F3
United
  Kingdom ■ 11 E5
United States
  of
  America ■ 67 F10
Unst 10 A6
Ünye 46 B4
Upington ... 58 D4
Uppsala ... 9 G11
Ural =
  Zhayyq → 29 E6
Ural Mts. =
  Uralskie
  Gory 28 D6
Uralskie Gory 28 D6
Urawa 32 B6
Urbana ... 72 D1
Urbino 20 C4
Urbión, Picos
  de 19 A4
Urganch ... 29 E7
Urla 23 E6
Urmia, L. =
  Orūmiyeh,
  Daryācheh-
  ye 46 C6

Uruguay ■ .. 94 C5
Uruguay → .. 94 C5
Ürümqi 34 B3
Usakos ... 58 C3
Usedom ... 15 B8
Usküdar ... 25 E2
Ussuriysk .. 31 E11
Ústí nad
  Labem .. 16 C2
Ustica 21 E4
Ustyurt,
  Plateau .. 29 E6
Usuki 32 C2
Utah □ ... 81 F8
Utica 73 C8
Utrecht ... 14 B3
Utrera 18 D3
Utsunomiya . 32 A6
Uttar
  Pradesh □ 42 F11
Uttaradit ... 36 A2
Uummannarsuaq
  ...... 68 C6
Uusikaupunki 8 F12
Uwajima ... 32 C3
Uzbekistan ■ 29 E7
Uzerche ... 12 D4
Uzh → ... 17 C10
Uzhhorod ... 17 D6
Uzunköprü .. 22 D6

Vaal → 58 D4
Vaasa 8 F12
Vadodara ... 43 H8
Vadsø 8 D13
Vaduz 13 C8
Váh → 16 E4
Val d'Or ... 69 D3
Valahia ... 22 B5
Valandovo .. 22 D4
Valdepeñas . 18 C4
Valdés, Pen. . 95 E4
Valdez 71 B5
Valdivia ... 95 D2
Valdosta ... 75 D6
Valence ... 13 D6
Valencia,
  Spain 19 C5
Valencia,
  Venezuela . 90 A5
Valencia □ .. 19 C5
Valencia, G.
  de 19 C6
Valencia de
  Alcántara . 18 C2
Valencia I. .. 11 F1
Valenciennes 13 A5
Vall de Uxó . 19 C5
Valladolid .. 18 B3
Valledupar .. 90 A4
Vallejo 80 F2
Valletta ... 21 G5
Valls 19 B6
Valognes ... 12 B3
Valozhyn ... 17 A8
Valparaíso .. 94 C2
Valverde del
  Camino ... 18 D2
Van 46 C5
Van Gölü ... 46 C5
Vanadzor ... 25 E5
Vancouver,
  Canada .. 71 D7
Vancouver,
  U.S.A. ... 80 C2
Vancouver I. . 71 D7
Vänern 9 G10
Vännäs ... 8 F11
Vannes ... 12 C2
Vanrhynsdorp 58 E3
Vanua Levu . 64 L12
Vanuatu ■ .. 64 L11
Vapnyarka .. 17 D9

Varanasi 40 E4
Varangerfjorden
  ...... 8 D13
Varaždin ... 20 A6
Varberg ... 9 G10
Varese 20 B2
Varna 22 C6
Vasilevichi .. 17 B9
Västerås ... 9 G11
Västervik ... 9 G11
Vasto 20 C5
Vasylkiv ... 17 C10
Vatican City ■ 20 D4
Vätter 9 G10
Vawkavysk .. 17 B7
Vega 8 E10
Vegreville .. 71 C8
Vejer de la
  Frontera .. 18 D3
Velebit
  Planina ... 20 B5
Vélez Málaga 18 D3
Vélez Rubio . 19 D4
Velika Kapela 20 B5
Velletri ... 20 D4
Vellore 43 N11
Vendée □ ... 12 C3
Vendôme ... 12 C4
Venézia ... 20 B4
Venézia, G. di 20 B4
Venezuela ■ 90 B5
Venice =
  Venézia ... 20 B4
Ventotene ... 21 D4
Ventoux, Mt. 13 D6
Ventspils ... 24 B1
Ventura ... 82 C3
Vera 19 D5
Veracruz ... 84 D5
Veraval ... 43 J7
Verbánia ... 20 B2
Vercelli ... 20 B2
Verden 14 B5
Verdun 13 B6
Vereeniging . 59 D5
Verín 18 B2
Verkhoyansk 31 C11
Verkhoyanskiy
  Khrebet .. 31 C10
Vermilion ... 71 C8
Vermont □ .. 73 C9
Vernon,
  Canada .. 71 C8
Vernon,
  U.S.A. ... 78 B4
Véroia 23 D4
Verona 20 B3
Versailles ... 12 B5
Vert, C. ... 55 F1
Verviers ... 14 C3
Vesoul 13 C7
Vesterålen .. 8 E11
Vestfjorden . 8 E10
Vesuvio ... 21 D5
Veszprém ... 16 E3
Vettore, Mte. 20 C4
Viana do
  Alentejo .. 18 C2
Viana do
  Castelo .. 18 B1
Viaréggio ... 20 C3
Vibo Valéntia 21 E6
Vicenza ... 20 B3
Vich 19 B7
Vichy 13 C5
Vicksburg .. 79 C8
Victoria ... 71 D7
Victoria □ ... 62 C3
Victoria, L. . 57 E6
Victoria Beach 71 C10
Victoria de
  Durango =
  Durango .. 84 C4
Victoria Falls 59 B5

Victoria I. ... 70 A8
Victoria Ld. . 96 B14
Victoria West 58 E4
Vienna =
  Wien 15 D9
Vienne 13 D6
Vienne □ ... 12 C4
Vienne → ... 12 C3
Vientiane ... 36 A2
Vierzon ... 12 C5
Vietnam ■ .. 36 A3
Vigévano ... 20 B2
Vigo 18 A1
Vijayawada . 40 J3
Vikna 8 F10
Vila do Bispo 18 D1
Vila Franca de
  Xira 18 C1
Vila Nova de
  Gaia 18 B1
Vila Real ... 18 B2
Vila Real de
  Santo
  António .. 18 D2
Vilaine → ... 12 C2
Vileyka ... 17 A8
Vilhelmina .. 8 F11
Villacarrillo . 18 C4
Villach ... 15 E7
Villagarcía de
  Arosa ... 18 A1
Vilahermosa 85 D6
Villajoyosa .. 19 C5
Villalba ... 18 A2
Villanueva de
  la Serena . 18 C2
Villanueva y
  Geltrú ... 19 B6
Villarreal ... 19 C5
Villarrobledo 18 C4
Villaviciosa . 18 A3
Villena 19 C5
Villeneuve-
  d'Ascq ... 13 A5
Villeneuve-
  sur-Lot .. 12 D4
Villingen-
  Schwenningen
  ...... 14 D5
Vilnius 24 C2
Vilyuy → ... 31 C10
Vilyuysk ... 31 C10
Viña del Mar 94 C2
Vinaroz ... 19 B6
Vindhya Ra. . 43 H10
Vineland ... 73 E8
Vinkovci ... 20 B7
Vinnytsya .. 17 D9
Viranşehir .. 46 C4
Virden 71 D9
Vire 12 B3
Virgin Is.
  (British) ■ . 87 C7
Virginia □ .. 73 F6
Virginia Beach 73 F8
Virovitica .. 20 B6
Visalia 82 B3
Visby 9 G11
Višegrad ... 20 C7
Viseu 18 B2
Vishakhapatnam
  ...... 40 J4
Viso, Mte. .. 20 B1
Vistula =
  Wisła → .. 16 A4
Viterbo ... 20 C4
Viti Levu ... 64 L12
Vitigudino .. 18 B2
Vitória, Brazil 93 G5
Vitoria, Spain 19 A4
Vitória da
  Conquista 93 E5
Vitsyebsk ... 24 B3
Vittória ... 21 F5

Vittório
  Véneto ... 20 B4
Vivero 18 A2
Vize 22 D6
Vladikavkaz . 25 E5
Vladimir ... 24 B5
Vladivostok . 31 E11
Vlissingen .. 14 C2
Vlóra 23 D2
Vltava → .. 16 C2
Vogelsberg . 14 C5
Voghera ... 20 B2
Voiron 13 D6
Vojvodina □ 22 B2
Volga → .. 25 D6
Volgograd .. 25 D5
Volodymyr-
  Volynskyy . 17 C7
Vologda ... 24 B4
Volos 23 E4
Volovets ... 17 D6
Volta → ... 55 G5
Volta, L. ... 55 G5
Volta Redonda 93 G5
Volterra ... 20 C3
Volturno → . 20 D4
Volzhskiy ... 25 D5
Voríai
  Sporádhes 23 E4
Vorkuta ... 28 C7
Voronezh ... 24 C4
Vosges ... 13 B7
Vouga → ... 18 B1
Voznesensk . 25 D3
Vrangelya,
  Ostrov ... 31 B15
Vrbas → ... 20 B6
Vrede 59 D5
Vredenburg . 58 E3
Vryburg ... 58 D4
Vryheid ... 59 D6
Vukovar ... 20 B7
Vulcaneşti .. 17 F9
Vulcano ... 21 E5
Vychodné
  Beskydy .. 17 D5
Vylkove ... 17 F9
Vynohradiv . 17 D6
Vyškov 16 D3

Waal → ... 14 C3
Wabash → .. 72 F1
Waco 78 D5
Wâd Medanî 53 F5
Waddington,
  Mt. 71 C7
Wager B. ... 68 B2
Wager Bay .. 68 B1
Wagga Wagga 63 C4
Wah 42 C8
Wageo 39 E4
Wainganga →
  ...... 43 K11
Waingapu ... 39 F2
Wainwright,
  Canada .. 71 C8
Wainwright,
  U.S.A. ... 71 A3
Waipara ... 65 E5
Waitaki → .. 65 F3
Wajima ... 32 A5
Wakasa-Wan 32 B4
Wakatipu, L. 65 F3
Wakayama .. 32 B4
Wakkanai ... 32 E12
Wałbrzych .. 16 C3
Wales □ ... 11 E4
Walgett ... 63 A4
Walla Walla . 80 B4
Wallis &
  Futuna, Is. 64 L13
Wallowa Mts. 80 C5

Walvisbaai

Walvisbaai .. 58 C2
Wanganui .. 64 C6
Wangaratta . 63 C4
Wangerooge 14 B4
Warangal .. 43 L11
Wardha → . 43 K11
Warmbad .. 59 C5
Warner Mts. . 80 B3
Warrego → . 63 B4
Warrenton . 58 D4
Warrington,
  U.K. 11 E5
Warrington,
  U.S.A. 74 D4
Warrnambool 62 C3
Warsaw =
  Warszawa . 16 B5
Warszawa .. 16 B5
Warta → .. 16 B2
Warwick ... 63 A5
Wasatch Ra. . 81 E8
Wash, The .. 11 E7
Washington . 73 E7
Washington □ 80 B3
Washington,
  Mt. 73 B10
Waskaganish 69 C3
Wasserkuppe 14 C5
Waterbury .. 73 D9
Waterford .. 11 E3
Waterloo ... 77 D8
Waterton-
  Glacier
  International
  Peace Park 81 A6
Watertown .. 73 C8
Waterville .. 73 B11
Watford 11 F6
Watrous ... 71 C9
Watson Lake 70 B7
Watsonville . 82 B2
Watubela,
  Kepulauan 39 E4
Waukegan .. 72 C2
Waukesha .. 72 C1
Wausau ... 77 C10
Wauwatosa . 72 C2
Waxahachie . 79 C5
Waycross ... 75 D6
Wazirabad .. 42 C9
Weddell Sea 96 A4
Weiden 15 D7
Weifang ... 35 C6
Weimar 15 C6
Welkom ... 59 D5
Wellesley Is. 60 D6
Wellington,
  Australia .. 63 B4
Wellington,
  N.Z. 64 D6
Wellington, I. 95 F1
Wels 15 D8
Welshpool .. 11 E5
Wemindji ... 69 C3
Wenatchee . 80 B3
Wenzhou ... 35 D7
Werra → ... 14 C5
Werribee ... 63 C3
Weser → ... 14 B5
West
  Bengal □ . 40 F7
West Palm
  Beach ... 75 F7
West
  Virginia □ . 72 E5
West Wyalong 63 B4
Westerland . 14 A5
Western
  Australia □ 60 F3
Western
  Ghats .. 43 N9
Western
  Sahara ■ . 54 D2

Western
  Samoa =
  Samoa ■ . 65 L13
Westerwald . 14 C4
Westland
  Bight 65 E4
Weston-super-
  Mare ... 11 F5
Westport,
  Ireland ... 11 E2
Westport, N.Z. 65 D4
Westray ... 10 B5
Wetar 39 F3
Wetaskiwin . 71 C8
Wetzlar ... 14 C5
Wexford ... 11 E3
Weyburn ... 71 D9
Weymouth .. 11 F5
Whakatane . 64 B7
Whale → ... 68 C4
Whale Cove . 70 B10
Whales, B. of 96 B16
Whangarei . 64 A6
Wheeling ... 72 E5
White → ,
  Ark., U.S.A. 79 C8
White → ,
  Ind., U.S.A. 72 E2
White Nile =
  Nîl el
  Abyad → . 53 E5
White Russia
  = Belarus ■ 24 C2
White Sea =
  Beloye
  More 28 C4
Whitehaven . 11 D5
Whitehorse . 70 B6
Whitney, Mt. 82 B3
Wholdaia L. . 70 B9
Whyalla ... 62 B2
Wichita ... 78 A5
Wichita Falls 78 C4
Wick 10 B5
Wicklow Mts. 11 E3
Wien 15 D9
Wiener
  Neustadt .. 15 E9
Wiesbaden .. 14 C5
Wildspitze .. 14 E6
Wilhelmshaven
  .... 14 B5
Wilkes-Barre 73 D8
Wilkie 71 C9
Willemstad .. 87 D6
Williams Lake 71 C7
Williamsburg 73 D7
Williamstown 63 C3
Williston .. 76 A3
Willowmore . 58 E4
Wilmington,
  Del., U.S.A. 73 E8
Wilmington,
  N.C., U.S.A. 75 B9
Wilson 75 B9
Wilsons
  Promontory 63 C4
Wimmera → . 62 C3
Winchester .. 11 F6
Wind River
  Range ... 81 D9
Windhoek .. 58 C2
Windsor, N.S.,
  Canada .. 69 D4
Windsor, Ont.,
  Canada .. 69 D2
Wingham ... 63 B5
Winisk → .. 69 C2
Winnipeg ... 71 D10
Winnipeg, L. 71 C10
Winnipegosis
  L. 71 C9
Winona 77 C9

Winston-
  Salem 75 A7
Winterthur . 13 C8
Wisconsin □ 77 C10
Wisla → ... 16 A4
Wismar 15 B6
Witbank ... 59 D5
Wittenberg .. 15 C7
Wittenberge . 15 B6
Wkra → ... 16 B5
Wloclawek .. 16 B4
Wodonga ... 63 C4
Wokam 39 F4
Wolfsberg .. 15 E8
Wolfsburg .. 15 B6
Wollaston
  Pen. 70 B9
Wollongong . 63 B5
Wolverhampton
  .... 11 E5
Wönsan ... 35 C7
Woodland ... 80 F3
Woods, L. of
  the 71 D10
Woodstock .. 69 D4
Worcester,
  S. Africa . 58 E3
Worcester,
  U.K. 11 E5
Worcester,
  U.S.A. ... 73 C10
Workington . 11 D5
Worms 14 D5
Worthing .. 11 F6
Wrangell ... 71 C6
Wrangell Mts. 71 B5
Wrath, C. .. 10 B4
Wrexham ... 11 E5
Wrigley ... 70 B7
Wroclaw ... 16 C3
Wuhan 35 C6
Wuppertal .. 14 C4
Würzburg .. 14 D5
Wutongqiao . 34 D5
Wuxi 35 C7
Wuzhou ... 35 D6
Wyandotte .. 72 D4
Wyndham .. 60 D4
Wyoming □ . 81 D10

Xánthi 22 D5
Xiaguan ... 34 D5
Xiamen ... 35 D6
Xi'an 35 C5
Xiangfan .. 35 C6
Xiangtan .. 35 D6
Xingu → ... 92 C3
Xining 34 C5
Xinjiang
  Uygur
  Zizhiqu □ . 34 B3
Xizang □ .. 34 C3
Xuzhou ... 35 C6

Yablonovyy
  Khrebet .. 30 D9
Yakima ... 80 B3
Yakutat ... 71 C6
Yakutsk ... 31 C10
Yalova ... 22 D7
Yalta 25 E3
Yam Kinneret 46 D3
Yamagata .. 33 G12
Yamaguchi . 32 B2
Yamal,
  Poluostrov 28 B8
Yambol 22 C6
Yamdena .. 39 F4
Yamethin .. 41 J11
Yampil 17 D9
Yamuna → . 40 E3

Yana → 31 B11
Yanbu 'al
  Bahr ... 47 F4
Yanji 35 B7
Yantai 35 C7
Yaoundé ... 56 D2
Yapen 39 E5
Yaremcha .. 17 D7
Yarkhun → . 42 A8
Yaroslavl .. 24 B4
Yaselda ... 17 B8
Yasinya ... 17 D7
Yatağan ... 23 F7
Yathkyed L. . 70 B10
Yatsushiro . 32 C2
Yavoriv ... 17 D6
Yawatahama 32 C3
Yazd 44 D3
Yazoo → .. 79 C8
Yecla 19 C5
Yekaterinburg 29 D7
Yell 10 A6
Yellow Sea . 35 C7
Yellowhead
  Pass 71 C8
Yellowknife . 70 B8
Yellowknife →
  .... 70 B8
Yellowstone →
  .... 76 B3
Yellowstone
  National
  Park 81 C8
Yelsk 17 C9
Yemen ■ .. 49 E3
Yenice ... 23 E6
Yenisey → . 28 B9
Yeniseysk .. 30 D7
Yeola 43 J9
Yeovil ... 11 F5
Yerevan ... 25 E5
Yevpatoriya . 25 D3
Yiannitsa .. 23 D4
Yibin 35 D5
Yichang ... 35 C6
Yining ... 34 B3
Yithion ... 23 F4
Yogyakarta . 37 F4
Yokkaichi .. 32 B5
Yokohama . 32 B6
Yokosuka .. 32 B6
Yonago ... 32 B3
Yonkers ... 73 D9
Yonne → .. 13 B5
York, U.K. .. 11 E6
York, U.S.A. . 73 E7
Yorkton ... 71 C9
Yosemite
  National
  Park 82 B3
Yoshkar Ola . 24 B6
Youghal ... 11 F3
Youngstown . 72 D5
Yozgat ... 46 C3
Yuan
  Jiang → . 35 D6
Yuba City .. 80 F3
Yübari ... 32 F12
Yucatán,
  Canal de . 85 C7
Yucatán,
  Peninsula
  de 85 D7
Yugoslavia ■ 22 B3
Yukon → .. 71 B3
Yukon
  Territory □ 70 B6
Yuma 82 D4
Yunnan □ .. 34 D5
Yuzhno-
  Sakhalinsk 31 E12
Yvetot 12 B4

Zabrze 16 C4
Zadar 20 B5
Zafra 18 C2
Zagreb 20 B6
Zagros,
  Kühhä-ye . 44 C2
Zagros Mts. =
  Zagros,
  Kühhä-ye . 44 C2
Zähedän ... 45 D5
Zahlah 46 D3
Zaïre =
  Congo → . 56 F2
Zaïre =
  Congo,
  Democratic
  Republic of
  the ■ 56 E4
Zákinthos .. 23 F3
Zalishchyky . 17 D7
Zambeze → . 59 B7
Zambia ■ .. 59 B5
Zamboanga . 38 C2
Zamora 18 B3
Zamość ... 17 C6
Zanesville .. 72 E4
Zanjän ... 46 C7
Zante =
  Zákinthos . 23 F3
Zanzibar .. 57 F7
Západné
  Beskydy . 16 D4
Zaporizhzhya 25 D4
Zara 46 C4
Zaragoza .. 19 B5
Zaria 55 F6
Zaskar Mts. . 42 C10
Zbarazh ... 17 D7
Zdolbuniv .. 17 C8
Zeebrugge .. 14 C2
Zeerust ... 59 D5
Zeitz 15 C7
Zenica 20 B7
Žepce 20 B7
Zézere → .. 18 C1
Zhabinka .. 17 B7
Zhambyl =
  Taraz 29 E8
Zhangjiakou . 35 B6
Zhangzhou .. 35 D6
Zhanjiang .. 35 D6
Zhashkiv ... 17 D10
Zhayyq → .. 29 E6
Zhejiang □ . 35 D7
Zhengzhou .. 35 C6
Zhigansk ... 30 C10
Zhlobin ... 17 B10
Zhmerynka .. 17 D9
Zhodzina ... 17 A9
Zhytomyr .. 17 C9
Zibo 35 C6
Zielona Góra 16 C2
Zigong ... 35 D5
Ziguinchor .. 55 F1
Zile 46 B3
Žilina 16 D4
Zimbabwe ■ 59 B5
Zion National
  Park 83 B6
Zlatoust .. 29 D6
Zlin 16 D3
Znojmo ... 16 D3
Zolochiv ... 17 D7
Zonguldak .. 46 B2
Zrenjanin .. 22 B3
Zug 13 C8
Zugspitze .. 14 E6
Zunyi 35 D5
Zürich ... 13 C8
Zwettl 15 D8
Zwickau ... 15 C7
Zwolle 14 B4